I D A _ _ _

LONERS

HERMITS, SOLITARIES, AND INDIVIDUALISTS

IDAHO LONERS

HERMITS, SOLITARIES, AND INDIVIDUALISTS

BACKEDDY BOOKS
Cambridge, Idaho

CORT CONLEY

For *Keats*, My Daughter

When one has lived a long time alone,
one wants to live again among men and women,
to return to that place where one's ties with the human
broke, where the disquiet of death and now also
of history glimmers its firelight on faces,
where the gaze of the new baby looks past the gaze
of the great granny, and where lovers speak,
on lips blowsy from kissing, that language
the same in each mouth, and like birds at daybreak
blether the song that is both earth's and heaven's,
until the sun has risen, and they stand
in a halo of being made one: kingdom come,
when one has lived a long time alone.

—Galway Kinnell
When One Has Lived A Long Time Alone

Other titles from Backeddy Books:

The Middle Fork: A Guide
River of No Return
Snake River of Hells Canyon
Idaho for the Curious
Gathered Waters
Ridgerunner
Last of the Mountain Men
Is Idaho in Iowa?

Idaho Loners was designed, typeset, and produced
using Apple Macintosh™ computers. Layout was
produced in Pagemaker 4.2™ and QuarkExpress™ 5.0.
The typeface is Sabon.

Designed by Fletcher Sliker, Sliker Communications;
Ada, Michigan.
Production by Roger Cole; Boise, Idaho.

Printed in U.S.A. by BookCrafters, Inc.

ISBN 0-9603566-5-7

First Edition

CONTENTS

PREFACE

As its title indicates, this is a book about a dozen Idahoans, ranging from gruff individualist to thorny hermit, all of whom are loosely corralled under the name "loners"—not a name meant to disparage. After all, the loner is a cherished figure in the Idaho landscape; so much so, in fact, that when a philosophy professor at an Idaho college learned I was at work on *Idaho Loners*, he quipped, "Isn't that redundant?" (On second thought, he may have said, "Isn't that a tautology?") In the event, there was tongue-in-cheek truth to his reply. I am persuaded by my reading and experience that Idaho has had more loners, for a longer time, than any other western state.

In spite of Henry Thoreau's "I never found the companion that was so companionable as solitude," each person in this book would have been (or is—three are alive at this writing) uncommon company, far preferable to solitude. Indeed, with the exception of Claude Dallas, I admire each character included here—they all, at the risk of sounding recklessly undemocratic, drank upstream from the herd—and they all had admirable traits, even Dallas.

Although the selections were personal, they were anything but arbitrary. If we know something of the world by knowing people (one justification for poking into the life of a loner), then we know people by knowing what they do or did. Occupation, however, was not a criterion for inclusion: whether one subject were a sheep-herder, another a forest lookout, and still another a Cistercian monk, it was simply coincidental. I chose persons who were largely self-sufficient, or who handled extended spells of solitude especially well. (In James Angleton's instance, readers will note that the solitude was mostly mental.)

Another criterion, of course, was sufficient information—records, incidents, informants—to trace a profile. As a result, some well-known Idaho loners were eliminated: among others, Johnny-Be-hind-the-Rocks, Andy the Russian, Cougar Gus Johnson, Hacksaw Tom, Red Harlan, James Castle, and Sasquatch.

To the reasonably curious, questions about the figures included here will surely occur. I can attempt to answer the most obvious. Is there something about Idaho that fosters or cultivates loners? And what traits, if any, did they share?

In China, where the hermit tradition goes back several thousand years, there is a saying, "The small hermit lives on a mountain. The large hermit lives in town." Idaho has always had more mountains than towns—large habitat for small hermits. Rugged landforms, so to speak, attract rugged individualists. By a current federal defini-tion (living in the vicinity of a town with a population of 5,000), Idaho is the most rural of the continental states. All but one of the loners included here lived in decidedly rural circumstances. In short, geographical isolation arguably nourishes the loner's temperament.

Idaho's endowment of live water is another relevant geographi-cal detail. Certainly the state is more favored in this regard than Utah, Montana, Nevada, Arizona, or New Mexico. All of the loners collected here settled on a creek or a river—perhaps because flowing water magnifies the reflective tendency of one's nature, or perhaps because all of them liked to fish, or simply, perhaps, for the easy access to water.

Moreover, in Idaho transportation was slow to arrive and slower to improve; this, too, made it a cradle for loners. In particu-lar, the late coming of roads forestalled the disruption of reclusive lifeways. Consider the hermit of Impassable Canyon, Earl Parrott, inveighing against the road being dozed down the Salmon River by the Civilian Conservation Corps; or the Ridgerunner, Bill Moreland, decrying the briarpatch roading of his Clearwater country.

Another aspect of Idaho life that carries a clue to the recurrence of loners is its independent political tradition: lack of party affilia-tion, frequent ticket-splitting, third parties. Coupled with maverick politics is a strong distaste for federal interference in state matters and for state interference in personal matters. More than half the loners chosen here had some sort of brush with the law. In addition, most of them had a mild mistrust or even outright resentment of the state and federal governments. Almost all of them lived on, or were surrounded by, federal lands (such lands comprise two-thirds of Idaho). It appears convoluted topography, delayed development, and quirky politics championed a frontier individualism—a potent compost for loners.

What then, if anything, can be said about them as a group? Three-quarters were men. Only two were born in Idaho. Only one of them had a regular paycheck and was well off; yet all but one practiced a pioneer work-ethic. All but two were readers, though only three went to college. They were all physically fit, at least until old. Almost half of them, unlike Idahoans who generally subscribe to strong family loyalties, had lost touch with their families. Just five of our sample were ever married; three of those more than once, and only two had children. At least half of them had a dog. All had a garden. And each of them at some point endured a newspaper reporter. So. You want to be a loner? Then come to Idaho if you are a single, childless, self-sufficient male with a dog. Better to know how to fish and garden. Lay in a cord of wood and two cords of books. Work hard. After twenty-five years, on average, when a reporter jangles the cowbell on your front gate, you will know you have arrived.

As change comes on the gallop to Idaho, the colorful figure of the loner inevitably fades into deeper obscurity. Our national forests are being roaded faster than an elk can trot, as anyone who glances from a peak or a plane can see. Even remote river canyons, the loner's last holdout, have been penetrated by numerous boaters. The loss of the loner and his space is a regrettable loss of variety.

Loners stand at the tail-end of a lengthy tradition—people who owned their own sunrise and sunset. A fugitive memory. Their aspirations, with the exception of the last two chapters here, seem to echo those expressed by the Chinese hermit Shan-chuan:

I have my place in the world. In winter, I wear skins. In summer, I wear hemp. In spring, I plow and plant and have enough to do. In fall, I harvest and gather and have enough to eat. When the sun rises, I get up. When it sets, I rest. I am free to do what I want in this world, and with this I am content.

Swap skins and hemp in 2200 B.C. for wool and cotton in 20th-century Idaho, and not much would be changed in ambition or desideration. Today, however, there is a different breed of Westerner and a different and diminished kind of country. Nevertheless, as the reader will note, every now and then the past seeps into the present.

—Cambridge, Idaho

RICHARD LEIGH, **BEAVER DICK**

SURVIVAL COUNTS FOR MORE THAN ONE CAN PROPERLY SAY.—BARRY LOPEZ

Idaho was barely open for business when Richard Leigh rode in from the south on his buckskin mare. The year was 1863. He was thirty-two and a long way from his boyhood home on the Irwell River, a tributary to the Irish Sea. Coming from a country short on mountains, he chose the most jagged geography in the West: the sun-rinsed and snow-pied spires of the Teton Range on the embossed border between newly named Idaho Territory and what would one day be called Wyoming.

In America, diaries and letters provide the genesis for any region; in Idaho, one recalls the journals of Meriwether Lewis and William Clark, of Wilson Price Hunt and John Work. For the Teton Basin (then Pierres Hole), however, the Leigh diaries are the taproot. When Leigh pitched his tipi between the forks of the upper Snake River, about forty miles northeast of present Idaho Falls, the fur trade had declined—as quickly as a species going into oblivion—but beaver had not been extirpated, nor Indians fought out of existence. In 1863 Richard and his wife Jenny were newly-weds. Jenny, an eastern Shoshone, was a daughter of Chief Washakie's band. (Leigh's marriage, performed by a Utah minister, may have made him a brother-in-law of sorts to Jim Bridger, whose third wife was a Shoshone from the same band.) And while the basin may not have been trackless topography at the time, undeniably it was frontier. The diaries that survive—1875-1876-1878—afford uncommon insights into daily life on the verge of settlements.

Many questions curl around Leigh's life—in fact, around most of his life not covered by the three diaries. Much of what we do know comes from his own pen, writing in a left-handed, methodical script. His spelling was phonetic; capitalization and punctuation were irregular or absent, the result of limited schooling. (His Cockney accent caused him to drop the *h* in words that began with that letter—for example, *have* becomes "ave"; *had* becomes "ad.") Nevertheless, his chronicle imparts an almost biblical rhythm to the satisfactions and afflictions of their seasoned life.

Teton Basin, 1875. In the reader's interest, some corrections in spelling and punctuation have been made.

May 20. I went into the woods and cut a set of timbers to bild myself a milk house.

May 25. Finished the milk house...watereng my garden, fixeng my saddles and geteng ready for the mountons.

June 21. It froze ard last night and nipped everything in my garden. only my peas and carrots were saved...

July 6. ...the flies and misqutos ad been so bad that i scarcely knew my own horses and cattle. my wife and children ad sufred more than death. they ad to keep big smokes all day and half the nights to keep the varmints off the stock....

Aug. 3. I went to see my garden and get some traps that i ad left there. The grasshoppers ad destroyed what the frost ad left. All I got for my springs work was a mess of peas.

Aug. 8. Grasshoppers came like a black cloud.

Aug.10. Gnats so bad that i could not mow hay.

Aug. 27. Mr. Davis man fetched Dicks stove [Leigh's son, who had traded his labor for it] home so his mother as got the first cook stove she ever ad and never saw but one before this one.

Sept. 6. The yellow jackets are in swarms by the hundreds for 15 miles the length of the timber on the North Fork. Me an Tom [Lavering] get stung very often while hunting fresh meat or fish. i ave never seen anything to equal them in all my life....

Sept. 8. a grizzly Bair killed one of Mr. Davis cows yesterday....

Sept. 19. Bannock Indians passed here yesterday on their way to hunt buffalo...i took my son John to camp with me for a few days.

Sept. 21. It fros ice in the water bucket last night and the Salmon River mountons west of here are white with snow....

Oct. 1. afternoon we ground our axes, trapeng hatchets and knives ready for another months trapeng. then i made a dining table for my famley. this is the first real table we ave ever ad in the mts....

Oct. 2. Some Indians came here. they ad shot a buffalo bull breaking his hind leg... this is the first buffalo that as beene seene since the spring of 1871....

Oct. 9. after supper i told John [Leigh's son] some hunting and war stories which amused him very much for this was Johns first camp hunt with me.

Nov. 6. Snowing hard at daybreak...it snowed in my face all day but i ad to cross the range or i might not be able to get them [11 horses] over tomorrow if the snow crusts in the night. i traveled 39 miles and camped on Sand Creek at dark. this is one of the ardest days work that i ever did. it was all i could do to make a fire.

And so it went—a government of two. For the first ten years of their marriage, Richard Leigh fathered hard: Jenny bore a child every other year. He supported them by hunting, trapping, and guiding. The diaries reveal a constant search for food: trout, ducks and geese, quail, grouse, and prairie chickens, marmots, beaver, bear, deer, antelope, and elk. In fall and winter he trapped: badger, mink, marten, muskrat, beaver (thirty-four one winter), otter, fox, lynx, wolverine.

Guiding was more tenuous. In 1860, Leigh met geologist F. V. Hayden, who was accompanying the Raynolds Expedition, in

Teton Basin. By 1872, Hayden had become the founder of the United States Geological and Geographical Survey of the Territories, and mounted a second expedition to explore and map large expanses of the Teton-Yellowstone wilderness. Two field divisions composed the expedition: one under Hayden; the other under James Stevenson guided by Richard Leigh.

Leigh met his division at Taylor Bridge (twenty years later, Idaho Falls) with his family. Expedition photographer William Henry Jackson took their picture.

Nathaniel Langford, who had been among the ambitious leaders of an 1870 Yellowstone expedition, and then was appointed first superintendent of Yellowstone National Park, was a guest of the Hayden Survey. In his journal, he wrote of Leigh:

> We must depend upon his guidance in fording streams, crossing mountain passes, and avoiding collision with unfriendly tribes.
>
> Dick is quite a character, and during the time he spent with us displayed personal traits that would make him a fitting hero for a popular dime novel. He is an Englishman, and has been engaged in trapping for 21 years [since 1851]; is familiar with all the accessible portions of the Rocky Mountains, and has adopted many of the habits and pursuits of the Indians. He, however, has made it a point twice a year to visit some civilized region in order to dispose of his furs and obtain supplies. His children are great favorites of our company, and his dusky wife seems a quiet inoffensive creature whose highest ambition is to learn how best to serve her lord and master.
>
> ...At Conant's Creek, Mrs. Dick and her children bade us farewell. She had won the respect of every member of our company for the care she manifested for her children and her attachment to her liege lord.

Richard Leigh guided the the party of thirty-seven mounted men through a landscape of hurdles and into south Yellowstone, where they rendezvoused with Hayden's division on the Firehole River. Stevenson's group then journeyed south into Jackson Hole. There, as the expedition wound down, two lakes at the knees of the Tetons were named in honor of the Leighs' services: Leigh Lake and Jenny Lake. (In later years, Leigh would frequently serve as local hunting guide, encountering such notables as Theodore Roosevelt, and escorting senators, doctors, and Vanderbilts.)

Through 1875 and October, 1876, Leigh's diaries portray a difficult, sometimes precarious, and occasionally cheery existence. No word of complaint, though, or even a gripe. This is a man living where he wants to live, doing what he wants to do, happy in his family. In January he notes that he has been too busy to keep his journal "agoing, but we are aving a nice open winter with only three inches of snow on the ground." On the Fourth of July he spends the night alone on an old campground of the Hayden Survey and at sundown drinks to everyone's health from a bottle of wine bitters. A few days later, with obvious parental pride, he says Little Dick caught a fine otter, and that Jenny is making a new lodge. In mid-month, after a filly destroys her pack saddle, requiring that he take son William's saddle in its stead, he writes that he fixed a pad with two feather pillows for William to ride on and "everything went lovely to Conant Valley." In late July, it is gooseberries plenty, fat roast ribs for dinner, no misqutos here. The first week of August he kills the largest buck antelope he has seen in over four years. By late August he is setting out traps along the creeks. Jenny and the children are digging yampa bulbs, a montane substitute for potatoes. In the evening, after dinner, on his way to check his traps, he remarks, "I passed Jinny and the children. they ware diggeng away like good fellows."

By mid-September, accompanied by his son Dick and their dog, he has moved camp clear down to the South Fork of the Snake and is trapping in earnest. He encounters some Shoshoni and parts peaceably; perhaps by now word of Custer's debacle on the Little Bighorn has filtered this far south. They gather wild cherries, and he says, "Fish are plenty here. We saw and heard the meadowlarks and doves today. the first since we left Teton Basin." Shortly, they go west to Taylor Bridge to sell their furs and resupply.

By September-end they are back at the homestead, cutting hay. Leigh makes a rope harness and a sled to help with stacking. Hitches up the jackass to it to see whether it will work. "Everything worked lovely."

The new cow for which he had traded cattle-watching duty provides a first opportunity to churn butter. He calls his attempt "passable." A few days later he concedes, "Jinny made some good Butter. the first time she ever tryed she beat me all hollow."

By mid-October the hay is stacked and fenced, the boat beached, the traps staked, and a pair of antelope hung by the lodge for meat. The basin sky is given over to the wavering lance-points of geese tapering south, imploring "carry on, carry on." Leigh's last entry for the year, October 14, is a haunting admixture, in retrospect, of hope and abidance: "Finished cutting house logs this evening. The days are very hot at this time of year and the nights are cold."

Richard Leigh's diary for 1877, the year of the Nez Perce War, has been lost. The next entry is January 22, 1878. It is a jolt. "Camped in the cabin that my cattle got into and died last year. The cabin is about a quarter of a mile from the graveyard of my wife and children." Wife and children dead and buried! When and how?

The loss of Richard Leigh's family is among the saddest narratives in Idaho history, rivalled only by the story of Nez Perce Chief Joseph. Leigh's account of the tragedy is unfolded in a long letter, undated, to friend Dr. Josiah Curtis, one of the hunters he guided:

> My Dear Friend:
> I set downe to give you an accont of myself and my lost famley. I moved up to the elbo of the Teton River on the 25th of April 1876. Thare I bult a log cabin and fenced me a farme and rased some little fegetobls. I also built a horse corall and a hay corral and put up 6 ton of hay in it. I also went and packed Tom Lavering and his partner and their camp and skins out of the mountons. I kept a diary up to August which I will copy and send to you some other time.

On the first day of August Tom and my son Richard started on a trapeng trip up the middle river while me and my wife hauled in the hay. Tom and Dick found nothing worth trapeng and came back the last of August and me and Tom went and trapped the North Fork of Snake with the boat. At my wife's request, I took hur and famley to camp. About the 25th of September we trapped down to a mile of my old winter cabin at the junction of the Teton River. When we got through trapeng my wife sade she would like to spend the winter in our old cabin as she might want some assistance during the winter and our old place was too far up from anybody. So I moved my famley and house goods to the old cabin at hur request. Tom bilt a cabin near me and then we went down to Warrens store on Blackfoot for supplies. On the 2nd of November I caught a bad cold and suffered from my old complaint whatever it is.

On the 11th of November we passed Humpys camp at the Point of Rocks 2 miles from John Adams place. Humpys wife came out and asked me for some bread. I told hur I ade none packed and went 6 miles to the foot of the Crater Buttes and camped. Wile we were eating supper by the light of the camp fire Humpys Wife and 3 year old Daughter came and sade Humpy had commited sueside and hur and hir child were starving. We gave hur someting to eate and blankets to sleep in. The next morning she came to where we were crosing our supplies with the boat and said she wanted to go over the river to see my Wife. I put her acrost. When we ad got everything acrost we went home. My wife told me that Humpys father ad died and her mother ad broke out in the face with little bumps. Tom sade it might be the small pox or measles so i told my wife to give the woman some provisions and tel her to go to the boat and camp and i would put her acrost the river in the morning so that she could go and tel the doctor on the resirvation. But when

I went to the boat i could not find hur. There was a Mr. Anes living near me and he was going to the South Fork to a Texas trappers camp for some harness he had loaned him. I told him to tell Tex if that woman came to his place to send hur off for we suspected she ad beene where the small pox was. Tex has a wife and 5 children. The woman was there already and Anes fetched hur back trying to get hur to go and live with him but she came to my camp and asked what i wanted hur for. I told hur i did not send for hur and told hur to go away. She said she was heavy with child and could not walk. So i told my wife to give hur our lodge [tipi] and some provishons and let her camp in the bushis my Wife and children keeping away from her untill she took in labor. Then my wife packed her eatibls and wood to the lodge door but did not go in.

Now none of us knew eny thing of the small pox and we suposed she was going to give birth to a child and if there was small pox in the camp she was clere of it as she had beene 10 or 12 days away from it. So me and Tom and Dick Junior went to the island to kill a large buck for mocksins and camped out one night. The next day when withen 2 mils of our home on our returne we met my wife and the rest of my famley coming to meat us. I knew what was the mater as soon as i saw them. The Indian womon was dead. When we got home we went and examined the womon and could see nothing suspisis about hur and came to the concluson that she had died in child bed. I asked my wife to take the little Indian girle to the house and wash and clene it. She sade not to do it. Something told hur that the child would die but at my request she took it to the house and clened it up. It played with my childron for four days as lively as could be and that night it broke out all over with little red spots. We thought it was a rash from being wased and cept it in a warme house as the child ad a cold at this time. At this time i had the bloody flux and was very weak from it. I had it for 5 days when it stopped on me.

The child appeared to be in no misery so when i felt better me and Tom took the wagon and went up to my ranch at the elbow of the Teton to kill deer for winters meat while it was fat. I killed 4 deer by noone the next day but my gun shot too low which caused me to miss several other shots. So we came down to resight my gun and Tom borrowed Dick Juniors gun for this hunt as his gun snapped very often and we did not want to take time to fix it. This was on the 13th day of December. We started up a gane on the 14th my famley all feling and looking wel only my wife she complaned of drowesnes but i thaught nothing of it in hur state [pregnant] she was often so. I told Dick he could come up there 4 days from then and take a days hunt with us. We went hunting the next morning, Tom on one side of the river and me on the other. The dogs ran some deer out and i kiled one of them. Wile i was dressing it i looked a cros the creek and saw some one with Tom. Thay was a long way from me but somthing told me it was my son Richard and that thare was somthing rong at home. I started for the cabin and thay did the same. When thay saw me Dick sade his mother ad a bad head ake and wanted me at home. He told me that himself and William were taken with a pain in the bely and my two daughters were unwell the day we left home. He ad rode from thair to hear in 2 hours 20 mils and i got on that same mair and went home in les time then that. When I got thair it was an aufull sight to see. My Wife was seting on the flore by the stove and my youngest daughter with hur boath thair heads tyed up and sufring very mutch. My oldest daughter was in bed complaning with a pane in her back and bely. Hur looks when she answard my qustons struck my hart cold. Williams legs ad wekned two hours before i got home and he was in bed. Just as i rode up to the dore of the house Johns legs gave way and i put him to bed. Tom and me was taken the same day and last night we did not sleep mutch. We were burning up aparently some times and chily other times. We ad both lost our appetites and did not eat. When we went to hunt we thought it was cold for we ave ad some very cold and bad weather the last 5 weeks. I left Dick to come down with Tom and the wagon.

Well my wife was in labor and i ad a hard time all a lone with my famley all night and nex day about 4 oclock my Wife gave birth to a child [the infant apparently died]. She had broken out all over with small red spots but after the birth of the child thay all went back on hur. I knew what the desise was as soone as i come into the house allthoe i ad never seene it before.

My wife felt better and i put her to bed. She slept well during the latter part of the night and i had a hard time with the children all night. In the morning my Wife sade she wanted to get up and set by the stove. I got hur up and as i layed her on a palit i had fixed for hur she fanted. She shook all over and made a rumbling noyse. When she came to she sade to me what is the mater dady? I told hur she had fanted from weknis that was all. I was satisfide that hur hours were numbard and i spoke incougenly to hur but my hart was ded within me. About noone she asked me to give her some Harpers magazines and those pictors that you sent to us. She wanted to look at pictors. She looked at them and talked and asked me qustons about them quite lively. It was hard work for me to answor hur without betraying my felings but i did so. The children ad got quiet and some of them aslpe and i told my wife i wold go out and set fire to a brush pile to signol for Tom and Dick to come home. Wile doing so my legs got weake and it was all i could do to get back to the cabbin. I ad beene back about 10 minuts when Tom drove up with Dick taken with the small pox. Dick went out and killed a large doe deer after i left them and he took sick that same night. Tom was the same as me. I got Dick in the house and to bed and Tom went over to get Mr. Aynes. While Tom and Anes were sounding the ice to see if a horse could cros my wife was struck with Death. She rased up and looked me streaght in the face and then she got excited and cursed Mr. Anes for bringing the Indian woman back to us. She sade she was going to die and all our childron wold die and maby i would die. Doctor this was the hardist blow i ad got as yet. She then layed downe and smiled to me. All at wanst she turned over to the fire place and comenced stireng the fire. She was cold. She was layeng betwixt the stove and the fire place but thare was no fire in the stove. I layed hur downe agane and at hur request i put 2 pare of my socks and hur shoose on her feet and coverd hur well with blankits and a roab. She smiled and sade she felt a little warmer. I then took my gun and shot a signol for Tom and Anes. They came and i told Tom what had happened but did not tell Anes all.

She was alayeng very quite now for about 2 hours when she asked for a drink of water. I was layeng downe with one of my daughters on eatch arme keeping them downe with the fevor. I told Anes what she wanted and he gave hur a drink and 10 minuts more she was ded. Dick turned over in bed when he hurd the words and he said God bless my poor mother! He then sade to me father maby we will all die. I was talking as incorigleny as i posably could to him when he sade well if we ave to die it is all right. We might as well die now as some other time. That remark was another hard blow on me.

We wrapped my wife up in a blanket and buffalo robe and put hur in the wagon bed. The next morning Mr. Anes started to the resirvation for the doctor or informaton how to treat the disease and Tom went 4 miles to get John Hague. Hague came over and chopped wood and carried water to us. He sade not to give any cold drinks to the children or drink any ourselves witch advice we followed until Anes came back from the doctor. He was gone 3 days. He sade the doctor sade to give them all the cold water they wanted for it would not hurt them. Myself and Tom did not know what to think or do about it but i sade i did not like the idea of cold water and did not give them any myself or Tom. I ad not slept one minuts since the time i got home from the hunt. Anes after taking one nights sleep came into the house and took a change of watching with me and Tom that was getting very low down.

I cannot discribe my felings or situaton at this time. I knew i must ave sleep and could not get it. While layeng down a few minuts to rest my legs i saw Anes giving the children cold water and asking them often if they did not want to drink. I begged of him not to do so. I could not sleep so i got up and adminestrad to my famley a gane with the ditermaton of doing all i could until i dyed witch i was shure could not [last] more than 24 longer for my eyes would get full of black spots and near blind me and death would ave beene welcome only for my children.

I saw the spots go back on William and Anne Jane my oldest daughter and was satisfied that it was the effects of cold drinks. This night about 10 Oclock i had to lay downe exhausted. Night before last i took 80 drops of laudanum inside of an hour at 2 doses but it had no effect on me. This night i felt some sines of sleep but with the sine came a heavy sweting and burning and tremors. My close and beding were ringeng wet in half an hour. When it left me i told Tom and Anes were everything was that thay might want and asked them to save some of my famley if it was posable and turned over to die.

I can not wright one hundreth part that pased thrue my mind at this time as i thaught deth was on me. I sade Jinny i will sone be with you and fell a sleep. Tom sade i ad beene a sleep a half hour when i woke up. Every thing was wet with presperaton. I was very weak. I lade for 10 or 15 minutes and saw William and Anne Jane ad to be taken up to ease them selves every 5 minuts and Dick Junior very unrestlas. I could not bare to see it.

I got up and went to elp Tom and Anes. I saw that the spots ad gone back on Dick. My detirmaton was to stand by them and die with them. This was Cristmos eve. Anne Jane died about 8 Oclock about this time every year i used to give them a candy puling and thay menchond about the candy puling meny times wile sick, espeshely my son John.

William died on the 25 about 10 Oclock in the evening. John and Elisabeth were doing well. They were ahead of the rest in the desise. The scales were out and drying up. On the night of the 26th i changed watching with Anes. I let Anes sleep until 1 or 2 Oclock then only for one or two hours with swet and tremors when i would get up. Tom was taken with dyarreah and was too weak to get up to assist us any more.

On the 26th Dick Junior died betwixt 5 and 6 oclock in the evening. Last night when i woke up the fire was out but some small coals the lamp burned down and the door of the cabin partly open. I was freezing apparently when i woke up and saw Anes leaning against the wall a sleep. It gave me a start that i cannot discribe. I woke him up then got up myself.

My son John had comenced to swell agane by day light and about 8 oclock on the 27 in the eveng he died. On the night of the 28th I woke up cold again and found Anes leaning against the bed fast asleep again. After sleeping 5 or 6 hours the fore part of the night, i got up as quick as my strength would let me and woke him up but it was too late. She [Elisabeth] was over all danger but this and she caught cold and sweled up a gane and died on the 28 of Dec abot 2 Oclock in the morning. This was the hardist blow of all. I was taken with the bloody flux this night and me and Tom layed betwixt life and death

for several days. Me and Tom ad to beg of Hague to stay
and get us wood and water every day.

Since Anes came back his plea was that his cattle
wanted looking after when there was a 15 year old boy at
home and nothing else to do but look after them. When
all my famley was dead and buried he was determined to
go when me and Tom was not able to do anything and
Anes arm was all sweled and sore from vacination. I
begged of him to take 2 of my horses and saddles and go
to Major Danilson [Fort Hall Indian agent] and cary a
letter from me asking him for some blankits and clothing
so that when we got well we could change and go
amongst people and not spread the disese. But Hague
could not see how he could go until i offered him $2.50
a day then he could go. It took him 6 days to make the trip
with 2 fat and as good mairs that are on the Snake river.
I had not slept more than 2 hours and that was a
miserable sweat and tremor sleep for the last 13 days and
i sent to Dr. Fuller on the Reserve for something to
promote sleep. The flux ad made me wakeful again. I did
not expect to live to see Hague return but God has spared
me for some work or other. I believe i am prepared to do
it whatever it is.

So he had burned life down to the socket, like lines from
Shakespeare: "What freezings have I felt. / What dark days seen. /
What old December's bareness everywhere." Emerging from the
deep twilight of his log cabin, he felt grief embedded in his bones.

He was well enough in late February, however, to take a span
of horses and a sled to the islands on the South Fork of the Snake
for ten days. Tom Lavering went with him. On their return to
Leigh's cabin—his homestead was three and one-half miles east of
Eagles Nest Crossing on Henrys Fork of the Snake River (Henrys
Fork enters the Snake just southeast of Rexburg)—they made
preparations to move to his other place, Hog Hollow, at a bend on
the Teton River. "I shall improve the place," he wrote, "and live and

die near my famley but i shall not be able to do eny thing for a few months for my mind is disturbed at the sight that i see around me and work that my famely as done wile thay were liveng."

Bereavement continued to dog him like a shadow. He finds he is not physically the man he was before the smallpox; yet he tries to stay busy. He burns his old clothing and blankets and washes his new ones; patches old moccasins and fashions some fresh ones. He makes a pillow from goose feathers. By mid-March he can notice, even appreciate, the balsamroot blooming yellow on the hillsides: "They look very pretty." But the enforced, unwelcome solitude gnaws at his spirit. "I am all alone and i kep doing at some thing from day light to dark every day. i am very lonesome."

In late April, as Leigh is saddling his horse to go check his traps, a horse gallops up to the house—the one he gave a man for helping him fence his family's graves. The man has left the country, but here is the horse that used to belong to Leigh's son William, come like a wind across his heartstrings.

Even the spark of the hunt is gone. His sensitivity to death has been sanded thin: "The antelope comes and looks into my little vally nearly every day. i dont kill any. dont want to. no one to eate the meat and i cannot waste with a good conshus."

May 22: "I am very lonesome alone. Am ruining my old ealth fast. i can work 4 or 5 hours a day tolerably ard...i ave not seen a living soul either white or Indian since the 20th of last month." In his situation, too little company did not beat the hell out of too much. By mid-June he pleads, "If i ad eny company to talk with i could stand it but i ave not seen eny person since the two men i gave my tobaco to in april last... i am so lonesome no matter how tyred i am."

A few days later, he takes his packhorse and a bale of beaver plews and lights out for the Sand Hole Trading Post twenty-five miles away. It proves to be a mistake. At the store he had not visited in almost two years, he sees a baby his wife had nursed as a newborn the last time they called. The infant is now a boy. "I nursed and played with him plenty this time while there," Leigh pens. "That night after going to bed my mind run a grate deele about my wife and that child so i could not slep and i must tell the truth i ad wet eyes that night. when i go over all a gane i intend to take a little filley 3 years old with me for the child. i intended braking it for my youngest daughter before she died."

On reaching home a couple of days later, he loses himself in the effort of scything hay. His diary entry that evening, however, turns pensive. "I ave got a large sack full of nice dried meat [antelope]. none and no one to eat it. someone will be along that is meat hungry after a while then it will do me good to see them eat it. this is a hard old county to deal with but there will be a railroad in this valley this year and then perhaps us working people can do some better. i am in hopes anyhow."

Like heartworm, the ache endures, but by the summer solstice he begins to revivify. "I am enjoying better health... if only i ad some good company i think i could be as happy as i ever expect to be in this world."

In mid-July the Bannock War crackles across the Camas Prairie. Leigh goes about his routines with rifle at hand and loaded and uses more circumspection than usual. "My being all alone makes it ard on me some times for want of sleep. i suffered last year for sleep thru trouble and illness. i suffer now for living in advance of settlements and aving to watch and protect the covewring to my ead. but i ave the pleshur of knowing that i ave led the setlements on snake river and showed them ware they could keep stock and farme..."

Time heals. The following year, Leigh married again. The former Susan Tadpole was the daughter of a Bannock couple, friends of Leigh since 1863. He was forty-eight; she was sixteen. They moved to his second homestead, on the Teton River about three miles north of present Newdale, on the east side of the river, and lived in a log house, eventually expanded to two rooms connected by a covered entryway. Over the next fifteen years, the couple had three children. Their remembrances sketch in further details about their father.

Leigh had a sandy complexion, wore a buckskin vest and a felt cowboy hat. He spoke some Indian dialects and always gestured when he spoke. He smoked and chewed tobacco. He liked to read, mostly magazines and newspapers. He was a closet hypochondriac, a sucker for patent medicines. Although strict, he was kind to his children, and considerate of his wife. He had an explosive temper, once striking his horse—after it shied and nearly unseated him—across its head with his rifle with such force that he bent the barrel. At the same time, he was generous to his neighbors, sharing food and hay whenever they were in need. His unfailing courage was dramatically demonstrated when he went to the rescue of an elderly couple whose bullying sons abused them shamefully. With steely resolve, he intervened at the risk of his own life and took the young men to Malad, Idaho, for trial. (In a wry sidelight, Leigh was also placed under a $300 bond for possible assault because he had leveled his rifle at the men. He recorded a prescient disdain for the legal profession: "the law in this section is only a Bilk and god keep me a long ways from it for i shall try and never Bother with such law a gane.")

In 1896 in a letter to his friend Nathaniel Langford, Leigh, while saying on one hand, "I am gaining in health and strength right along now," says on the other, "I see that many...of my old friends and acquaintances have crossed the line. Well it is no use complaining. It is a debt we all have to pay."

Three years later, Richard Leigh, "Beaver Dick," paid in full, dying of a stroke after several months of illness. He was buried in accord with his wishes on the bluff overlooking his homestead. About fifty neighbors attended the Mormon service.

Eventually, Leigh's land was forfeited to Madison County because of unpaid taxes. (In 1976 the same land was scoured by floodwaters when Teton Dam failed.)

Leigh's summation of his own life is scarcely seventy words:

> i am the son of Richard Leigh formerly of the British navey and grand son of James Leigh formly of the 16 lancers england. i was borne on Jenury 9th in 1831 in the city of Manchaster England. come with my sister to philadelphia u s a when i was 7 years old. went for the Mexcin war at close 48 atched to E co [company] 1st

infentry 10 months then come to rocky mountons and
here i die.

Not quite. This transplanted Englishman, Idahoan by conviction, has his most admired memorial just across the border in Wyoming: two lakes connected by a narrows, each with the inverted
dragon-spine reflection of the Grand Tetons—one named Leigh, the
other Jenny. In a poem about names on the land, Kim Stafford says,
"A place is a story happening many times." Each time those lakes
are called by name, the Leighs' star-crossed story happens to mind,
and always will.

1 RICHARD LEIGH WITH HIS FIRST FAMILY IN FRONT OF HIS TIPI : JOHN, ANNE
JANE, JENNY WITH WILLIAM IN HER LAP, DICK JR. BAREBACK; OCTOBER, 1878.
2 LEIGH'S LODGE, 1878.

3 LEIGH'S TIPI PHOTOGRAPHED BY WILLIAM HENRY JACKSON
AT FORT BROWN, WYOMING, IN 1878.
4 RICHARD LEIGH'S SECOND FAMILY: WIFE SUSAN TADPOLE,
WILLIAM, ROSE, BEAVER DICK, EMMA.
5 LEIGH'S DIARY.

that did not want me to
see thair poses i set on my
horse and talke a with them
for a half hour i had an
obeseclt tha was all well
arme a and eld thair
guns in readyness as well
as my self I used my
Banock frinds name
and told them he was
at my house & i had an
obgect in this also when
I was satisfide that he
was out of reach and
they could not over take
him i bid them good by
for i told them in answer
to thair questions that I
was sending lettes to
the major by him but
did not tell them

what i had an obgect in
this also i burevle rune
to my lodge at the mouth
of the telon got my dogs
and arrived at home at
4 Oclock the sun a 1/2
hour high i signald
for my frend my old
bending bow and 80 roun
of cartriges as been my
Bedfellow for the last
8 months a companays
with my old hunting
knife but wether it will
aveale me eny thing sem
anes to be seine my
being all a lone makes
it hard on me some time
for want of sleep i
sufred last year for

6 INTERIOR, LEIGH'S LODGE, 1878.

WILLIAM HISOM, **THE COVE RECLUSE**

WE NEVER TOUCH BUT AT POINTS.—RALPH WALDO EMERSON

Nothing much stirs at Halverson Bar nowadays. The graveled point bar—once called the Cove—along the middle Snake River is merely a bend like many others, furred with cheatgrass and sagebrush and rucked with untidy piles of lava rock which shelter their share of snakes and lizards. Skunk and coyote visit more often than bobcat and deer. Solitary cottonwoods, stands of hackberry, and thickets of ubiquitous willow impede the upstream afternoon wind, while the torpid Snake, come from the farthest corner of Wyoming, takes its own sweet time to Oregon. A lonesome, uncultivated spot, it is too far from town for anyone to want to live there now.

When William Hisom settled at the Cove (his partner, William White, had staked the twenty-acre claim by 1907), it was less desolate or isolated than at present. The railroad bridge three miles downriver was scarcely ten years old. The settlement of Guffey, a mile from the south end of the bridge, was home to railroad workers and sheepshearers; proud of its store, saloon, stables, boarding house and barns. Guffey was intent on serving the gold and silver mines and miners of Silver City, twenty miles south.

Five miles upriver from the Cove, workers at recently completed Swan Falls Dam intended to meet the electrical demands in Silver City.

In 1912, adding to the abundant optimism, Melba was platted astride the railroad tracks six miles northwest of the Cove because irrigation water was finally available from Arrowrock Dam on the Boise River to the northwest. Homesteaders filed under the Desert

Land Act for 640 acres "which will not, without irrigation, produce
some agricultural crop...."

The West is a great place for turnover, however. Within a few
years, the desert reclaimed its own. When the Silver City mines
declined, the railroad south from Melba was derailed well short of
its lodestar; Guffey faded like a rainbow: post office closed, saloon
shuttered, ferry shorefast. Hisom's pard left for parts unknown.
Other riverside rock houses soon housed only the wind. Doc Hisom,
all unintentionally, had become the "Hermit of Snake River Desert."

Hisom's story, at least in Idaho, begins in 1900 with the census
taker at Banner Precinct (Idaho City), Boise County. Hisom stated
there that he was born in 1858 in Chicago, Illinois; that his race was
black, his occupation veterinarian surgeon, and that his parents
were born in New York (which made him a second-generation
freeman). Since these replies were given under penalty of perjury,
and well before Hisom's age became a source of esteem, there is no
cause to question them.

In 1900 Hisom must have been en route to the Snake River,
accompanied by his partner William White, six years his junior.
Both of them were miners, at the time unemployed for several
months. How or why they chose the shore of the Snake at the Cove
is unknown now (White said he had visited the area in his early
twenties as a rider for cow outfits and had mined there since 1897).

Snake River gold is flour-fine: it defies mechanical recovery and
is separated by pan or sluicebox only with difficulty. Miners along
the river could earn a dollar a day—but not every day. So maybe
gold was the sole reason for their arrival and their residency. Maybe
not.

Although Hisom had practiced his veterinary skills in Kenesaw,
Nebraska, for several years before his arrival in Idaho, and carried
his case of instruments with him to the Cove, there is no evidence
that he ever doctored after he reached the river.

Hisom and White placer mined in the winter; however, their
survival demanded other work as well. They tended a substantial
garden (their root cellar, fifteen feet long and proportionately wide,
was a potato throw from the cabin), kept chickens, toiled for nearby

rimrock farms, and winter-trapped for pelts and the one-dollar bounty on coyotes and bobcats.

Some time after 1913, White severely injured one of his legs—perhaps in a farm accident—and left for good. Hisom stayed on, footed to his shadow, alone as a blue heron.

He lived in a basalt-stone cabin with a dirt floor, a single-story retreat with a slightly gabled roof of planks and sheetmetal covering two rooms. The walls were two feet thick, tempering extremes of heat and cold, and troweled with clay on the interior. The front room (twenty by twenty) accommodated a stove, two beds, a table, a rocking chair, and high shelves along the walls; the rear room (ten by fifteen), used for storage, admitted a fireplace in its west wall. Each room had a window. The front door faced south and opened toward the placid face of the river.

Outside, a lean-to angled from the house front, offering the friendship of shade. In summer the rocking chair sat east of the doorway and provided a pensive evening perch overlooking the glide of clay-colored water—river-watching is a patient art.

A set of four-point deer antlers forked from the roofpeak above the front door. Just west of the doorway, Hisom had a milking platform for his goat. A few feet in front of it, he had placed his tanner's bench, where he softened leather hides. He hauled his drinking water from a crease in the bank, halfway between the door and the river.

On at least two occasions the law in all its majesty pried Hisom off his roost and into town; much of what has been recorded about him resulted from those summonses.

In September, 1913, Hisom and White traveled to Boise in order to testify in a U. S. Land Office hearing on behalf of their friend Warren Mace, who had a Desert Land entry at the elbow across and upriver two miles from the Cove. The transcript of Hisom's testimony (twenty-five pages of direct examination) reveals remarkable diction and extensive knowledge.

In the course of his testimony, Hisom said that he had been at the Cove since 1897; that he and his partner could excavate and wheelbarrow up to five cubic yards of gravel to the river—where they washed it in a rocker—in a day; that the least they made in a ten-hour day was ten cents and the most was two and a half dollars. He added that trapping, or even a garden, paid better than mining. "Sometimes you couldn't make chewing tobacco." (Their friend's agricultural entry lost out to the defendant's earlier mining claim, however.)

The second time the law came knocking, in October, 1921, it at least provided a free automobile ride. Hisom's testimony in a probate case was needed by his nearby rancher friend Halvor Halverson, for whom he occasionally worked. Hisom's arrival was noted by a Boise newspaper reporter.

INDIAN MINER, 71 YEARS OF AGE, HAS FIRST AUTO RIDE ON VISIT TO BOISE

"Doc" W. E. Hisom of Riva [renamed Guffey], Idaho, 71 years and six months young, celebrated his second visit to Boise in 21 years by taking his first ride on a street car Monday evening, when he started on the return trip by the interurban route to Nampa. "Doc" enjoyed his first automobile ride last Friday, when neighbors brought him to Boise as a witness in a probate case.

"Doc" Hisom, of Indian and Negro parentage, and a well educated graduate veterinarian, has for 36 years lived the life of a recluse on his placer mining claim, 20 miles south of Nampa on the Snake River. In that period he has visited Boise but twice, once 21 years ago, and again seven years ago, when he came to the city for a few hours.

Everything was new and novel to the sprightly old man, and though doubtful of the wisdom of living in a city, he told friends he had enjoyed the visit. In fact, he is seriously planning a future visit, "if there isn't too much to do at home."

Electric lights, crowded streets, rapid transit—it all

enthralled the old man, while visits to the exhibits of the state historical collection probably proved the greatest treat of all.

"Why, I've got a lot of curios down at the camp which you folks do not have, and I'll just have to send some of them up here," he told attendants. The list includes reed matting of Indian manufacture, "fire" sticks, wooden root diggers, whole arrows, rubbing stones and fish skewers.

Thirty-six years ago "Doc" came to southern Idaho from Nebraska and Chicago, where he had formerly practiced his profession. Since then he has been engaged in mining and prospecting, until the last few years, when he has been content to do a little photography, farm a little in his vegetable "patch," trap and fish a little, and act as host to the children of the neighborhood, who gather almost daily to hear his quaintly flavored tales of Indians, woodcraft and nature, with which he mixes his own philosophy of the golden rule both to men and animals.

"Doc" is especially proud of the guests whom he has at various times housed within his lava rock cabin...[many of whom] have made his lodge their headquarters for fishing and hunting trips.

Among some of his avocations the old man numbers the mastery of seven musical instruments, expert photography, taxidermy, and nature lore to a remarkable degree. He is well read and can converse on any subject. He is also an expert manufacturer of obsidian arrow points, which he chips by hand from the native rock.

He returned to Nampa Monday night, where he will visit friends for four days before returning to his home on the river.

By now Hisom was actually sixty-three, but his credentials as a recluse had been established. Race may have been a factor in this notoriety-verging-on-celebrity. (In 1900 there were fewer than 300 blacks in Idaho.) Al Zeyer, who lived in Melba most of his life, as a boy rode horseback down to the river to visit with Hisom. He was drawn to this black man living by the river among deserted rock houses, with only cliff swallows and Canada geese for company. "He was the first colored man [I'd seen], and he wasn't real black, but he was dark, and for that reason we were always kind of intrigued with him...and to see a colored man, why, that was really kind of exciting to us. We really appreciated it...He was a mystery man. And as boys we'd go away wondering 'well, why did he come out here? Who is he?' It was always a big question mark in my mind...'til this day."

Hisom's lifeway was that of a bee in clover. In summer he worked his garden. He had a wooden boat and fished. He hunted birds, rabbits, and deer, trapped coyotes and badgers, tanned hides, used a sewing machine to make leather (beaded) gloves, moccasins, and jackets which he sold. As an amateur photographer he took scenic photographs, tinted them, and offered them for sale as well.

Leona Comstock lived on a rimrock ranch over a mile from Hisom, and she and her husband often hiked down to see him on Sunday afternoons in spring and fall. When she encountered him at work tinting a photograph, she expressed an interest in learning how it was done. He offered to teach her and later went to her house to give her instructions. He worked on the porch and, though invited, refused to eat in their dining room, although he agreed to be served on the porch. (At *his* house, however, which was consistently neat and clean, his rustic hospitality always required that visitors come inside.)

As Hisom's fame increased, the flow of visitors grew from freshet to stream: schoolchildren, Boy Scouts and, of course, irrepressible journalists. In June, 1923, Nona Zeigler, of Boise's *Capital News*, visited and then wrote a report of interest, despite its sentimentality and condescension.

THE HERMIT OF THE SNAKE RIVER DESERT INTERVIEWED AND PROVES TO BE A MOST INTERESTING CHARACTER

The people about Melba and Glendale often speak of the old Hermit who lives "Down on Snake River." I had seen him sometimes, for he bought his few groceries at Melba, and as an especial favor to some of his friends, helped them during the haying season. There are greatly exaggerated stories about Doc Hisom, as he is called. Some maintain that he was a college man and a very brilliant scholar. At last I determined to visit this wonderful man and find out what I could.

It is not an easy journey. The cliffs are hundreds of feet high along the canyon, while the road is so close to the Snake River that I walked most of the way, leaving my husband to pilot the car either safely into camp or to go down alone to a watery grave. The sand is deep, but only once did we have to pull the car out, that was on our return trip.

Doc Hisom's place is four miles up the river from the railroad bridge going to Murphy, and it must be about four miles this side of Swan Falls. The road is full of rocks and altogether it is no place for timid souls to venture, although the trip is worthwhile. The canyon of the Grand has nothing on the Snake for scenery. When we were almost in despair and marital relations were becoming a little strained, owing to the remarks made by a friend's husband in regard to 'the inherent curiosity of women in general and one woman in particular,' we came in sight of the cabin that shelters this strange man, for he is, when all is said, a remarkable person.

His house sets in a little wide spot in the canyon, there are no trees, just a clump of willows and about 60 feet from the sullen unresponsive waters of the Snake, that never smile or unbend to answer the call of man. We come to it. Never does it grant us favor. The house is built of rough, unhewn stone, a little porch at the side. On the top is a deer's head and antlers. The yard is swept clean and there are some homemade chairs, a work bench, a blacksmith's bellows and a pile of wood.

Doc Hisom himself came up to greet us, a load of wood upon his back. He is not a large man, medium rather, but he is straight and although not black, decidedly brown with wavy grizzled hair and mustache. He is three-quarters negro and one quarter Black Hawk Indian and looks the Indian most. His eyes are black, piercing and kindly. In them the pride and sorrow of the Redman, but none of the snap and jazz of the American son of Ethiopia. His apparel is overalls, khaki shirt and red handkerchief. He is scrupulously clean, I saw a toothbrush lying in the window before I entered the cabin. Inside the house everything was clean, [and] although the floor is dirt and the walls are plastered with mud, he has tried to conceal their ugliness by hanging many pictures upon them, cheap pictures but well chosen. One was of a rather handsome man dressed in the regalia of an athlete. It was Ad Santel, who once visited the old man and often sends him tokens of friendship, although Mr. Hisom is not interested in athletics. Another picture was that of a little white child and I asked if he had ever been married, to which he answered, 'No, I never had time.' At this I commenced to have faith in some of the vaunted wisdom which is accredited the old hermit. I call him old, he is in fact 72 years old but looks 50. He has a few books and innumerable magazines, *Field and Stream*, *Popular Mechanics*, *Technical World*, and loads and loads of Elizabeth Towne's magazine, *Nautilus*, of the cult of new thought of which he is a devout follower, and a library of the literature left by a comrade who died. I questioned him closely and found him well grounded in his philosophy, although he had never heard of Emil Cone, who has stolen Mrs. Towne's thunder of late. [Elizabeth Jones Towne, born in Portland, Oregon, moved to Holyoke, Massachusetts, in 1900, where she became a publisher and lecturer for the International New Thought Alliance. New Thought, also called 'the religion of healthy-mindedness' or 'the mind-cure movement,' was or is a popular philosophical and mental therapeutics movement that began in the mid-19th century. It is an individualistic, nonliturgical religion that emphasizes the power of constructive thinking. God is Universal Mind or Infinite Wisdom; man is one with God and has creative power in his own sphere.]

Mr. Hisom is a veterinary doctor and when I asked him if he ever practiced New Thought on dumb animals, he quickly replied:

'No, New Thought is the triumph of mind over matter. Horses have no mind.'

'Will you tell me about your life?' I asked.

'Very gladly,' he replied, 'My father died when I was small and my mother married again. I quit school at 12. Mother was New Thought although she did not know it. She always told me to send out good kindly thoughts, and I would be repaid in the same way. All I have learned has been acquired through study alone. I can read music and play several different instruments, can paint a little in water and oil. I do not like poetry nor Harold Bell Wright's novels. [Wright, the most popular writer in America from 1909-1921, was a master practitioner of the craft of sentimental romance. Written in a simple, pseudo-biblical style, his comforting stories told a middle-class white America that its homes and values were safe from the alarming spectacle of modern life. By the mid-1920s, however, Wright lost his audience to the movies.] I am never lonely. I trap and tan hides and placer mine for a living. Every day through the summer there are crowds of people who come to see me. I don't know why.

I have lived here 18 years. I had a partner, a white man, who stayed with me many years, but he lost a limb and could not work. His family wished him to come home. My dog is my companion and friend. I drink coffee once a day, my eyesight is good and I never drink whiskey. I do not take a daily paper to bias my judgment, have no politics and am glad to answer any question you may ask.'

He paused.

'Will you tell me about your friend, the white man?'

A shade of sadness and a great dignity came over the Hermit's face as he spoke slowly and as though it took immense self-control to keep his voice steady.

'Never men were better friends, for 25 years,' he said. 'White and I were partners, he stayed here off and on. White was his name, color and soul, we toiled and studied together and then he lost his limb and had to go home. I cannot tell you how I miss him, I have only my dog left.'

The Hermit's wonderful dark eyes softened almost as tender as a mother's and dimly I sensed something of the power to love in this old man's heart. I could not fathom his desire for solitude or how civilization had driven him back among the cliffs far from the haunts of man.

I love the crowds and noises of the city streets. I see no beauty in Snake River and the desert silence, only at sunrise and sunset does it relent a little, but I could understand his friendship and love for his comrade. I looked around the room, four fishing rods, a cook stove, two beds, one long unused, mute reminder of the absent friend, the pictures, a banjo lying as though just put down and as we went away I turned and looked back. There are three or four other cabins standing near Doc Hisom's home now, for Anglo Saxons are restless seekers after gold, have filed on mining claims and for brief seasons sometimes fitfully placer mine, but all through the bleak wind-swept winters he is alone, and I saw him alone

today, save for his dog, silent and erect, his swarthy face
reflecting the sorrow of the two disinherited outcast races
whose blood flows through his veins. He had said he did
not like poetry, yet unconsciously he is a tragic poem. He
was never lonely, yet the loneliness of all the "Great
Alone" is stamped indelibly upon his countenance. I
thought of his love for his white companion who had
shared his home, and Kipling's lines, "The Ballad of East
and West" came to me.

> Oh East is East, and West is West
> and never the twain shall meet.
> Till Earth and Sky stand presently at
> God's great Judgment seat;
> But there is neither East, nor West,
> Border, nor Breed, nor Birth,
> When two strong men stand face to face,
> though they come from the ends of the earth.

The collective recollections of visitors, some of them children at
the time, provide other insights into Doc Hisom.

He was of medium height, about 145 pounds, sported a mustache and smoked a pipe. He usually wore a long-sleeved shirt and
wash-faded coveralls, a neckerchief, and in sun a wide-brimmed
straw hat. If he was wearing pants instead of overalls, he might also
wear a vest.

Because he was an adept flintknapper, he often made arrowheads for children when they visited. He might play the trumpet or
the banjo. A man accustomed to doing things for himself, he could
sew and knit, mill his own grain and bake his own bread.

Amos Burg, while on a canoe trip down the river in 1925,
stopped to visit. He recalled that Hisom had acquired something of
a regional reputation as a riverbank philosopher, and local people
sometimes sought his advice as a marriage counselor. Burg also
remarked on his retentive memory.

One visitor as a child was impressed with Hisom's ability to
extract venom from rattlesnakes and find a market for it. Another

heard that reputedly Hisom used his savings to help bright, indigent students go on to college. Still another, a scoutmaster, recalled that the hermit had mentioned running away from home and being in vaudeville. The scoutmaster added that Hisom mesmerized scouts with his campfire talks about Snake River lore and the Indian burial ground across the river (where petroglyphs were clustered). Each year the scoutmaster took his troop for a visit at the Cove.

Wendell Chase recalled an incident indicative of Hisom's sense of humor. "I think I was seventeen at the time. There were four of us, high school kids. He invited us in. I was sitting there with my arm on the sewing machine, and these other kids were around the room. We sat there (visiting) for quite a while. On the sewing machine he had a pair of coyote trap springs. He had whittled out some wood to put on the springs and wrapped them with rawhide so he wouldn't hurt his hands. I picked one up and asked him, 'Doc, what do you use these for?' 'Well,' he said, 'I exercise my hands with them.' So, being young kids, we had to try them. I've got pretty big hands. I tried it and could just barely make it click with the right hand but couldn't get it clear down with my left. So these other kids, great big husky football players, had to try it, but they couldn't do any better than I could. So we said, 'Doc, let's see you do it.' 'Well,' he said, —you must remember he was eighty-five years old at this time—'You must remember I'm kinda old.' He tried and he could only get it down about an inch. Then he said, 'But when I was your age, I used to make them click just like this.' He just made them click like there was nothing to it. You see, he had fun. A great sense of humor."

The T. E. Halversons regularly looked out for Hisom's needs. Visitors brought their own lunch and something extra for him. Fishermen on their way back from nearby Halverson Lake would often stop to share their catch. Although Hisom was resourceful enough to survive the agricultural depression of the 1920s and the Great Depression of the 1930s, in later years he may have received assistance from friends. In January, 1942, he wrote a friend in Middleton, "Thank you for the Christmas letter containing five bills. I'm flued in and snowed in. Doc Hisom at Camp."

In spring, 1944, the sturdy would-be recluse who enjoyed company began to lose his health. His vision started to fail and knapped away at his independence. Members of the Friends Church in Melba moved him to a boxcar-apartment in Melba in order to take care of him more easily. (He had not been to town in years.)

In December he suffered a stroke and was driven to the hospital in Nampa, Idaho. He was unable to speak. One of his nurses recalled his "beautiful personality" and lamented that she was unable to visit with him. He died at night December 26, after a three-day stay.

When the Melba Friends Church learned that Doc Hisom was going to be buried by Canyon County, it organized a collection among members and friends. He was, however, buried in Nampa, where he died, instead of Melba—perhaps because wartime gas rationing was in effect. His remains rest in the children's section of Kohlerlawn Cemetery there. An obituary stated that he had no known kin.

In March, 1945, William Hisom was in the Boise newspaper for the last time. His meager living arrangements were casually autopsied. The *Idaho Daily Statesman* carried a "special" from Melba:

FRIENDS OF 'OLD DOC' GATHER AT AUCTION OF PIONEER GOODS

All the worldly goods of "Old Doc"—Dr. William C. Hisom, beloved character in this community since he first settled down in a cabin on the Snake River in 1890—were auctioned off here Wednesday afternoon from the back of a truck in his own backyard.

"Old Doc" died the day after Christmas, taking with him memories of 94 years that began in Chicago and ended in the little two-room house on this town's main street.

"Old Doc" came by his title legally. He was a veterinarian in Kenesaw, Nebraska, for many years before he came out to the Snake River valley. [Wendell

Chase recalled Hisom telling him that he attended Oklahoma State University. Oklahoma Agricultural and Mechanical College, as it then was called, opened in 1891, and it was 1913 before the College of Veterinary Medicine was established. Ohio State A & M, the closest to Chicago, opened in 1873, with a veterinary medicine program in 1883.] He was born in Chicago October 6, 1850, the son of a Negress mother and an Indian father.

Several of his friends—all old-timers—were there at the auction Wednesday, recounting some of the things that "Doc" used to do. One of them, Fred Perry, lived with him for a time in his cabin on the river, and he recalls that "Doc" used to sit out in the sun, and tan hides for buckskin gloves.

When he wasn't busy at that, he was placer mining, and collecting Indian relics, Perry recalled. He made quite a collection of arrowheads, and shortly before he died last year gave part of them to the Idaho State Historical Society in Boise, and the remainder to another friend, Albert Parsons, a farmer near here, to be added to the latter's collection of 4,000.

"Doc" was a bachelor. He ran away from home when a youngster and lived out a long life without ever glimpsing a member of his family again. But in his younger days he was quite a musician with the banjo—and one of the pictures up for sale Wednesday was a brown-and-white print of him in the middle of a musical circle of friends.

Mining, tanning and banjo-playing weren't the only things that evidently interested old "Doc." Shoe and boot making and sweater and sock knitting must have occupied much of his time, for shoe lasts, a wooden knitting machine and yards and yards of wool yarn were auctioned off Wednesday.

Then there was a lot of old photography equipment, including a camera patented in 1904, and an old radio battery set and telegraph key. One Melban bought a shotgun and commented as the clerk handed it to him, 'I bet this has ended the life of a lot of jackrabbits.'

People from all walks of life interested old "Doc." There was a photograph there of Ad Santel, autographed by the boxer with the date given as "April 3, 1920, Boise." Neighbors also recalled that Bayard F. Griffin, the Boise jeweler, was on his list of friends and that Cornelia Hart Farrer of Boise once made an oil sketch of him. Old "Doc" lived by the river until about a year ago when his friends persuaded him to move into town. He kept house for himself until he got too sick—and all his household belongings, including a coffee grinder, and jars for making sassafras bars—were also sold. His clothing will go to the Red Cross, neighbors said.

Last October 6 was his ninety-fourth birthday anniversary and the T. E. Halversons of Melba and their family made him a gaily decorated cake and took it over to him. "Doc" thanked them from his sickbed, but said he'd rather not hear the song "Happy Birthday," because he felt it would be his last.

Doc Hisom's house has long gone to ground, although the outline of its tumbled walls remains. The spring still wells near his doorway; wild rose pollinates his garden site. Mourning doves call from the head-high greasewood.

His memory lingers among those who knew him and loved him. Wendell Chase again: "To a young guy, we didn't pay too much attention to the things [he was saying]. It was just to the point that we worshipped him. We loved him because he was that kind of guy. You didn't look at his skin, you know, you were just so impressed with him that you just liked him, and that's the way everybody else felt around here."

As for the meaning of his life to those who simply have come to care about him as part of Idaho's folk history, historian Kathy Hodges has summed it well:

Even though he was physically separated from the town of Melba by about six miles, he played a role in its mental world. Doc Hisom was important for the farmers up on the rim. Perhaps as they milked the cows, went to church on Sunday, and carried on with all their routine chores, they liked to think of him sitting in the doorway of his cabin, watching the Snake River slide by. Maybe they just liked knowing that there was some diversity in the world, that their lives had touched the life of someone so different from themselves, and that both sides had been better for the exchange.

7 HISOM AT HIS HOUSE; MAY, 1926.
8 HISOM MINING ON SNAKE RIVER.

9 HISOM AT HIS FRONT DOOR.

10 HISOM PHOTOGRAPHED BY MRS. HALVERSON.

11 AMOS BURG WITH HISOM, WORKING A DEER HIDE; AUGUST, 1926.
12 DOC HISOM PHOTOGRAPHED BY AMOS BURG.
13 HISOM WITH HIS GOAT; SUMMER, 1926.

14 VISITORS PLAYING MUSIC INSIDE HISOM'S HOUSE. (DOC AT FAR LEFT.)
15 DOC WATCHING VISITOR PLAY SOLITAIRE; MARCH, 1920—IF THE
CALENDAR IS CURRENT.

Melba Idaho
Jan. 7th 1942.
W. G. Cowden
Caldwell Idaho
Dear Will
I Recived the Xmas letter
containg Photo and Five Bills
many Thanks I am Flu' ed In
and Snowed In. Will write as soon
as I can get out
Happy new Year to you
Come when you Can
Yours Truly
Doc Hisom
At Camp

16 A HISOM LETTER.

17 HISOM'S PARTNER, WILLIAM WHITE, AND THEIR FRIEND, WARREN MACE, FOR
WHOM THEY THEY BOTH TESTIFIED IN A DISPUTE OVER PROPERTY RIGHTS. THE
STURGEON, CAUGHT IN THE SNAKE RIVER NEAR MACE'S DESERT LAND ENTRY,
WEIGHED ABOUT 450 POUNDS. HISOM TOOK THE PHOTOGRAPH.

18 & 19 Ruins of Hisom's house on Snake River.

20 Handstitched deerskin gloves made by Hisom and given to
Wendell Chase in 1931, when he was a teenager herding cattle
down at the Cove.

DAVE LEWIS, COUGAR DAVE

WATER IN THE SUMMER AND FIRE IN THE WINTER IS ALL THE NEED I NEED.
—CORMAC MCCARTHY

Mountain lions are loners. Elusive and evanescent. They live at the top of the food chain, shy survivors, solitary and cautious. Like the mountain lion, Cougar Dave Lewis was a loner. He, however, killed lions in order to live a notch above them.

Lewis claimed to have served in the Union army at the siege of Vicksburg in 1863; to have been a volunteer at the Modoc Indian uprising in northern California in 1872; and to have been a scout with 7th Cavalry Captain Frederick Benteen (also a Vicksburg veteran) in Montana Territory in 1876.

The tapestry of known fact concerning these claims is threadbare. That Lewis was born in 1844 in Wales and brought to New Orleans at age four is beyond doubt. So are his whereabouts in summer, 1877, when he traveled from Oregon, where he had been prospecting and trapping, with the Henry Jones family to Idaho's Camas Prairie near Grangeville. (It was at least his second visit, since years later he said that he first came to Idaho in 1867 from Arkansas.) He probably hired out as a civilian packer during the Nez Perce War that year. During the Sheepeater War of 1879—a four-month running battle between U. S. troops and a handful of mountain Shoshoni—he handled the ammunition train (two mules) for Lieut. Henry Catley. Lewis was on Big Creek, a tributary of consequence cleaving the west side of the Middle Fork of the Salmon River, when the Indians, weary of the three-month pursuit, ambushed the soldiers in a defile there, killing Pvt. Harry Eagan, who was shot through the legs.

After the end of the war in October with the surrender of fifty-one Indians, Lewis settled on the Jewett Ranch at Slate Creek, near Riggins, Idaho, and from 1881 to 1894 raised horses. Then, with fifteen-year-old memories of Big Creek's sawtoothed seclusion, he rode back there and, finding Conyer Bar, a sizeable flat among endless-looking inclines, occupied, he squatted downstream at Goat Creek, at the head of Big Creek Canyon, and built himself a small, foursquare log cabin. When John Conyers and his wife abandoned their bar in 1909, Lewis moved west up-creek three miles and took possession, hosting a housewarming party there at age sixty-five.

Lewis largely supported himself on Big Creek by hunting cougars for the state bounty and whatever he could get for the pelt. He always had three or more dogs that slept beneath his bunk, and he used them to track and tree lions. There is no sport or skill to shooting a creature impotent and at bay in a tree—Lewis killed lions for the money. In 1922 the *Statesman* in Boise reported that he had collected $1,400 in bounties for the year. "Mr. Lewis brought to Boise the pelts of 14 cougars, 15 coyotes, 2 bobcats, 2 foxes, and 4 mink, all of which were caught last winter." He saved the bounty "tokens" as his currency. Cougar Dave maintained that he and his cross-terriers had killed at least 500 cougars in his hunting years. State records cannot verify his claim—he might have been stretching the blanket.

In 1907, the state game warden was authorized "to devise and put into operation such methods and means as would best secure and attain extermination of wolves, coyotes, and cougars." The department employed a number of hunters and trappers for this purpose, but Lewis was not one of them. At that time, a cougar's bounty and pelt brought about thirty-five dollars. Still, in 1928 and 1929 only fifty-two cougar were taken statewide. Not until the forests were heavily roaded did the count jump to its present annual average of 200. (In winter, lions are thinly distributed: a single male may require twenty-five square miles of snow-covered slopes to survive.) Thus his tally seems improbably high.

Perhaps there was something more than money in Cougar
Dave's quest, however. Harley Shaw, an expert on mountain lions,
softly explains, "You follow them step by step, and then you relate
to them. They're out there alone, without tools, without shelter,
without food. Down deep I have an image of myself as being totally
wild, and I know in comparison I never will be." Another writer
observes, "Above all, the lion is fundamentally the cat that walks
alone...it is the symbol of the instinctive and royal individual self."

Lewis did have other means of eking out a living: he packed for
miners and for the Forest Service during the fire season; he sometimes guided sheep hunters (in 1913 he guided W. A. Edwards to a
mountain goat whose horns proved to be a national record); he did
blacksmithing on his forge for neighbors; he looked after John
Conyers' cattle during the winter; and he received a small pension
for military service.

At times during the summer and fall, pining for a visit, he would
hike, according to a newspaper account, "to the Salmon River
between Obsidian and Challis [sixty air-miles] for a smoke and a
chat with a few genuine old sourdough bachelors who spoke his
language and lived the same sort of life. Without reservation they
acclaimed him the patriarch of the tribe and the best man among
them."

In summer, 1922, the *Idaho Statesman* carried a column on its
city news page:

PIONEER TRAPPER HERE FOR FIRST TIME IN
FORTY YEARS

'You know it has always been a mystery to me to
know how all the people you see in a big city like Boise
make a living,' said David Lewis, pioneer trapper of
Idaho who came to Boise Tuesday night after an absence
of 44 years. Mr. Lewis has not been in the capital city
since 1878.

Mr. Lewis is a little man and speaks with the slow
drawl of the mountaineer. 'You know,' he said, 'You see

the same folks on the streets every day and it just makes a fellow wonder what they all do to make a living.' He was told that the many offices of the city provided employment for the city's inhabitants to which he answered that his office for the past 50 years has been the wild forests and his living has been the wild animals inhabiting his "office."

With the exception of two years, 1908-1910, spent at White Bird, the veteran trapper has not been out of his forest home since 1900. He never saw or rode in an automobile until two years ago and Tuesday when he rode from Cascade to Boise was the third time he had been in a car.

He was brought to Boise by Leroy Lisenby, a deputy game warden, who intends to show him the city. All Mr. Lewis can remember of Boise is a building which he referred to as the "Pioneer Hotel" and a little post office.

Of Welsh parents, Lewis was not tall—five feet, seven inches, 130 pounds. His politics were decidedly Republican. Less taciturn than a lion, he was friendly without being loquacious. He had a sense of humor, and one celebrated remark deserves repeating: "Anyone who says he's been et by a wolf or a lion is a liar." He was an avid reader in winter; books filled a dark hole in his isolation. He lived alone in his log fifteen-by-fifteen foot cabin under a roof insulated with six inches of dirt. (Visitors noted that rather than buck firewood, he simply fed log lengths into the fireplace: pushwood.)

In 1923 he was visited by Forest Service surveyor Francis Woods:

> We rested at his cabin for a couple of days. The cabin, I remember, had an outside kitchen area, a living quarters built of logs, and an additional room.
>
> The second day he said he was going to take his cougar dogs and hunt for some meat for them. [Lewis fed

his dogs venison.]

We noticed that he never went into the second room of the cabin. While he was away, we looked into the room through a window. There were cobwebs and dust every-where. On the wall near the door was a large framed picture with its face to the wall. We just had to see the picture. We cut a small pole, four or five feet long, and opened the door to the room very carefully and pried the picture away from the wall, but not far enough to make it fall. It was the portrait of a beautiful young woman. For the past sixty years I have been intrigued by the picture with its face to the wall. What a mystery!

The portrait was that of a woman on a ranch in Oregon who had received and rejected the marriage proposal of a young Dave Lewis over fifty years earlier. How he packed the framed picture unscathed from Oregon to Camas Prairie and then to Big Creek, eight miles up-trail from the Middle Fork is an equal mystery.

In 1928, Lewis, with the assistance of friends, finally received a homestead certificate for his sixty-three acres. (Filing papers required his first trip to McCall, Idaho, in over twenty years.) The homestead spans the mouths of Rush, Trail, and Sheep creeks, although the last two names have been changed to Pioneer and Cliff creeks.

Five years later, by chance he met Jess Taylor, an eastern Idaho rancher and Boise building contractor, when the two of them were hunting above Big Creek. They got along like salt and pepper. Taylor was invited to stay at the cabin. In fall, 1934, he bought the homestead for $1,200.

The sale was witnessed by Walt Estep, who had mining claims on nearby Ramey Ridge and assisted Lewis in legal matters. Estep agreed to carry the deed to Cascade, Idaho, to record it. Three miles west of the ranch, he was murdered—perhaps for paying too much attention to another man's wife. The Valley County sheriff had to ride in to recover Estep's body; he found the deed and had it recorded.

In June, 1936, Lewis felt the wind of age press hard against his chest. He contracted pneumonia, yet managed to ride horseback, accompanied by two of his dogs, over twenty-five miles to Big Creek Ranger Station for help. He fell off his gray horse at the end of the airstrip, and was helped inside the warehouse, where he rested for a couple of days. It was his last trip up Big Creek. When his condition did not improve, an ambulance, with Lewis lying inside, sped for Cascade by way of Yellow Pine. En route it had a head-on collision with a truck. Lewis died the next day, age ninety-two, at the Veteran's Administration Hospital in Boise—his only visit to a hospital. He was buried in Yoncalla, Oregon, where his surviving brother lived.

In its obituary notice for Cougar Dave Lewis, the *Idaho Statesman* reported:

> Last fall he complained that the country was settling up too fast. 'A man don't have no privacy no more,' he told his nearest neighbor—five miles away. He planned to spend a few years knocking down on the Oregon cougar crop around Rogue River where a brother lives. Snow came on, however, before he got over the Edwardsburg pass and he stayed on for his final season in the valley he frequently said would find him baking sourdough on his hundredth birthday.

Thirty-two years later, the Taylors sold their ranch to the University of Idaho as a field station for wilderness research. The sale was brought about by Dr. Maurice Hornocker, who had used the site as a base for his five-year study of mountain lions while associated with the university's Cooperative Wildlife Research Unit. Over forty lions were captured and marked in the Big Creek drainage, then recaptured at intervals, and their kills examined. Hornocker's study concluded that deer and elk populations were limited by winter food, and that predation by lions was inconsequential in determining the size of the herds.

In 1972, persuaded by his evidence, the state finally stopped funding the bounty system. Instead, lions were classified as big game animals, and hunters were given a season and tags. So the animal whose slaughter had long been the mainstay of the old homestead became the means for its preservation, along with Cougar Dave's cabin. And the mountain lion—mysterious, seldom seen, surveyor of deer herds, long-tailed ghost of the Rockies—still leaves its pug tracks along the sandy banks of Big Creek.

21 LEWIS ON HIS IRON GRAY MARE, "OLD BELLE," IN 1932.
22 "UNCLE DAVE" LEWIS AT SOLDIER BAR IN 1935.
23 LEWIS WITH HIS CROSS-TERRIER HUNTING DOGS.

24 Looking east down Big Creek toward the Taylor Ranch.
25 Lewis with his dogs at his cabin.

Clydeus Dunbar, **Wheelbarrow Annie**

I DID NOT CHOOSE SOLITUDE. WHO WOULD? IT CAME ON ME LIKE A
VOCATION, DEMANDING AN EFFORT THAT MARRIED MEN CAN'T PICTURE.
—Mary Adare

A lot of good luck is undeserved but then so is a lot of bad luck. Both visited Annie Dunbar.

In November, 1931, as she trudged north into Hells Canyon—the border between Idaho and Oregon—towering cumuli billowed upward, trailing soft shadows like large unmapped lakes across the cliffed slopes high above Snake River. Dunbar struggled along the track that hugged the river, alone and unencumbered as if she had fallen off one of those clouds. The canyon walls pinched inward; heat that matched a bake oven in summer had given over to winter's cast-iron cold. Grim going.

Dunbar was, at that point in her life, what would later be called a bag lady. But this was the Great Depression and, along with millions of other societal castaways, she moved in search of a better shore.

She lugged two rag-wrapped bundles: one carried as far as her strength allowed, then dropped it and walked back for the other. In this manner, tracing each advance three times, she muled her meager possessions into the reaches of Hells Canyon.

Where she came from and why, and why she chose this remote region is now past knowing; she never volunteered, and in a still-young West where manners mattered, people did not ask. At Thorn Flat, four miles upriver from Homestead, Oregon, she did pause to request a glass of water from Mrs. Baker. After providing the drink, the postmistress offered Dunbar a wooden wheelbarrow with an iron tire in a gesture of compassion meant to ease her burdens. She accepted gratefully.

Then on she moved, like driftwood, farther and farther into the canyon. The river grapevine reported her progress: she forded Irondyke Creek, Ballard Creek, McGraw Creek. Perpendicular slopes abounded. Sounds of the Snake River chorded the gorge below.

The lava heights had begun to make shadows, and the day's cold was deepening, when Thomas Benjamin Van Cleave found Wheelbarrow Annie in the trail. She was at the end of her rope, literally: a rope ladder connecting the trail to the bench above Fisher Bar brought her to a halt, even forced a retreat. She turned back toward Leep Creek; then, with no shelter or prospects, gave out for the day.

Thomas Van Cleave knew well enough himself what it was like to be acquainted with the bad end of the stick. Born in Holland in 1862, he had immigrated to America and followed the mining boom to Golden, Colorado. There he became an estimable handdriller, swinging a four-pound singlejack with either hand.

Eventually, he and his wife Mary Anne, fourteen years younger, moved farther west to Burnt River, thirty-five miles south of Baker, Oregon, where they lived in a log cabin and supported seven children.

The Van Cleaves had borrowed against their river ranch, and during the Depression had to let it go for the loan payments. They moved to Baker and built a new house. Thomas farmed during the spring and summer, then labored as a driller at hardrock mines during the winter: at the Red Boy near Granite, west of Baker; at the Rainbow near Durkee, east of Baker; and later at the Red Ledge, near Homestead but on the Idaho side of the river. The same summer that Annie Dunbar came into the canyon, Thomas' wife died at age fifty-seven.

Van Cleave owned the bench at Leep Creek, where he hayed the fields with a pair of teams and ran a few cattle and horses. He had hammered up a two-room house, as well as a hay barn and a hen house. But he still spent most of his time in Baker. He suggested

Dunbar be the winter caretaker for his place—an updraft offer to her grounded spirits.

Over the next ten years, Annie Dunbar lived alone at Leep Creek and knitted her torn life into thin but serviceable fabric. Her loneliness remained unbending, however.

In May, 1936, Thomas Van Cleave died in Baker. Dunbar continued to look after his place, now owned by his sons. Stories began to collect around her the way weather collects over mountains. (Among the more fanciful: She came down the river in a boat, lost her oars, was rescued by Van Cleave who was dying of silicosis, nursed him unto death, then inherited his place as a gift of gratitude.) Along with the stories, she acquired the reputation—as a solitary often does—of being a person whose bolts were a bit loose.

Dunbar was about six feet tall, not a woman who would be noticed, straggly gray hair, husky but not heavy. Most of the time she wore jeans and button shoes and, in the garden, a felt hat, although Hugh Smith remembers that her hat was often fashioned from a paper bag. She made some of her own clothes out of white canvas. Despite being troubled with emphysema, she smoked roll-your-owns. (She often slept in her barn because she found it easier to breathe there.)

Although set in her ways, she was usually rather pleasant. She liked animals, including horses, which she handled competently but did not ride. On at least one occasion, however, she was upset with beaver—then protected by federal law—that felled shade trees at Leep Creek. (At river level the canyon has only splashes of trees.) Ralph Turner, who had spent a year in the canyon as a miner, recalled the incident in 1942 for the Sunday Portland *Oregonian*. The peculiar slant of this piece is better understood in context: it is excerpted from an article titled "Hells Canyon Defense Corps. Old Generalissimo Frank Lauzon [foreman of the Red Ledge mine] And His Sharp-Shooting Cronies Are Ready—Let the Japs Come!" Turner wrote:

> Itinerant trail riders and boomer miners can tell how

she takes care of herself. Last autumn, provoked by the depredation of a beaver colony which destroyed some of the trees sheltering her rude shack, the wheelbarrow woman set out for Portland to demand the Forest Service for relief.

It was cold and her clothing inadequate. For garments she built an overall cloak of gunny sacking artistically tailored with feather-stitched edges. With a lighted lantern she took the trail at midnight and in eight hours had covered the fifty miles to Richland [Oregon], where auto traffic begins. Her pipestem legs drive her at a walk much faster than a pack train.

Met on the trail at midnight she might be wearing a gunny sack cloak. But Miss C. R. Dunbar is human, understanding and wise. She will extend a helping hand and do much for a friend; but she would be terrible in her hates. She likes rattlesnakes, and woe to any man who kills a pheasant on her property.

At Leep Creek, Dunbar pursued a stoic economy. She kept a garden and canned its produce and the fruit from the orchard. She packed her root cellar with potatoes. She continued to hay the field in order to sell to Toby Warner at Big Bar any that was not required for her horses or cow. At times, she used Van Cleave's plank rowboat to cross the river to Idaho, where a gravel road led south to the Interstate Ballard Bridge and back across to Homestead and its store. (There was also a fifteen-mile trail over Horse Mountain to Bear, Idaho, a copper-mining community.)

In 1937 Amos and Bernice Robinette leased Big Bar on the Idaho side of the river across from Dunbar's place. Amos trucked mail from Robinette, eleven miles south of present Brownlee Dam, where the train still arrived from Baker, to Homestead three times a week. He often brought along groceries to Big Bar, and Dunbar would row across for them. Bernice, who spoke to her often, recalled that she said she was a nurse who had cared for a doctor's invalid wife in New York until the wife died. Thereafter the doctor sent Dunbar a monthly pension—Amos saw the envelope each month.

"She was a worker and a walker; odd but educated," Bernice recounted. "She scythed her hay by hand. She raked it with a garden rake, pulled it into shocks and turned it, then took it to the barn in a wheelbarrow. Put up thirty tons. You'd see her from morning till pitch dark."

In winter, Toby Warner would pasture his horses on her place, and she fed them from her barn and took good care of them. In the spring, he paid her cash before he swam them back across the river to Big Bar.

With a smile, Bernice recalled another of Dunbar's rituals. "She adored her dog. Bought canned dogfood for it. Nobody did that then. She wasn't hurting for money. Paid cash for everything. Amos would bring the dogfood from Robinette. Annie would row over with her dog. She'd open a can with her knife, slice off a piece for herself, then feed the rest to the dog."

The dog had belonged to Shirley Smith Edmundson, daughter of Jess and Mary Smith, who ran a lumber mill at Bear in the mountains above Big Bar. Shirley recalled as a girl in 1931 seeing Annie Dunbar arrive at her parent's house on a snowy November night. She told the Smiths her name was Barbara. She had walked nine miles from Lafferty Camp, her feet wrapped in rags. (To get there, she must have come from Weiser to Council, Idaho, on the Pacific and Idaho Northern railroad.) Dunbar refused a bed and slept on the floor, leaving the next morning for Hells Canyon. She seemed to know her destination.

Shirley remembered other details. Van Cleave kept a wagon at Big Bar and had driven it up the Kleinschmidt Grade to Bear for lumber to build his cabin, as though preparing for someone's arrival. Perhaps he knew Dunbar or was distantly related to her. He took Shirley's pesty dog at her mother's urging, and left the disappointed girl a can of pork and beans in return. (The dog became Dunbar's "Towser.")

Shirley also heard later that Dunbar often took the trail, on the Oregon side of the river—rougher than the Idaho side—to the

Homestead post office, beating the heat by going at night with a kerosene lantern. She took along a gunny sack for groceries.

Lawrence Warner, Toby's brother (both lived in Hells Canyon at the time), recalled the first time Dunbar tried rowing across the Snake:

> She made several trips to Homestead for groceries by foot on the trail. No one liked traveling that trail, and the wheelbarrow woman could see cars going up and down the road on the Idaho side. In late spring of 1934, Roxie decided to take the boat across the river and catch a ride to Homestead. She succeeded in rowing across the river; however, when she landed, she drew in the oars and walked to the front of the boat. The rockered bottom caused the boat to go backward because she had not rowed it fast onto the sandy beach. She just sat back down and let the boat drift down the river! I don't know why she didn't take up the oars and try again.
>
> My brother Toby was riding for cattle on the upper end of Big Bar, and he had watched her row across the river and land unsuccessfully. He kicked his horse into gear and rode as near as he could get to the river, jumped off his horse at the road, crawled through the fence, crossed the road, crawled through another fence, ran a hundred yards across some level, open ground, and down a steep bank for fifty yards to the river's edge, where he saw the boat and Roxie. The boat was in the rapids and moving right along. Toby saw his timing was just right, and by wading into the river chest-deep, he was able to grab the boat as it drifted by and pull himself in and row to shore. Roxie said, "I knew God had heard my call for help when I saw you coming down that bank."
>
> The two of them got the boat towed back up the river to where it could be rowed upstream. Toby started rowing back upriver and Roxie sat on one side of the back seat. Toby asked her to sit in the middle of the seat so the

boat would level out and make it easier to row. Roxie
said, "Oh, my 115 pounds surely wouldn't make any
difference!" So Toby explained about the boat and how
to beach it so the boat would stay put on the sand.

(Lawrence also remembered that Old Man McIntyre made
Dunbar a two-wheeled cart out of old buggy wheels but did not
believe she ever used it because he saw it abandoned on the upper
end of the bar for a couple of years.)

In May, 1939, Edith Clegg from Vancouver, British Columbia,
came up the Snake River on her way across the continent by water
(another story altogether). She traveled with two wooden boats
powered by ten horsepower outboards, and was accompanied by
four boatmen. Her diary, and that of head guide Buzz Holmstrom,
carry descriptions of an encounter with Annie Dunbar.
Buzz Holmstrom, May 31:

> Clarence [Bean] and I walk up two miles and visit
> Roxalure Dunbar commonly known as Wheelbarrow
> Annie—supposed to be crazy—about sixty years old—
> dirtiest person I ever saw—hates most everyone—uses
> wheelbarrow to haul hay. Dog named Towser "Towsy"
> who has tapeworm and she has fed dog eight pounds of
> lard to cure it. Gets mixed up—referring to dog as he and
> worm as she. Worm moves around—once got twenty-
> two inches out of dog but can't get head. Chicken pet
> Black Boy got sheep dip and got sick. Finally ended by
> freezing to death in hog pen.

Edith Clegg was considerably more sympathetic:

> Buzz and Clarence went up to see Wheelbarrow
> Annie, a local celebrity—who lives about a mile up
> stream. They said she was incredibly dirty, but not crazy
> as the locals say. Devoted to animals. Looks about

seventy. They said she talked well, like a person with a good education and a good background. But farouche [withdrawn temperament coupled with cranky, sullen charm].There must be some story behind her. She lives absolutely alone in the poorest way, dresses like a tramp (or very much in my own style of the moment) but seems to have money to send away for things. She doesn't like her neighbors up the creek (apparently she doesn't like anybody, and I gather has a persecution complex about the post-master at Homestead). These neighbors have made a bridge across the creek. But when Annie goes to Homestead, she carries her big boots as far as the creek so as to be able to ford it instead of having to be beholden to the people she dislikes by using their bridge. It doesn't sound quite sane. Annie's real name, she says, is "Rosalure," and she doesn't like being called "Annie."

June 1st: When we passed "Rosalure's" place this morning, she was down at the river to wave to Buzz and Clarence. She wears a white cloth folded rather like a nun's coif to keep the sun off instead of a hat. I thought she looked rather pathetic and would have liked to have stopped and talked.

In early winter 1941, Dunbar's age and health required a move to Baker. Richard Neuberger, a popular Oregon senator, recounted the move:

> Some of Mr. Van Cleave's people came in from Baker and moved all her belongings there to care for her. They had to go down by car on the Idaho side of the river, as her cabin was in Oregon, and boat across the Snake River.
>
> Several men helped Mr. [Newton] Van Cleave of Baker, using two boats to cross the river: Henry Titus, George Degit, and Amos Robinette of Homestead.

They made several trips across the river, and on one of the boat loads she had a big box of old shoes, and when loading up the boat, Van Cleave said dump those old shoes in the middle of the river if you get a chance. But Miss Dunbar watched with an eagle's eye while they rowed across, so they didn't have a chance to dump the box.

After crossing and loading things in the car, the wheelbarrow woman asked the fellows from Homestead how much she owed them for helping her move. They told her, and she went over to this old box of shoes and dug down in the box and pulled out a roll of bills that would choke a cow. All one hundred dollar bills. What if they had thrown them in the river? Motto: Don't throw anything away if it belongs to old folks.

In Baker, Dunbar lived in a crude little cabin owned by Elizabeth Van Cleave (daughter of Thomas), whose house was in front of the cabin. The Van Cleaves looked after her.

In January, 1945, after several weeks of illness, Annie Dunbar died at the home of Ted Morin on Balm Avenue. Local doctor Thomas Higgins found that malnutrition had caused her death. The funeral service was held in the Morin home.

Her effects revealed that Roxanne Dunbar's first name was Clydeus; her birthplace and her past, however, were secrets she took to her grave.

Twenty-three years later, the diversion tunnel at Hells Canyon Dam was plugged, and the flat at Leep Creek gradually submerged beneath 300 feet of water. Now shadows of powerboats skate over Annie's old anchorhold; fish glide through her garden. But at campgrounds and campfires along the reservoir her story still surfaces with questions cleaving: who was she? where did she come from? why Hells Canyon? And all the straightforward answers recline where they settled in 1945—in an unmarked grave at Mount Hope Cemetery in Baker.

26 THOMAS VAN CLEAVE AT LEEP CREEK IN 1930.
27 TED MORIN AND EMMA MARIE, THE OLDEST VAN CLEAVE DAUGHTER, WITH
DUNBAR'S BOAT AT LEEP CREEK.

28 THE VAN CLEAVE-DUNBAR FARM AT LEEP CREEK BEFORE HELLS CANYON
DAM WAS BUILT.
29 THE VAN CLEAVE-DUNBAR SITE TODAY.

30 WHEELBARROW SIMILAR TO ANNIE'S.

EARL PARROTT, HERMIT OF IMPASSABLE CANYON

LIVING IN TOWN
ONE MUST HAVE MONEY
EVEN TO MELT THE SNOW DOWN.—ISSA

Earl Parrott was the hermit of the Middle Fork of the Salmon River, and his hermitage was a log dugout just above the rim of Impassable Canyon. Of all recluses in Idaho, his story seems to contain the most imaginative appeal and much of that appeal must lie in the beauty of the place in which he chose to hide—a hideout so remote even a guardian angel could hardly find him.

As with most hermits, the details of his life are elusive, but this much is now clear. Parrott's parents, Joseph and Sarah (nee Sacareeton) married in 1850 and immigrated from Yorkshire, England, to Canada, where three of their children were born between 1851 and 1854. The family must have returned to England, because four children were born there (in Hull) between 1855 and 1862. In 1866 the Parrotts came to America. According to the census of 1880, they resided in Wilsburg (now Blanchard), Iowa, just north of the Missouri border, where five more of their children were born. The town of 150 persons had been platted a year earlier and was located on the Omaha and St. Louis Railroad (later Wabash).

Joseph Parrott, educated in England and Germany, was the town's first postmaster and druggist. His wife tended shop as well. In 1880 he was fifty-two, she was forty-nine. Altogether, the couple had twelve children: eight boys and four girls, ranging from five to twenty-nine years. (Two infants died.) Earl was the seventh sibling.

Blanchard was known for its excellent school, and Earl, who was then nine years old, attended. When old enough, he assisted at his father's store. In 1888, at age sixty, Joseph sold the drugstore and moved the family to Orange Park, Florida.

Earl, now nineteen, and his brother Allen, younger by two years, engaged in truck farming with fruits and vegetables. During their spare time, they taught themselves telegraphy with a wire run from the house to a shed.

Although the first telephone exchange had opened ten years earlier, the telegraph had been around for fifty years, and Western Union was the first monopoly and largest corporation in the country. Its most valuable and inseparable partner was the railroads, which had agreed to lay telegraph lines along their right-of-way and provide office space in depots for telegraphers employed by the railroads and Western Union. In return, Western Union transmitted messages regarding the railroad business without charge and gave their messages priority. This marriage made the railroads a safe and efficient transportation network.

After two years' practice with a telegraph key, Earl obtained employment with the Jacksonville, Tampa, and Key West Railroad, and Allen joined him a few months later. According to Allen, Earl left the railroad business in 1898 because he became color blind (being able to discern the color of railroad signals was a necessity for such telegraphers).

The rest of Earl's story—pieced from letters, diaries, newspapers, and interviews—becomes less certain. Earl alleged that the telegraph carried early word of the Yukon Gold Rush (1897-1898), and he went north to seek his fortune. Parrott's name is listed in the Klondike registry kept at the border near Skagway by the Royal Canadian Mounted Police.

His brother said he thought Earl went directly to Idaho in as much as he heard from him in 1898 by letter addressed from Dixie, Idaho (just north of the Salmon River), and from Warren, Idaho (just south of the Salmon), a short while later.

Earl did go to the Yukon, but it was a brief stint. He was seen in Lewiston, Idaho, about 1900, and he may have gone to Warren at the invitation of saloonkeeper Charlie Bemis. In November, 1905, Grant Humes' diary states several times that Parrott, while engaged in trapping, was sleeping nights on the floor at Mitt Haynie's cabin at Rattlesnake Creek on the Salmon River. Parrott filed on a homestead (later known as the Rushton place) in 1908 on Rock Creek, a tributary of the South Fork of the Salmon, but did not patent it. He had a cabin and barn there. One clue suggests that around 1910 Parrott may have gone home to Florida for a visit.

Following the sale of his Rock Creek acres to Earl Rushton, Parrott spent the winter of 1916 at the mouth of Elk Creek on the South Fork of the Salmon with Brad Carrey, uncle of Johnny Carrey of Riggins, Idaho. Although Johnny remembers that Parrott was intelligent and industrious, he was also aloof, stubborn, and lacking in humor. Nor was he fond of children. He lived in a sturdy tent with his possessions kept in wooden boxes, and his chief occupations during those months were tanning hides and panning gold. He left with the melting snow.

Some evidence implies that Earl Parrott located his roost above the rim of the Middle Fork in the early 1900s, perhaps at the time of the Thunder Mountain boom, and began preparations for full-time residency. Certainly he was established there by 1917, living like a hawk with wind under its wings. At that time he had a little brown riding mare, half a dozen burros, and a dog. Perhaps he liked animals. In any event, for the next twenty-five years Earl Parrott became about as self-sufficient and self-reliant as it is possible for a person to be.

In early April, 1919, he visited the town of Salmon in the company of August Motzell and Jess Root. Root had a homestead at the head of Whimstick Creek in Chamberlain Basin (about seventeen air miles west of Parrott's place), and needing witnesses for the final proof on his ranch, brought the two men along to testify to U. S. Commissioner Merritt. They had come four days upriver on foot to Shoup, where they caught an automobile ride to Salmon. The town newspaper took note:

They are sturdy men, just as would be looked for in

the last frontier of the wilderness where they have set up homes. They told *The Recorder* that most settlers like themselves in that country live lonely lives of bachelors, always in hopes, however, that they may be able a little later along to induce life-partners to come and make real homes...After arriving here they ascertained that Capt. Harry Guleke would have a transport down the river [Salmon] early this week, so they waited for passage that way.

Earl does not appear again until summer, 1923, when Francis Woods was working as a member of a Forest Service survey crew along the Middle Fork. As the three-man mapping party hardscrabbled through the country, locating the mouths of tributaries entering the Middle Fork, they had an encounter of interest:

> One day we spotted a small cabin and noticed smoke coming from the chimney. We decided to stop and have lunch with the occupant. He was busy at a stove cooking some kind of berries. The mixture had not come to a boil. Above the stove, lying on a shelf, was a big cat. When he saw us he made a pass at the cat, knocking it into the fruit. Reaching into the pot, he pulled the cat out and ran his hand over it, draining the berries back into the pot. He then threw the cat out the door. Needless to say, we did not stay for lunch.

Another chance meeting was recorded April 11, 1928, by Jim Gipson, who was bivouacked at Nolan Creek (five miles up the Middle Fork from its confluence with the Main Salmon) with Henry Weidner, the two of them having left a scow at the mouth of the Middle Fork. It was a cold and windy day, blowing snow before breakfast was over, and Gipson decided to stay in camp. A stranger, who must have spotted his smoke, joined him.

An old prospector by the name of Parrott, who makes

his headquarters on the Middle Fork a couple of miles above where we are camped, came down and spent the day with us, an odd character of about 65 who hates to leave his hills. Like most of the Salmon River settlers he is a southerner. His trip to Mountain Home [Idaho] after wild burros. Dates everything by the Thunder Mountain Boom. Another nick in his gun when he gets hurt or sick. Wes [Weidner] and I try our hands at panning gold, but find it too cold and tiresome. I talked with him by the fire and rather sympathize with his philosophy of life. He says coyotes increasing. Believes my project for stocking the Salmon River country with buffaloes is a good one and thinks well of the idea of heavily salting the licks. No coyotes in the hills when he came here 35 years ago.

Jack Killam, a lawyer, who for reason of his health moved to the Salmon River in the 1930s, built a cabin at Bear Bar, below Corn Creek, on Parrott's side of the river. According to his son Alvin Killam, Jack had numerous visits from the hermit; the two of them would sit up most of the night talking.

It was the boating parties that came down the Middle Fork in the 1930-1940 period, however, that revealed most of what is known about Parrott's lifeway.

In mid-July, 1936, the Hatch-Swain-Frazier expedition was floating past Nugget Creek when someone spotted a small log structure and what appeared to be bear tracks on the beach. They rowed ashore and were incredulous at finding a tiny shed with a note on the door:

> Dear Oliver, the cork came out of that bottle of Poison and alot of it spilled in here all over this stuff. I don't know if it would be safe to use it, but be careful. Better not monkey with it. Come on up. Parrott. You remember what the druggist said, a very little of it would kill a horse. Be careful how you stir things up, you can

breath enough to kill you.

Inside the small, crude shed the men saw cornmeal, a frying pan and plate, a gold pan and blanket. Finding a trace of trail leading to a ladder which stood against a rock wall, they climbed the rungs and began the two-mile, 1,000-foot ascent to the canyon rim. Log ladders along the way helped them up the steep cliffs.

The men came up into a hanging valley that fostered a stream, and followed the trail with rising curiosity and taut expectancy. Coming around a turn, they suddenly saw a small cabin and a garden that looked like an exhibit at a state fair. No one in view. On approaching closer, they found the cabin was actually a partial dugout, rumped into the bank. Smoke feathered from the chimney, and another note was tacked over the door:

> Some of everything in this garden is poison. Nothing in the house is poison. Help yourself.

Swain called several times but received no answer. The men sat down outside the cabin to await the owner's return. One of the party went over to pull a carrot from the garden and was startled by a voice from the sky: "What do you men want down there?" Peering from a crow's nest of poles and goat skins in the fork of a ponderosa pine was the hermit. Persuaded that they meant him no harm, he came down with the agility of a marten.

The parties surveyed each other until Swain broke the silence by saying, "Dad, you sure have a beautiful place here." "I like it," Parrott replied. Everyone relaxed as the hermit moved his hand from the butt of a thumb-buster Colt .45 slung under his arm.

The boatmen explained how they had rowed from Bear Valley and recounted their adventures. Preternaturally shy, Parrott learned more about them than they discovered about him.

Parrott was about five feet, four inches, muscular, blue-eyed, and clean shaven. He wore an old buckskin visor, buckskin shirt, tattered denim trousers with buckskin suspenders, and shoes with tire-tread soles and buckskin tops.

Most gardening is solitary, requiring attention and perception. All of the men agreed that Parrott's garden was the most extraordinary they had ever seen. Obviously, he benefited from his experience with truck gardening as a youth. He irrigated from the creek, fenced with poles to keep out the deer, and raised corn, beans, potatoes, sweet potatoes, cabbage, beets, carrots, peppers, squash, cucumbers, raspberries, strawberries, watermelons, peaches, and apricots. He selected the best from each crop for next year's seeds, and dried and stored all the produce, even the berries. He kept his potatoes in a small root cellar. His major storage containers for corn and beans were large yellow pine logs, which he split and hollowed. He would put one half on top of the other horizontal half, having smoothed the faces where they met so perfectly that not even an ant could get between them. For meat, he would kill a deer with his .30-30 Winchester from his platform in the trees.

Elaborating, Parrott said that the only supplies he needed were salt, matches, tea, and bullets, and when the unshruggable need arrived, they were obtained by a seventy-mile trip to Shoup once a year. (In earlier times, before the Salmon River road, he hiked to Warren.) Parrott would go down canyon to the mouth of the Middle Fork, making the trip in two days. Later he used the Stoddard Creek trail to the pack bridge across the Salmon River.

For these necessities, he traded the gold dust he panned. In 1936 Doc Frazier estimated 100 cubic yards of placer tailings had been worked on the Nugget Creek beach. He said Parrott "worked his placer every day in the summer, including Sundays," but such seems highly unlikely, given the demands for growing and storing food. "The most he ever got out of one pan of gravel was $97. At first he thought we were there to rob him of his gold, but reasoned we would not come in a bunch and in daylight." He revealed little else about his mining, as though to say more would be like drawing a map to his diggings.

His cabin, though small, with a three-by-four-foot bed, was "neat and clean, he swept the dirt floor with pine boughs, his bed was out of poles covered by a bear skin, his cover was a mountain sheep and a great white goat's skin, his pillow was a mountain goat kid's hide." The door hinges were wooden, set in knot holes.

The only tools observed on the place were an axe and a cross-cut saw. (In 1946 Hack Miller found a brace and bit.) Parrott would cut enough wood from dead pines to last all winter. He said he did not move around much once the weather turned icy for fear of getting hurt; at such times he would turn dormant— sleep almost twenty hours a day. They pictured him: casehardened by cold, clamped in silence, pupating toward spring.

Although he had never heard a radio, Parrott knew the day of the month. Frazier again: "I had seen no calendar and asked him how he kept the day and the month. 'What else have I got to do?' was the terse response. He had a sundial out in the yard that told him the time and the equinoxes." (No one else reported a sundial. Hack Miller on a later trip said he saw a pocket watch in good repair in a tobacco can and a current almanac on a shelf.)

When a camera was explained to Parrott, he consented to have his picture taken, though he called it "a peck of foolishness."

The rivermen learned that the following day was Parrott's birthday, so they invited him to join them for dinner at the boats. To their amazement, he ran down the ladders face-out, beating them to the boats by twenty minutes.

Parrott obviously enjoyed their food. "Frank opened a Hormel canned ham, and did his eyes bug out, again the biscuits, canned butter and canned milk, canned pears for dessert." They gave him what items they could spare: cigars, some salt, surplus containers, a spade for his garden. As they said their goodbyes, Parrott told the men that they were his first visitors in thirty-seven years (he'd forgotten the surveyors). His hermetically sealed world had been perforated; his unbreathed air breathed by others.

After their completion of the 1936 trip, Dr. Frazier, with Mack Corbett, published an article in *Field and Stream* magazine about their meeting with the "Hermit of Impassable Canyon." Earl Parrott's brother Allen, now in eastern Washington, read of the encounter in the July 24 edition of the Portland *Oregonian,* and promptly wrote Frazier and got the name of a packer who could take him to see his brother—he had not heard from Earl for twenty-four years.

In August, 1936, Ray Mahoney packed Allen to the Stoddard Creek lookout and then went down to inform Earl, who told the packer to have Allen come down to his place if he wanted to visit; he was not going up to the lookout.

In September, from Starbuck, Washington, Allen Parrott wrote of his encounter to his sister-in-law Julia in Barre, Vermont.

> Dear Sister,
> I do not remember whether I owe you a letter or not, it has been so long since I heard or wrote. [I've] got about as bad as Earl. By the way, I have located Earl and was over and saw him last month. I was laying off when I saw a piece in a Portland, Oregon, paper wrote by a man that had gone down the Middle Fork of the Salmon River in Idaho in a boat. It is a very hard river to go down, and impossible to go upstream. On account of the current and rapids it is called the River of No Return. I am going to send you a couple of newspaper clippings which I have.
> Now for my trip. I was going by train, then decided it would cost me more on account the railroad does not run close to where he is located, so drove auto. It was about a 600 mile drive the way I had to go. At first I expected to have to pack back to where he was, some 70 miles. But found later I could drive within about 15 or 17 miles of him. This proved to be far enough for me, as the country is very rough and all mountains, climbing as high as seven and eight thousand feet. I was not accustomed to that kind of traveling, it was hard. I was going to hire a man with horses to go with me, but I decided that would be worse than walking, as I had not rode a horse for years, so I hired a man to go as guide and carry most of our stuff that we had to have, for it was a two-day trip going. On the way I got awfully tired the first day, but we found him. He is well, seems happy and says he always feels well.
> He has a fine garden. Raises most all the stuff he eats,

as it is too far to pack it in. Plenty of potatoes, strawberries, corn, wheat, squash, pumpkins, and in fact everything that grows.

As a rule, he told me, he had not been coming out but once a year, and a few years ago wouldn't come out only once every two or three years. (He) gets plenty of game, deer, mountain sheep, goats, fish, birds, etc.

You know it has been over 38 years since I saw him, and he said he would have known me and I would have known him, but I must say that I think he is somewhat of a wild man, or might say good old frontier days folk, and not to be wondered at when you think he has lived back there all this time by himself. Probably not seen another person once in six months or a year.

Had a nice visit, hated to leave him in there alone. Tried to persuade him to come out with me even for a short time, but no use, he just would not hear of it. He did say that he might come and see me this winter or next spring. Still I doubt it if he does. And if he is really contented and happy, I don't want to make him otherwise, but as I told him, he is getting too old to stay in such a place alone, so far from anyone to help him in case he needed it.

He raises his garden and washes gold. It is placer mining on those rivers. In the winter when it is froze up, he traps some bear etc. He did not say it to me, nor could I seem to find out whether he had accumulated anything much or not. Sometimes he said he would make pretty good and then again not much. Said he lost five hundred dollars in bank at Salmon, Idaho, several years ago. [Salmon's Pioneer Bank and Trust collapsed in May 1929; Citizen National Bank in May 1932.] He's got no use for banks now, so I don't know what he does with his savings or if he has any much. Some think he has, others think not. He don't talk much, but as I told him he could come and live with me while I had.

Well, Julia, it is quite a long story. You might know he was awful surprised to see me, going in on him and he not expecting me for 23 years. We neither one could hardly realize it until it was all over.

He was 67 last July 16. If you could, I wish you might send Ruth this clipping, so she could see. I tried to get more but newspaper seemed to have no extras. I must try to write Ruth too.

Now Earl's nearest post office is Shoup, Idaho. He does not come out often. I told him to write me, and he said he would if he thought of it and told me he didn't think it any use me writing because he probably [would] not get it. So he has got out of the way of writing and maybe don't care if he hears. Living too much alone so long has made him that way. All them old timers are the same. Seem to want to be left alone. Don't want roads built in to them. I am going to write to him and try to get some of my letters to him. I got a little acquainted in that little town of Shoup and probably can get word to him through some of them. Of course he had not heard of Fred's death [older brother] nor Mary's [oldest sister] nor Tom's [older brother]. He asked me about all the folks and we talked about many old times things, but our visit was comparative short. And [it] had been so long since seeing each other that it takes time to get acquainted again, but if I could get him to come out he might get over that kind of lonely life.

You know his accommodations are very poor. You and I would not like it. He does not have any stove, his cooking is all done on open fire, he has a fireplace built with rocks and mud, no bed spring, and you know to us it would be awful inconvenient.

I want to try and go back and see him next summer if I can do it some way. Especially if he will not come to see me.

Well, Julia, guess I have told you about all. We have

had a very hot summer. Will soon have fall now. Then it
will rain. I was off duty a month and that means pay stops
when we are off. I had a photographic picture taken of
that sheet which has our births on it. So I think I am
through with it and will return.

The railroad retirement plan act is still tied up in court
as I guess you know. May be nothing come of it anyway.
I hope this finds you all well. I will close.

Bro Allen B. Parrott

You will see by one of these clippings how I first heard
of Earl. Then I wrote this doctor Frazer and got more
information. The pictures of Earl are pretty good of him.
You will see in one with hat off hair makes him look a
little wild like.

Three months later, Allen Parrott wrote to Ruth.

Dear Sister Ruth,

Long time since I wrote you. I managed to write Julia
some time ago and sent her some newspaper clippings
about Earl and asked her to try and get word to you about
him.

I layed off last July, and when I heard about a man by
the name of Earl K. Parrott being back in the hills or
rather mountains in Idaho, I started out to find out if it
was my brother. I drove and it was some 900 miles as far
as I could go with a car. I could not get very near him with
a train and was afraid it would be expensive and
troublesome getting from the end of the railroad to where
I could drive. That was why I took a car from home.

Well, I had some trip both in the car and on the trail.
After I got to the end of the wagon road it is a very rough
mountainous country. Just climbing up mountains was
hard on me, for I was not used to it. About 15 or 17 miles,
not so far on level roads but climb up and down is worse.

But I found him and had a nice visit. Tried hard to get

him to come out with me but nothing doing. He did say finally that he might be out this winter or next spring to see me, but do you know I have my doubts if Earl ever will come out. I am afraid he has been back in there so long all alone that he will never care to come out. He is mentally and physically all right. Of course he has changed but looks much like he always did. He asked about you and in fact about all the folks. Carry, Rex, Lettie, Ella, etc.

I had not heard from him in 23 or 24 years, and had not seen him for over 38 years. That's a long time. Of course he had not heard of any of the family for over 23 years. He said after father died he quit writing. Being alone so much, [he] just got out of the way. Strange one would bury themselves like that.

I have written him since I came out and asked him to answer but have heard nothing yet. He does not come out to the post office often. Maybe once a year, unless there is something he must have, although the wagon roads are being built toward him. Slowly a little each year. They are about as close now as they will be for years to come.

He has a fine garden, raises about everything he eats except game. Plenty of game. Goats, sheep, deer, bear, lots of fish. He washes out gold, but how much I could not find out. He did say that he had washed out as much as $30 in one day, but those days were maybe far between.

I tried every way to get him out that I could think of then. I only told him if he was happy I guess that was the place to stay. He is pretty much set in his ways. Been his own boss for so long one gets that way. I may go back to see him again next summer and stay longer with him anyway. If I get any encouragement from him.

Well, Ruth, how are you Republicans back there? Vermont and Maine seem to be about the only Republicans left, but I don't think the Democrats are going to get us very far. I still stick with Socialism and think if we ever get anywhere they will all have to come to it.

Well, I am still with the railroad, but if retirement act goes through I guess I will be thrown out as I am now 65—but I do not look for it to pass the 9 Gods on the bench.

We are having quite cold weather. About 10-above is the coldest. Awfully dry. Not much rain. Farmers cannot seed on account of it. Be short crop if we do not get rain soon.

Well, guess I have told you all. Probably enough for this time, so will close hoping you are all well.

Your Bro. Allen

Earl's closest post office is Shoup, Idaho. If you should write him, send it in care of Emmet Reese, Shoup, Idaho.

Because of this unwanted publicity, Parrott was most unhappy with Dr. Frazier.

Unaware of the hermit's acquired animosity, Frazier and Swain stopped to visit him when next they ran the Middle Fork, in early July, 1939. Doc Frazier recalled the meeting this way:

As we rounded the bend above his diggings, we saw the old man bent over his gold pan, he did not hear us because of the roar of the rapids until the prow of our boats landed at his feet. In an instant he had whipped out his gun and had us covered. Recognizing who we were he started to lower his gun. His expression changed, and he said I have a notion not to let you come ashore. On being asked why, he said you told that brother of mine where I was and I had to lie to him about coming out last winter. Besides that he brought two of those forest fellers in with him. We told him we had brought him some salt and other supplies. Let me see the salt was his immediate reply. We undid the waterproof hatch on the boat and set out a 5 gallon keg of salt. When he saw it he gathered both hands full of 'sal' [salt], and as he let it trickle back into the keg through his fingers, he said, now I will not have to go back to that old store for years. As he repeated handling the salt, tears came to his eyes and he said he was sorry about the way he had greeted us. Wait here and I will go up and get you some garden stuff. We camped with the old gentleman that night. Sitting on a rock after supper I pecked [Morse code] his name on a rock with my geologist hammer, two or three times before I attracted his attention. I'll be dammed, I have not heard that in 40 years. How did you know I knew the code? Your brother told me. That was enough to set him off. I'll have to leave this place for it will be overrun now.

Since Hack Miller recalls a stiff, cold rain sliding down the canyon, and consequently states that the group hiked up to Parrott's cabin and met him there, Frazier must have resorted to literary license.

Charles Kelly's diary from the same trip has additional useful insights:

July 5—Parrott's cabin on the river is very small but weather tight. Looks like a boar's nest. He lives above during the growing season to look after his garden. In the fall he works his placer here or above about a mile (up river), and climbs the cliff twice a week to see that everything is all right above. We found his trail overgrown and dim. Climbed the face of the cliff about 1500 or 2000 feet, very rocky and narrow, with ladders in several places. His garden is very fine. All kinds of vegetables. Has had no new seed since 1900. Potatoes that weigh more than 1 lb. each. Strawberries growing wild. Wild roses all around his garden. No domestic flowers. Cabin is small, built half in the hillside, but is tight. Makes his own shakes. Two very small windows, no glass. Fireplace and bunk, a few dishes and tools. Bunk is about 4 feet square. No supplies in cabin except a few potatoes. Soap covered with dust. [Since Parrott was clean-shaven, if he did not use soap, one wonders how he shaved.] Everything made of split logs. No sawed lumber. Few nails. Makes his own shoes and buckskin clothes for winter. Enjoys tobacco but don't drink. Goes out once a year. Packs in about 30 lbs. of stuff—overalls, tobacco, ammunition, salt, etc. Lives on 8 cents a day outside expenses. Pans enough gold to buy necessities, but no more. Said if he knew we were coming he would have hidden out. Don't like company. Says he used to go two years without seeing anyone, but now hunters disturb him every few months. Deer eat lettuce out of his garden sometimes, but otherwise don't bother. Game not so plentiful now. He eats meat only in winter. Don't like dried meat. Kills a bear in the fall for its grease. Has to go five miles now to hunt deer in the fall. There is a new forest guard station [Stoddard Lookout, 1933] 5 miles from him. Country is getting too crowded. Used to go 70 miles for supplies. Now goes 10 miles to CCC camp [on the Salmon River] and bums a ride to town. Gets mail at Shoup, Idaho if and when. Has not seen a movie in 15 years. Dying calf expressions of actors make him sick. Don't like radio. Would rather hear the coyotes howl. Only question he asked us was 'Who is going to run for president?' [Parrott inveighed against Roosevelt because he felt the CCC was going to ruin the river and fishing; he said he was going out to vote for Landon.] No taxes to pay. Gov't makes him sell gold dust through buyers, they take $3 an oz. He gets only $17 to $19 for his gold. Once made 2 oz. a day for 7 months on the Salmon River. Cunningham says he was once disappointed in love. Also lost his money in a bank failure. That's why he's a hermit. [Parrott told one informant that he put his money in the Weiser, Idaho, bank and it went broke. He would have taken his money via Warren, and the distance would have given him more privacy than the Salmon bank. Both banks in Weiser failed in 1924.] Drinks tea but no coffee. Dries all his vegetables. Raises corn every 3 years. Eats only corn bread. Has no use for women. Won't live with his brother because he would be bossed by a woman. Uses no candles or artificial light. Reads little. Sleeps outside between two big trees in summer. Carries .45 Colt with him everywhere, to kill himself in case he falls and gets broken leg.

July 6—Parrott had supper with us last night, then climbed back up to his cabin. Came down again just as we finished breakfast. Seemed more friendly. Doc gave him a keg of salt, and some gallon tin cans with lids. I gave him a box of cigars. Seemed to enjoy them. Posed for pictures. Panned some gold for us... [He] came down to Butts Bar [Salmon River, below the confluence] and met John Cunningham [sweepboat pilot].

And Willis Johnson notes a few details more:

...It is almost unbelievable how he exists. About all he has to buy is 30 lbs. of salt, tea, and tobacco. He uses one box of matches a year and makes his own shoes; wears no socks or underwear and doesn't own a coat. Just a dirty pair of overalls and shirt and his shoes which are made of buckskin and old tires, which he never takes off. His garden is very neat and well-kept, his potatoes are the most perfect ones I have ever seen...he cooks in an open fireplace.

In addition to the salt, the men gave him fishing line, hooks, and Corona cigars.

Parrott must have sensed that his way of life was fast becoming an anachronism. The following summer his domain was invaded yet again, and visitor hours were becoming ever less tolerable. In August the Zee Grant party with three foldboats was boating through Impassable Canyon at 10:00 p.m., having grievously miscalculated the length of the canyon. In his article about the trip, Zee recounted the unexpected meeting:

>...Just as we were positive that at last our objective was at hand, a campfire gleamed on the east bank [Parrott Placer camp], so we quickly beached our boats and hailed it. But no answer came in reply. Aller left his boat and walked up to the fire. At first he could not find its maker, but shortly he sighted an old man quivering behind a rock. The man did not speak until Aller strode over and touched him. "Hello! Hello! Hello! Who are you?" The poor man surely thought Aller was a river ghost. In ten years, he might have seen other men four or five times in the Impassable Canyon. Now, here was someone coming up out of the river itself, in the middle of the night. During this brief conversation the old man never stopped shaking. He told Rodney of five rattlesnakes he kept there, which, we later learned, was a story he had told before to others that he might be rid of them. Although it was difficult to get any information from the terrified old man, we did learn that the junction with the Salmon was still six to eight miles away [actually ten], and so we decided to camp at the next available spot. We discovered later that the man to whom we had given the scare of his life was Earl K. Parrott, famous hermit of the Middle Fork, who has lived there for years, eking out a meager existence by placer mining.

As surely as a placer streak, the old hermit's stay on the Middle Fork was playing out, along with his solitude.

In March, 1942, Parrott appeared at a mountain sheep study-camp on Reese Creek on the Middle Fork. He was in pain from what was to be diagnosed as an enlarged prostate gland. One of the men rode to Stoddard Creek lookout and telephoned Shoup, Idaho, upriver on the Main Salmon, for a packer. Earl Poynor, who was packing for the crew, took a packstring to the Reese Creek cabin on the Stoddard Trail. Parrott was waiting there with a small tote bag. As the packer guided him out, Parrott confided that while some people thought he was rich, he had never accumulated more than $600 in gold dust.

The men followed the Stoddard trail down to the Stoddard pack bridge and crossed the Salmon River below the confluence with the Middle Fork. The doctor from the CCC camp at Ebenezer Bar (upriver) met them at the mouth of the Middle Fork, and Parrott was taken by car to Salmon.

It is not clear whether Parrott had surgery, but he lived with sweepboat pilot Cap Guleke for a period until alcohol and arguments required other arrangements. Parrott went downriver to Shoup, where Mr. and Mrs. Emmett Reese provided a comfortable home for him in a little cabin at their ranch on Pine Creek. There he remained until his health failed and he had to be nearer a doctor. He was transported back to Salmon and cared for by the Department of Public Assistance. Dr. O. T. Stratton of Salmon noted that Parrott had, since 1942, "lost compensation." Then he was moved to Lewiston, Idaho, in the hope its lower elevation would prove beneficial.

Before long he was back in Salmon; the Salmon *Recorder*, February 24, 1943, reported:

> A sanity hearing was conducted before Prosecuting Attorney Fred Snook in probate court Monday morning. C. W. Lyons was appointed to represent Earl Parrott, and Dr. Owen Stratton and Dr. John Mulder were the examining physicians. They pronounced the defendant sane.
>
> The case was the result of an episode that disturbed Mr. Parrott's neighborhood one day last week. He claimed that dogs were running across his porch and were bothering him at night, so he fired at them with a rifle. The bullet glanced and went through Captain Harry Guleke's house, allegedly narrowly missing Mr. Guleke. The sheriff was called and a complaint resulted.

Mercifully, no trial was reported. Later in the year, Parrott had a cerebral hemorrhage, followed by hemiplegia (paralysis on one side of the body). In September, 1944, he suffered another stroke. Thereafter he was unable to walk or talk, but he was well cared for at the Silbaugh nursing home until his death on August 15, 1945. On the certificate of death, Dr. Stratton listed the cause as "Occlusion of coronary artery. Had lesion of aortic valves." Parrott had been at the Silbaugh home 300 days. He was seventy-six years old.

Funeral services were held at the Doebler chapel on the afternoon of August 20, and then his body was laid to rest in the Salmon cemetery.

In 1945 Frank Swain and Doc Frazier again floated the Middle Fork. Doc Frazier wrote:

> When we came to the old hermit's place, no work had been done on the bar, weeds had grown up around the little overnight shack, the trail had not been used. We went up the canyon wall to his cabin, the garden had dried up, the cabin door was ajar, and we were sure we would find the old gentleman's body. We looked around the place and over all of the ledges as we went back to the river, not a trace was found of him. We were sure that his good "Doctor" [pistol] had not let the old man suffer. Enough to say—we were sad.

Hunters who used Parrott's place after his death vandalized it while looking for his gold. Lee Bacos, a river guide, burned the storage logs for firewood. When outfitter Bob Sevy first visited the cabin in the mid-sixties, he found letters wedged between cabin logs that revealed Parrott had a paranoid fear of woodrats. Sevy left them and they too disappeared. The shelter largely went to ground, finished off in 1989 by a forest fire; grass and brush have taken the garden, but three dwarfed peach trees still bear fruit on their gnarled limbs.

In 1988 Bruce and Diane May, having made a Middle Fork trip and learned of Parrott's life, decided to have a tombstone made for his unmarked grave. It was in place, along with flowers, for Memorial Day that year.

Earl Parrott's memory lives in the name of a creek, a lake, and a river campsite.

31 EARL KING PARROTT IN FRONT OF HIS CABIN IN 1939.

32 Frank Swain carries some spuds down one of Parrott's ladders.

33 PARROTT IN 1939, PANNING GOLD ON THE MIDDLE FORK.

34 PARROTT BY HIS GARDEN.
35 PARROTT'S IRRIGATION DITCH FROM NUGGET CREEK TO HIS GARDEN.

36 PARROTT WITH HIS PISTOL DOWN BY THE MIDDLE FORK, SALMON RIVER.

37 PARROTT AT THE MIDDLE FORK, PHOTOGRAPHED BY HACK MILLER IN 1939.

WILLIAM MORELAND, **THE RIDGERUNNER**

WITH SOME PEOPLE LONELINESS BINDS HARDER THE LONGER IT HOLDS ON,
LIKE BEING TIED DOWN WITH STRIPS OF GREEN RAWHIDE IN A DRYING WIND.
—H. L. DAVIS

The ins and outs of rumor warranted a wild man was padding through the pine-dark forests of the St. Joe and Clearwater drainages in northern Idaho. In the crossroad communities walled in by national forests, the stories were something to savor, especially on long winter nights, growing like antlers in velvet, each story another point. Forest Service district rangers, on full cock to nail him, discovered he traveled like a deer or an elk aware hunting season was open: at their approach, he disappeared as if witched into mist. At least he was one shade shy of invisible—he left tracks now and then.

March 15, 1941. Halfway between Avery and Red Ives—more clearings than settlements—on the shadowy St. Joe River, the lock on the Peewee Cabin, property of the U. S. Forest Service, is forced open and personal belongings of a Forest Service employee vanish.

May 2, 1942. Forty miles south of the Peewee Cabin and fifty miles from the nearest town, at Roundtop Ranger Station the district ranger discovers the woodstove has been used and a radio taken. Footprints are evident by the building, but not a single track leads away from it.

June 9, 1942. Thirty-five air miles southeast of Roundtop, two men on a Forest Service trail crew working alone out of a tent on Isabella Creek lose a packsack, sleeping bag, and food from their camp. Pursuing, they quickly lose the thief's trail.

July 11, 1942. Northwest of Isabella Creek, two small smokes below Goat Ridge (6,300 ft.) lure the lookout from his tower to extinguish them. On returning, he finds someone has bathed in his quarters, shaved, then departed with a mackinaw, raincoat, tobacco, and a .32-caliber pistol, together with a box of shells.

August 7, 1942. Twenty-five miles southwest of Goat Ridge, District Ranger Roy Lewis discovers a theft at Collins Creek Cabin: firefighter's food pack, packsack, maps and compass. No sign the padlock was disturbed.

August 11, 1942. Goat Ridge revisited. While fire-spotters sleep on the second floor of the lookout, an intruder enters the ground-level storeroom below them and departs with food and flashlight.

September 12, 1942. Seven miles southwest of Goat Ridge, at Smith Point Lookout, Ranger Lewis finds footprints around the vacant tower. Another sleeping bag and more food gone.

March 20, 1943. Thirty miles northwest of Goat Ridge, newly assigned ranger Merrill Oaks rides horseback to Roundtop R. S., arriving toward evening, and spots a man fleeing like a felon across the frozen snow between building and brush. Oaks' mare rears; he dismounts and sprints after the indistinct figure. In the dusk he is unable to gain on the man, who tops one ridge and then another. The dark figure hits the trail down into the canyon of the Little North Fork of the Clearwater just as Oaks stumbles and falls. By the time he is up again and running, he can no longer see or hear his suspect. Darkness forecloses further pursuit.

Oaks returns to the station and radios for assistance. Two search teams spend the next three days combing the canyon. They find a hollow cedar tree where the fugitive hid, but no trace from there that they can follow. Oaks names his escapee "the Ridgerunner."

May 5, 1943. Binoculars and food are removed from Roundtop R. S.

May 15, 1943. Thirty-seven air miles southwest of Roundtop, on the North Fork of the Clearwater at Canyon Ranger Station, a pane is broken out of a window, candlewax spatters the rooms, more food is packratted away.

July 7, 1943. Ten miles northeast of Canyon R. S., near the lookout tower on the Nub, a Forest Service dispatcher spots footprints in the snow.

September 6, 1943. Six miles east of Canyon R. S., at Skull Creek Cabin, a .22-caliber rifle goes missing.

September 8, 1943. Over forty miles northwest of Canyon, Roundtop R. S. is hit again: a backpack is carried off with fifteen fire rations, ten pounds of flour, eight cans of corned beef, beans, bread, and crackers.

October 17, 1943. Five miles north of the Skull Creek Cabin, Forest Service packers find a window open at the Collins Creek Cabin. The visitor departed in haste, leaving binoculars and flashlight behind.

November 30, 1943. At Roundtop, Ranger Oaks learns twenty pounds of flour and twenty-five fire rations have been borrowed without asking.

The Ridgerunner, ephemeral as a cross fox, had the Forest Service mad enough to chew stumps. In makeshift settlements on both sides of the St. Joe-Clearwater divide, in Headquarters and Weippe, Avery and Calder, and in towns such as Orofino, Pierce, and St. Maries, the will-o-the-wisp woodsman stirred conversation, speculation, and even admiration. As reporter Richard Ripley has put it, "The idea that a man was living year-round in the rugged divide caught the imagination of the residents of the timber towns, many of whom made their living in the woods. They knew the snow drifted to twenty feet deep in the divide in the winter, and wind gunned ice crystals over the ridgetops."

Fact, fantasy, and folklore mixed. Some thought he was a draft dodger, others that he was an escaped convict, still others that he was a murderer. Among people who worked without wearing neckties, however, the fact that the Ridgerunner raised all grades of hell for the Forest Service was not a character defect. It was a case of necessity being the mother of contention: the Ridgerunner simply used shelter and supplies required to survive. The cabins had been paid for by the people; by tradition they served in emergency.

March 30, 1944. Clyde Cole and Louis Holt, USFS, hike southeast thirteen miles up the North Fork of the Clearwater from Canyon R. S. to Flat Creek Cabin, on their way to Bungalow Ranger Station. Intent on spending the night at Flat Creek, the midway point, they arrive at dusk and are startled by the sight of smoke drifting from the cabin chimney. They tiptoe onto the porch, then rush the door. A surprised, slight figure faces them, seated at a table dimly lit by a single candle on the floor beneath it, his hat pulled low, his mouth frozen open in the middle of an unspoken word. They cannot see his face, but they know he is the Ridgerunner.

"Why are you using this cabin?" demanded Cole.

The man stood, slung his rifle over his shoulder, replied, "I've got to feed my horses, then we can eat," pushed past them out the door and was gone with the sunset.

Cole and Holt radioed Pierce Ranger Station, south of Headquarters, for instructions. The forest supervisor told Cole and Holt to proceed to Bungalow the next day and on out of the woods. In the morning, as replacements, he sent employees Moton Roark and Mickey Durant to pursue the Ridgerunner. Roark was an experienced tracker, an indefatigible hiker, and a crack shot. Most important, the North Fork country was as familiar to him as his own face.

Roark and Durant reached the Bungalow that night. At daybreak they set out for Flat Creek and arrived well before noon. They picked up the Ridgerunner's tracks and followed them northwest down the North Fork for thirteen miles to Canyon R. S. He had made no effort to disguise his route—probably moving at night— but once he reached the bridge across the North Fork, he left the trail and cut down to the riverbank. Roark found food scraps on the bank where he had eaten, but no further trace—as though he had entered or rafted the river.

The trackers spent the rest of the day walking downriver, with no results, in search of footprints. After a night in the Canyon R. S., they renewed their hunt, intent on scouting the slopes along the river, but they were halted only a hundred feet from the cabin door by a new set of tracks obviously left in the trail while they slept. The men dropped their packs to expedite their pursuit.

The next morning, when they overtook their quarry on Collins Creek, fourteen miles north, he proved to be the wrong man—a fellow who had not been long in the woods but who had entered one Forest Service cabin. Roark and his partner took him to Headquarters in the Ridgerunner's stead.

During the summer and fall of 1944 B'rer Ridgerunner, he lay low. A new supervisor, Ed Barry, was appointed to the Clearwater National Forest. On learning the saga of the Ridgerunner, he requested that the sheriff of Clearwater County deputize Roark, then arranged for Roark to occupy Forest Service cabins while he winter-trapped coyotes east of Skull Creek, a south-draining tributary that empties into the North Fork five miles east of Canyon Ranger Station.

Another trapper and woodsman, Lee Horner, an Oregonian, worked the area west of Skull Creek. The two met once a week, and agreed to inform the other if they cut any sign of the Ridgerunner.

February 2, 1945. Roark and Horner met for lunch at the Flat Creek Cabin, where Cole and Holt had cornered the fugitive ten months earlier. Lunch talk confirmed that no trace of him had been seen over the previous two months. After eating, they put on their webs and slogged downriver toward a parting at Skull Creek. A mile short of the confluence with the creek, they suddenly came upon snowshoe grids imprinted on the the trail. A rifle butt had left its oval in the snow alongside the prints, which were imposed over Horner's, meaning they were no more than a few hours old. It was Groundhog Day!

The trappers gave chase immediately. They shoed downriver, rifles in hand, following the trail like wardens after a poacher. The corded tracks circled the Skull Creek Cabin, then continued down the North Fork.

Roark and Horner paused to check the cabin's interior. They found food scraps and an alarm clock wound recently. Roark, figuring their options, concluded the Ridgerunner was headed for

Canyon R. S. for supplies and shelter. They decided to wait at Skull Creek until dark, then try to hook the renegade at Canyon downriver. While Holt fashioned a palouser—a horizontal candle-lantern— from a paint can to supplement the light of a fingernail moon, Roark cooked dinner.

Dinner done, they started down the trail again, breath billowing, cheeks numb. Cold had cramped the temperature down into single digits. They shoed at an even, practiced gait. Abruptly, half a mile from the Skull Creek Cabin, the Ridgerunner's tracks frayed out, then ceased altogether. Ended. From the last track the men searched outward in concentric circles. Nothing. Gone like a ghost at dawn.

Perplexed, they decided to go on to the Canyon R. S., figuring he might be there, and if not, they could still radio the Pierce R. S.

Roark and Horner reached Canyon at 9:00 p.m. and stopped to scout the clearing. No smoke. The sky was a lake of stars. A meteor flared like a sulphur match. No tracks. Only the sound of some elk across the way pawing through snow in search of forage.

The pair entered the office cautiously but found no sign of recent occupancy. Baffled by the lack of evidence, they decided their quarry had somehow side-hilled north of them and escaped east back to Collins Creek Cabin, five miles upcreek from Skull Creek Cabin. They radioed the ranger at Pierce, asking for a portable radio with which to maintain communication once they resumed their search in the morning.

The ranger replied that the new forest supervisor had directed a team of four rangers from Pierce by rail speeder car to the logging camp nearest Canyon R. S. Meanwhile a plane would drop supplies to Roark and Horner, then fly patrol over the mountain ridges.

That night the cold knocked the bottom out of the thermometer; the wind would have shivered an arctic fox. At dawn the temperature remained below zero. A Travelaire from Johnson Flying Service in Missoula, Montana, made a pass over the cabin and parachuted a cargo box with the radio. Roark recovered it, tested it, and then both men strapped on their packs and started back up the river trail, rifles in hand. They set an eager pace.

At the junction with Skull Creek, they turned north up the creek and after another five miles, they sighted the Collins Creek Cabin. Cautious, they snapped their radio off. A circle hike around the cabin failed to intersect any tracks in the deep snow, and their spirits nose-dived.

"Well, the Jesus wept," said Roark. "How do you catch a man who can winter out with only his back for a mattress and his belly for a blanket?" Horner shook his head in disbelief.

They flipped on the radio and called Canyon R. S. The Forest Service reinforcements had arrived there. District Ranger Lewis, who was with them, ordered Roark and Horner out of the Skull Creek drainage and back down to Skull Creeek Cabin for the night—fifteen miles of snowshoeing for the day.

Since the river, naturally, marked the low center of the valley, Lewis reasoned that the Ridgerunner was trapped on the slopes somewhere between ridgetop and the North Fork. He planned to have the plane patrol the ridge during the day, while Roark and Horner traveled the river trail between Skull Creek and Canyon R. S., and while the other rangers covered the reach between Canyon and Isabella Creek to the west.

Monday, the patrol began. No sign surfaced. Tuesday, more of the same. Wednesday, colder and more of the same. Thursday, still nothing. Roark and Horner, thoughts akimbo, decided to overrule Lewis and trail back up Skull Creek to the top of the drainage, then stalk their prey by contouring down the slopes and through the draws.

After six hours of climbing, they were ready to begin their descent. It was midday. They moved with an eagerness reined by caution. To increase their stealth, they alternated sweeps leapfrog-fashion, one man moving forward, then the other. Within two hours they were halfway down the mountain and nothing flushed. Of a sudden, Roark glimpsed a fleeting scarf of smoke before it dissipated in a stand of pine. He waved frantically at Horner, then pointed downslope.

Horner quickly angled down to his partner. "Smoke," whispered Roark. "Come on." The men crept downhill. They spotted tracks—the first they had seen in a week. They continued their stealthy approach, confident they were closing on their quarry.

Roark suddenly came to a standstill. A green tarp was tented over a rope strung between a pair of stout pines just below them. The silence was palpable. They strained for any sound or movement. Opposite the tent-tarp, a small, ragged, deliberately inconspicuous fire licked away from the upslope draft. The stalkers had a hurried, whispered exchange. Roark was confident their man was out of sight behind the canvas. They agreed to charge the shelter from each side, rifles ready.

At a nod, they bolted downhill. Horner stubbed his snowshoe on a covered limb and went ears-over-tincup. Roark kept his feet and spotted a small man hunched over the fire like a mantling hawk, cooking. The noise of Horner's sprawl caused the man to glance toward its cause. As Horner sought to flounder up and recover his rifle, Roark arrived from the blind side, prodded the fellow with his rifle barrel, and said, "Hello." Their arrival was as unexpected as a chinook. The man regarded his captors for a moment without moving, then replied, "Hello. I guess the dear rangers have been looking for me for a long time."

Roark nodded emphatically. It was February 9, 1945, and the Ridgerunner had run out of aces. Had it not been for the plane, however, the cards might have fallen otherwise.

Horner retrieved the Ridgerunner's rifle leaning against a tree a few steps away. Then he and Roark hunkered in the snow to talk with their captive. A wiry man, five feet, two inches, 130 pounds, he was clothed like a detained refugee: brimless wool hat, blanket poncho, sleeveless mackinaw, canvas stagged pants, laceless cracked rubber boots, feet wrapped in dishtowels. One would have to be off his hinges to live like this, thought Roark. He urged the Ridgerunner to finish frying his meal of hotcakes and corned beef.

Once the little man had complied and finished, they had him empty his pockets. The contents resembled those of Tom Sawyer's: pocketknife, fishline, .22-caliber cartridges, vials of boric acid and oil of cloves, a tobacco pouch with a tin-can key for Forest Service locks. At this point Roark informed him that they were taking him to Skull Creek Cabin. They assured him he would not be hurt if he did not attempt to escape. With no other choice, he consented.

As they shoed downhill through the snow, the conversation turned to answers for which all three hungered. The Ridgerunner revealed that his name was Bill Moreland; that he had run low on food and was ready to move again—at night because that was when he preferred to travel (spooked animals would alert him to another's presence) and because of the airplane; that he had eluded Roark and Horner below Skull Creek a week earlier by removing his shoes and wading up the four-inch-wide rill that came down the hill and across the trail; that he had cut some small trees and tossed them in the river with the hope his followers would assume he had fashioned a raft and gone downstream. He confided that a severe toothache had driven him to distraction just before his capture. Most astonishing, though, was the revelation that he had been in the woods since 1932—thirteen years. (He had so lost track of calendared time that he was surprised to learn he was a year older than he had thought!) He learned from them that they were not forest rangers, and that Roosevelt had been re-elected.

At the cabin, Roark gave Moreland a pair of wool socks, which he pulled on thankfully with the comment that his last pair could have been put on from either end. Roark used his radio to notify Ranger Lewis at Canyon R. S. of the situation. The threesome ate dinner, then pushed on downriver to Canyon, arriving after nightfall.

More questions. Ranger Lewis was rather stiff-necked with his interrogation, perhaps understandably since the Ridgerunner had been an exhausting opponent. If Lewis was expecting a fellow with a loose shingle, however, he was soon disabused. The Ridgerunner's memory sidetracked here and there, but as his replies filled in the puzzle, it was evident that he was highly intelligent, and that before settling in northern Idaho he had traveled in at least half of the forty-eight states.

Once inside the Idaho woods, he had never visited a town; he preferred government cabins and logging camps, wearing his solitude the way a turtle wears its shell. He had ranged north 230 miles from the Sawtooth Mountains to the St. Joe River. He had buried caches in the Canyon R. S. front yard and north all the way across the St. Joe-Clearwater divide.

He confessed to stealing candles from the Forest Service cabins so that no one could follow him in the dark. He said he used sticks inside his removed shoes in order to make reverse tracks over his trail. He knew the mountains and their drainages, including those of the Salmon and Selway rivers, better than any Forest Service cartographer. "I wanted to live like a coyote, just live from day to day...."

On the morning after his capture, the Ridgerunner was marched to Potlatch Forest Industries' Camp 14. The group ate canned rations and bedded down for the night. (Roark and Horner remained behind in the mountains.)

The next day they hiked six miles to the PFI rail line, where they were picked up by a speeder car. At Headquarters a crowd gathered to stare at the captive as though he was a prize hog at the county fair. He was hustled into an official car and driven southwest two hours to Orofino, where the sheriff fingerprinted him and lodged him in the Clearwater County jail.

The next morning the *Spokesman Review* in Spokane, Washington, headed a front-page column, "Phantom Fugitive of the Forest Caught At Last." The *Clearwater Tribune*, Orofino's weekly, carried a similar tale: "Forest Service Hunt Nabs Woods Hermit. Three Year Hunt Ends With Jailing of Wild Man."

On his first day in captivity, Moreland underwent intensive interrogation by an FBI agent and a law enforcement officer from the U. S. Forest Service. The outcome was a typed memorandum-for-file for a trespass action by the Forest Service, and a signed voluntary statement (confession) for the FBI. Since the two "autobiographical" documents overlap, what follows is Moreland's confession supplemented with five parenthetical inserts from the memorandum.

My name is William C. Moreland. I was born October 1, 1900 in Wolfe County, near Landsaw, [eastern] Kentucky. My father was W. L. Moreland and my mother was Emmie Stone Moreland. I have a sister Stella, and the last I heard she lived in Morgan County, Kentucky. I believe she is married. I think she is a year older. My family was separated when my sister and I were small. My father took my sister, and I went with my mother. I was raised by my grandfather, Bill Stone, who had a farm in Wolfe County, near Landsaw, Kentucky. (My mother is dead, and I have not heard from my father in over twenty years.)

When I was about nine or ten years old, I went to Indiana and lived on a farm there with my grandmother Corrie Stone. As I recall, the farm was partly in Indiana and partly across the river in Kentucky. I cannot recall the name of the town which was near the farm in Indiana.

Later I went to Covington, Kentucky [near Cincinnati], where I lived with some people who I believe were related to my grandmother. I went to school about four miles out of Covington. I think I was in the fifth grade there.

From the time I was twelve to sixteen years old [1912-1916], I was in a lot of reform schools. I ran away from the people I had stayed with in Covington, Kentucky, and I recall being in reform or juvenile schools in Lancaster, Ohio, and in the states of Kentucky, Michigan, Wisconsin, Texas, and a few others. I was picked up a few times in Oklahoma.

During the last war [WWI], I worked for about one year for the Stevens Lumber Co. near Wells, Michigan. I believe we were paid on this job out of Wells, Michigan. I recall this because a bunch of us went out to register for the draft, but I was too young. I must have been about seventeen years of age.

I stowed away on an ore boat near Sault Ste. Marie on the Great Lakes. Later I got on a freighter [McCormick Steamship Co.], probably at a port in the Great Lakes near Pennsylvania. This freighter took me to Seattle, Washington. I believe I was on the boat about three months and earned my way by washing dishes. The First World War was over [November 11, 1918] when I arrived in Seattle. I cannot recall what year it was.

I worked around Seattle for about one year, during which time I washed dishes in a lot of restaurants and in a Coast Guard boat. I went to St. Paul, Minnesota, from there and worked on farms for a Nelson and a fellow named Olson. I believe Nelson lived near some division point on the Chicago, Milwaukee Railroad.

For several years I traveled around doing odd jobs in towns in Washington and Oregon. (This was in the fall of the year, and I left there about the following July. My work in Tacoma was hauling fuel, putting wood in basements, and mowing lawns. I lived between two bridges near a sawmill. I think this was about the time Hoover was President. Times were tough, and I could only get twenty-five cents for unloading a full truckload of wood.

When I left I went to Vancouver, then on to a place called Washam, where I stayed about a week, then to Bend, Oregon, where I bummed around town for eight or ten days, then to Klamath Falls, then on to another place, I don't remember the name, then back to Washam, then to Pendleton, probably on to Pasco next, then to Umatilla and Lewiston, Idaho, but there was very little work anywhere. I drifted like this for four years.)

I got down to Arkansas and got in trouble over a horse and was given two to five years, I believe, in the state prison at Little Rock [1921]. Before going to Arkansas I had been in prison in the state prison in Arizona [Florence] on a grand larceny charge. I broke into a grocery store.

I bummed around the country a lot after getting out of prison in Arkansas. I never held any job for any length of time, just doing odd jobs and once in a while doing some farm work. (I also did some work in fruit harvesting and digging potatoes in the Yakima and Wenatchee [Washington] valleys.)

I recall when Roosevelt was running for election the first time that I was at Mountain Home, Idaho, on a little place where I worked for a sheepherder who was a German. He had a little farm, and I did the irrigating for him and skinned some sheep for him. I believe I was there forty-two days.

Mountain Home was the last town I was in of any size before I went into the mountains. I stopped at some little mining town, probably Atlanta, Idaho, and bought some supplies before going into the mountains.

I spent the first winter in the Sawtooth Range, living largely on venison. I think I got some Forest Service food but can't recall where. I might have spent two winters in this area. From this area I went to Chamberlain Meadows on the Salmon River [via Gibbonsville, Shoup, Dixie, Riggins]. I reached this place in about June. About July of this year I saw two airplanes in the Meadows and one night I got in them. I found the keys in one of them, and although I do not know how to fly an airplane, I tried to start it with the idea of flying it. I spent the winter along the Salmon River.

I spent the next year around the Deep Creek area. I made a key which I first used to get into Forest Service cabins in this region. I entered these cabins to get Forest Service food. I believe I spent two winters in this country. I made several keys out of the tin from cans. I made these keys so that I could get into Forest Service cabins and lookouts. I used my keys to go into Forest Service cabins at Deep Creek Ranger Station, Bear Creek R. S., Three Forks R. S., and the cellar of the ranger station at Meadow Creek. I also entered two buildings at the Powell R. S. on the Lochsa River [1935-1936].

From there I went to the Cedars on the North Fork of the Clearwater. I stayed about eight days at a building at the Cedars. I spent about ten days in a Forest Service cabin at Chamberlain Meadows, at the mouth of Meadow Creek which flows into the North Fork of the Clearwater.

I went into the ranger station at Red Ives on the St. Joe River a couple of times. I went into the cook shack there. There was no road in there at that time, but later I have been in there and have seen the road.

I have entered ranger stations at Roundtop, Canyon, Collins Creek, Skull Creek, and numerous cabins in the vicinity of these.

I do not recall how many winters I spent in the vicinity of the last named ranger stations. (I believe I spent the winter of '42 and '43 on Snow Peak and on Rutledge Creek. Was also on Freezeout, Pincho Mountain in Floodwood drainage, and built a small cabin on Rutledge Creek. Obtained most of my food supplies from Roundtop.)

One spring I entered a cabin and a tent on Isabella Creek. I took some food, a pair of overalls, and a pocketbook. I took a shirt and in the shirt pocket was a draft card. I kept the card for a while but later lost it. I knew good and well that I had to have a draft card if I met anybody.

During the time I was in the mountains I entered almost every Forest Service lookout and cabin in the North Fork of the Clearwater area, and also entered cabins in the Salmon River area, the St. Joe River area, and in the Sawtooth Mountain area. I used a key I had made to make all these entries. I knew it was unlawful because I saw Forest Service signs which said it was unlawful to break or enter. I usually took food from these places but also took other supplies such as flashlights, blankets, sleeping bags, and sometimes clothing that happened to be there. I once took a portable radio. I think

I was in the hills about twelve years.

(I spent most of this past winter between the mouth of Gold Creek and Gold Creek lookout. I made a lean-to out of some boards about a mile up from the mouth of Gold Creek at an old camp. I lived mostly on venison and cereals which I had taken from Camp T.)

Before going into the hills I worked on a sheep ranch around Mountain Home or Jerome, Idaho. I believe it was south of those towns or reservoirs. I thought some persons were trying to frame me with a girl named Rose Baker, claiming that I had raped her, so I pulled out as I figured that having a prior prison record, that I would have a hard time explaining it. A German and the girl's mother were trying to blackmail me. They told me that the girl's mother was going to have the law after me; so I left. I caught rides to Mountain Home, and then went up to some mining town which might have been Atlanta, and from there I went into the woods and never came out until the Forest Rangers caught me.

I think it must have been about the time Roosevelt was running for President the first time that I went into the mountains. I recall that the German was against Roosevelt and wasn't going to vote for him.

This is a true statement to the best of my recollection.

FBI agent Mayer filed a federal complaint, charging Moreland with failure to register for the draft, and neglecting to have a draft card in his possession. He was arraigned before the U. S. Commissioner, waived his right to a preliminary hearing, and tried to plead guilty, but the commissioner, who was not a district judge, rejected his plea. Bail was set at $600.

On Valentine's Day, unable to meet bail, the Ridgerunner was taken to Nez Perce County jail in Lewiston, Idaho, where federal prisoners were held. A doctor's examination there revealed he was suffering from malnutrition. (During his incarceration, Moreland told fellow prisoners, "If I had known how good it would be here in jail, I'd have given up last fall." Officers said he gained six pounds over the next two weeks.)

Because the U. S. District Attorney was persuaded that he had insufficient evidence to prove Moreland knew of the draft requirements, or had forcibly entered government buildings, the FBI had to drop all charges.

Nonetheless, Moreland was transported back to Orofino to await trial by the state on burglary charges. On October 4, 1945, he pleaded guilty, was given a five-year suspended sentence, and was released. Within days he was back on the North Fork of the Clearwater.

Perd Hughes, a trapper and surveyor who had lived on the river since 1929, invited the Ridgerunner to winter at his lodge, which was twenty miles east of the settlement of Elk River. The men got along like cartridge and clip.

The pair were once out on a ridgetop unfamiliar to Hughes and far from his cabin when a blinding fog rolled in. Darkness fell, but the Ridgerunner led Hughes home with an unerring sense of direction. Hughes was impressed.

As Robert Parker has written, "One of the good parts to being alone is when you move out no one minds. It's also one of the bad parts." When spring arrived, the Ridgerunner moved out.

Over the next few years he worked for Potlatch Forest Industries three times, and for the Clearwater Timber Protective Association at least as often. The association manned fire-fighting camps, one of which, Boehl's Cabin (a collection of buildings), was at the confluence of Little North Fork and the North Fork of the Clearwater, just west of Hughes' place.

The Ridgerunner knew the woods the way a tree knows its bark and branches. Camp bosses colluded to keep him employed and thereby out of their hair. He proved a tireless worker—whether setting chokers for log drags or greasing Cats or packing TNT for powder monkeys who blasted stumps. But he seldom cashed his checks.

When the camps folded with the onset of wet weather in the fall, the Ridgerunner went off to winter on his own in the mountains;

sometimes he lived in a cave. He would show up for work in the spring, looking like he had been outfitted in a wind tunnel. Occasionally, at dinner, he became the object of teasing, and when the jokes went too far, he could become touchy as gunpowder. Generally the loggers knew when to back off.

In 1948 he worked for PFI as a flumewalker: he patrolled the wooden trough that snaked through the forest, keeping it clear and in repair, so that logs could be floated down to the river. The job dovetailed with his inclinations. He performed creditably and wintered in a cabin at Elkberry Creek on the North Fork, ten miles south of Hughes' place.

The following year, Moreland's advances (gifts and notes) to two of the girls who worked as cook's helpers in camp were rebuffed, and he turned moody and took to wearing his pistol.

In the summer of 1950, about two months after the Ridgerunner was fired by a PFI boss for pulling a gun during an argument, the camp was awakened by an explosion. On the landing at the edge of camp, a D-8 Caterpillar bulldozer worth $15,000 was completely destroyed.

The Ridgerunner was, of course, the chief suspect, but he had vanished like a spark in wet grass. PFI, USFS, and the Clearwater County sheriff made a coordinated effort to catch him. After two weeks nothing more than tracks had been found. Bloodhounds did not help. Then unexpectedly, the Ridgerunner strolled into the PFI warehouse in Headquarters and casually remarked, "I hear you've been looking for me."

The sheriff took custody and jailed him in Orofino. He was charged with malicious destruction of property. Bail was set at $5,000; trial for October 17.

Orofino attorney Raymond McNichols, as competent and decent a lawyer, and later judge, as ever graced the Idaho bar, was appointed to defend the Ridgerunner.

McNichols, no friend of PFI, could argue the hind leg off a mule. He decided to let the Ridgerunner testify on his own behalf.

During the three-day trial, Moreland admitted being in the vicinity of the bulldozer on the weekend of the explosion, but he said he was sleeping on a nearby hillside when the blast occurred. Courtroom witnesses enjoyed his frankness and sense of humor. In his closing argument, McNichols said, "Just because he does not live like you or I does not mean he is any more of a criminal than you or I. Mr. Moreland may have a packrat attitude, and he may be different, but he's not charged with having a packrat attitude or being different. He's charged with blowing up a bulldozer, and the state has an obligation to prove [that] beyond a reasonable doubt."

The jury deliberated four hours, and in the belief PFI had tried to frame Moreland, voted for acquittal.

The Ridgerunner resumed his life in the woods. Two years later, while working at a mill near Pierce, he quarreled with a fellow worker, left briefly and returned with his pistol, and fired at the other millworker to frighten him.

Moreland was jailed again. Following his psychiatric evaluation, a doctor wrote, "He is apparently unable to adjust to adult society, and in my opinion, it may be reasonable to assume that because of the unsatisfactory environment of his boyhood and youth he entertains some hostility toward society...."

On October 28 Moreland had a one-day trial. He insisted on acting as his own attorney. "He who serves as his own lawyer has a fool for a client." After an hour of deliberation, the jury found him guilty. Again, however, his sense of humor was not lost on the court. He was sentenced to six months in jail; with time off for good behavior, he served five.

In spring, 1953, the Ridgerunner moved into a gap-boarded, abandoned cabin at Milk Creek on the North Fork of the Clearwater, about six miles west of Canyon Ranger Station. Supervisor Stillings of the Clearwater National Forest adopted a "live and let live-in" attitude toward him. Unable to get a job with either logging outfits or the Forest Service, the Ridgerunner gardened, fished, hunted, and panned for gold. He still pilfered articles from camps and cabins.

The Forest Service understanding with the Ridgerunner frayed in June, 1954, when new supervisor Ralph Space replaced Stillings. Even though he had never met the Ridgerunner, Space regarded him as a burr in the fur of the Forest Service and was determined to comb him out. He figured Moreland for a full-bore looney and schemed to get him committed to State Hospital North, Orofino, an institution for the mentally ill. Second-hand reports that Moreland referred to Space as "Old Horse Face" and to himself as "Acting Ranger, Milk Creek Sub-station" did not smooth any feathers. On the other side, the Forest Service policy of burning serviceable cabins did not sit well with the Ridgerunner.

In 1955 the accommodation unravelled entirely. The Canyon District Ranger found the Ridgerunner living in the Skull Creek Cabin and ordered him out. He left, growling like a sow bear with a sore toe.

The following March, when a backcountry pilot reported seeing smoke coming from the chimney of one of the buildings at Canyon R. S., Space ordered District Ranger Floyd Cowles to go in and arrest the Ridgerunner. Cowles obtained a John Doe warrant, had the county sheriff deputize him, and strapped on his .357 Magnum pistol. A helicopter pilot flew him in.

Cowles found the Ridgerunner in the ranger's residence, mopping the kitchen floor. The pilot joined them and they had a cup of coffee together. Moreland had been cooking on the heating stove and feeding raccoons indoors—the place looked like he had bedded down in it for several weeks.

The Ridgerunner told his visitors how he had shoveled snow from the roof, killed packrats and porcupines in and around the buildings, and shot coyotes preying on elk calves. Nonetheless, Cowles told him he had to take him in. Moreland stated that he was not going and sulled up like a possum.

At this point, the pilot had a spark of inspiration and asked Moreland if he had ever been in a helicopter. He replied that he had not, obviously piqued by the possibility.

During the flight, Moreland was all observer, naming every peak and creek all the way to Orofino. Once again, he was billeted in the county jail there.

As Cowles was leaving Canyon R. S., he confiscated four letters written by the Ridgerunner, thinking they might serve as evidence. Actually, the letters were evidence—but evidence of an uncommon

mind. In their own way they were as startling as hearing a rock
marmot stand up and whistle "My Old Kentucky Home." A few
passages will suffice:

This evening I watched the thick mass of white fog as
it slowly disappeared revealing these beautiful and almost
inaccessible green mountains surrounding the Canyon
Station.

When arriving at this observation point [Thompson
Point Lookout], forest travelers or nature loving humans
can if they wish see and admire some of Idaho's most
beautiful works formed by Nature's molds and the age of
time. As one climbs the steps leading up to the little cabin
fifty feet above the ground and perched on four long
cedar poles, the view becomes so impressive the observer
feels as if they were becoming strangely intoxicated by the
airy stimulants evaporating from such a beautiful nature
created scene.

Obscured from all earthly creatures and screaming
with unsurpassed delight each time he glances at his
elementary control room, the Great Elementary Director
spent almost twenty-eight days amusing himself by way
of creating misery for earthy humans. I for one would
almost think he had created a switch that would alternate
from rain to snow. There could also be a possibility that
the switch that controls the sun was jarred loose by an
atom bomb test. Personally I believe he is just testing to
see what people can survive under....

Snow, more snow, then more snow. Few hours rain.
These two things were causing the Great Elementary
Director considerable worries as it was apparently impossible for him to form a decision until the eighth day of
March, when he must have screamed to his assistant and
asked him on the sake of Mankind [to] shut them both off
for a spell. Anyway, it was while these two elementary

factions were dealing out everything they had on reserve, while striving with utmost skill to win precedence, that friendship between me and the deer and elk ripened to such a memorable state. This friendship was always in evidence throughout the long winter months each time I would stop at the Canyon Station. On each trip I would feed them some hay from the mule barn. Not only would they permit me to pet them, but there was outstanding proof of existing jealousies as they would quite often push and butt each other trying to place themselves in the position of the one being petted.

After Moreland had spent sixty days in the county jail, the county prosecutor decided that this was a federal case and refused to file charges. Then the U. S. attorney also decided not to file charges. The Ridgerunner was set free.

Supervisor Ralph Space was livid. He wrote the Forest Service attorney, "Locally, the people are rather amused by the difficulties Mr. Moreland causes the Forest Service. To them, it is some kind of a game and they get a kick out of seeing Moreland escape punishment for offenses that do not directly concern them."

A month later, the Ridgerunner sent Space a bill for twelve dollars he claimed was owed him for clearing trail. Space seethed.

In May, 1957, when the new district ranger learned a pistol had been taken from the Canyon R. S., and a chainsaw from the Skull Creek Cabin, he informed the FBI, and two agents flew to Milk Creek. The Ridgerunner admitted he had the pistol and saw. The agents took the pistol, and once it was identified in an FBI lab, they returned and arrested him. He was helicoptered to Boehl Cabin (perhaps it was all a ruse on his part to get another such ride), then driven to Lewiston. Following arraignment, he was taken north to the Clearwater County jail.

Moreland was held until mid-January, 1958, awaiting a sanity hearing. No psychiatrist testified. Space, who still had never met the Ridgerunner, but whose prejudices slipped like a greased key into the lock of his preconceptions, stated in an affadavit that Moreland was, "mentally deficient...of such low intelligence that he cannot properly handle his business and personal affairs and has been and can be exploited."

On this unsupported showing, Judge Ben Bear found the Ridgerunner insane and ordered him committed to State Hospital North, Orofino.

At the asylum, Moreland lived in an open ward, worked in the laundry and the garden, got along with everyone, and was locked up at night.

August 2, 1963. Pre-dawn. A wiry figure shoulders through a small window, drops to the ground, and darts away from the hospital grounds like a boy just getting out of school. That afternoon a Catskinner spots the Ridgerunner walking down the road to Canyon R. S.

The next afternoon a Forest Service worker meets the Ridgerunner on the trail along the North Fork of the Clearwater. He asks the Ridgerunner where he is headed.

"I came back to see if these mountains were as beautiful as I remember them, or if I just imagined it all. I'm not going to stay."

December, 1963. Some food disappears from the cookhouse at the Canyon R. S. The cook, with sympathetic suspicions, says nothing.

April, 1964. John Altmiller is sawing logs at a landing south of Canyon R. S. and the Ridgerunner passes with packsack on his back, walking toward the morning sun. Altmiller shuts off his saw and asks the Ridgerunner, whom he recognizes, where he is going.

"I'm leaving."

"I thought these mountains are your home."

"They were, but there's too many people here now. I'm leaving for good."

Altmiller wished him luck.

No one ever saw or heard of the Ridgerunner again. Idaho has no record of his death, nor does Kentucky.

Since then, most of the stretch has gone out of the Clearwater country. The forests have been roaded and eroded. Lookouts have been abandoned for a policy of larger and more frequent fires. Forest Service cabins have been burned. In 1973 the Army Corps of Engineers closed the gates on a colossal straight-axis dam (717 by 3,000 feet), thereby flooding fifty-four miles of the incomparable North Fork of the Clearwater, including the flat at Milk Creek. And for those who knew it when, the question goes echoing: those beautiful mountains and rivers—did we just imagine it all?

Received 3-4-56
Floyd R. Cowles

UNITED STATES DEPARTMENT OF AGRICULTURE
FOREST SERVICE
CLEARWATER NATIONAL FOREST

Snow more Snow then more Snow few
hours Rain these two Things were Causing
the Great elementy director Considerable
worries as it was apparently impossible
for him to form a decision until the
eighth day of march when he must of
Screamed to his assistant an asked
him on the Sake of mankind Shut them
Both of for a Spell it was while these
two elementary factors were dealing out
every thing they had on reserve while
Steuring with utmost Skill to win
Precedence, that friendship Between me
and the elk and Deer Ripened to Such
a memorable State this friendship
was always in evidence thorough out
the long Winter months each day.
when I would feed them Some of the
goats Hay from the Mule Barn

38 WILLIAM MORELAND
39 PAGE FROM ONE OF MORELAND'S LETTERS.

40 MORELAND, WEARING HIS PISTOL AND FISHING ON THE NORTH FORK OF THE
CLEARWATER.

SYLVAN HART, **BUCKSKIN BILL**

TO DARE TO LIVE ALONE IS THE RAREST COURAGE, SINCE THERE ARE MANY
WHO HAD RATHER MEET THEIR BITTEREST ENEMY IN THE FIELD, THAN THEIR OWN
HEARTS IN THEIR CLOSET —CHARLES COLTON

Although the clock has stopped for Sylvan Hart, his story seems no less hardy than the bunchgrass and mountain mahogany that encroach upon his grave, and although Five Mile Bar on Idaho's River of No Return may be silent now, his memory still vibrates there, as endlessly persistent as the whispered story of the river itself.

Sylvan Ambrose Hart was born in 1906 in a dugout near Carmargo in western Oklahoma Indian Territory. His father Oliver "Artie" Hart from Kansas was of German descent (Hardt). His mother Malissa Tuck from Missouri may have been part Choctaw. Sylvan was the oldest of six children.

Artie Hart owned a small clay farm, but his real interest was horses: raising them, racing them, betting them.

Malissa Hart eventually sold their Angus cattle and bought and managed a boardinghouse near Stone, Oklahoma. A devout woman, she professed to be a Free Methodist, which Sylvan was fond of pointing out meant "free to do almost nothing: no smoking or drinking or dancing or singing." After twenty years, she and Artie split the blanket.

As a boy Sylvan hunted with his lever-action Winchester shotgun in order to help his parents feed the family. In his words,

> I had a small creek to play in, with cutbanks some fifteen feet deep. A twine string, a bent pin, and a piece of

salt pork got me many crawfish. I cooked and ate their tails. Mourning doves don't nest very high, and I collected fat squabs about ready to leave the nest. My first hunting was with bare hands. I got catfish...in the manner of a varmint. You put your arm underwater into a hole in the bank, and there is likely to be a catfish with sawtooth horns, a snapping turtle, or a water moccasin. I got three and four-pound catfish.

Ducks were a big help in preparing a meal. I killed ducks, picked and cleaned and cooked them for my parents. Canada geese were a little too much for a kid...but people thought nothing of running down young rabbits. The last few swathes in a wheat field held quite a few cottontails and jackrabbits that you and your dog could easily get.

Like many boys, he collected small reptiles and animal skulls for the room he shared with his brother and sister; less common, he also collected books.

Sylvan was a determined and committed student:

My memory of going to school is just of being terribly cold. It was two miles uphill into a blizzard, and when you got there it took half a day to thaw out [he survived the influenza epidemic of 1917-1918, though severely afflicted].

I had a very good grade school teacher. His strong point was English, and he taught you to diagram sentences. In a one-room schoolhouse you could learn all grades at once.

High school and college just repeat what you should have learned in grade school. In high school [Carmer, Oklahoma], if your grades were good you need not take the monthly examination. On those days I went squirrel hunting or field butchering with my father.

After high school, Hart rode freight trains to follow the wheat harvest in Nebraska and Texas. He visited southern California briefly.

In 1925 he traveled north for his first years of college at Central Academy in McPherson, Kansas. The academy was a small religious institution, and his choice was undoubtedly influenced by his mother. While there, he served in the Field Artillery of the National Guard, and frequently wore his uniform—not popular apparel so soon after World War I. Hart also spent part of the summer at an encampment at Fort Sill as a special private and second cook, paid $1.29 a day.

The college yearbook reveals that he was commonly called "philosopher"; that his favorite hangout was "sitting on campus"; that he spent enough time in the library to be nicknamed "book-worm." Most prescient, however, is the quotation that accompanied his freshman photograph: "I envy them, those monks of old, their books they read, their beads they told."

In his sophomore year he moved to nearby McPherson College, where he was known as "Hart"; and where he appears to have been popular: vice president of the literary society on campus; librarian of the Young People's Missionary Society; member of the Anti-Tobacco Association. The yearbook reports "reputation, information bureau; occupation, dissecting bookworms; aspiration, to be a colonel."

For his last two years of college, Hart turned homeward to pursue a B.A. in English Literature at the University of Oklahoma. Upon receiving his degree, and with the Depression gathering overhead, he began a year of graduate school in petroleum engineering that he failed to complete. (His penciled field notes were still in his possession at Five Mile Bar.) He tried roughnecking in the east Texas oil fields—"there was danger, crime, bad air, and poor housing"—then in 1931 he drifted north to Moscow, Idaho, where he took elective courses at the University of Idaho for the winter semester.

In spring, 1932, at age twenty-six, Sylvan Hart left the university for good, but he never lost his love of learning. Joined by his now-divorced father, he headed for the Salmon River, the River of No Return. "I wasn't trying to run away from anything. I was just a natural born student, and I could study there, investigate for myself, and I could experiment with different things. I'm not going to give up education. It doesn't pay to stop. Once you get really dumb there's no redemption for you."

The pair fenced a garden plot at the apron of a hill on Five Mile Bar on the south side of the river, and lived in an abandoned one-room cabin a few hundred yards downstream. They grew some tobacco—a laborious and soil-depleting crop—to barter with other river refugees who were also riding out the Depression. (In winter tobacco was almost more precious than food, certainly more precious than money.) They caught fish, and shot deer, elk, and mountain sheep.

> My reaction to the Depression was to find a place with natural resources to defeat it. I could have found no better place than Salmon River. I spent some $50 a year then for what little I needed to buy. I always had a garden. It was easy to get fruit, and I made moccasins and clothing out of animal skins. There were copper plates lying around at Painter's mine that I made into cooking utensils.

Artie Hart eventually forsook the canyon for town work as a carpenter. He never returned to the river. Sylvan stayed.

Over the next ten years Sylvan Hart lived alone most of the time—though not a hermit except by an indulgent standard—always busy without running on a timecard. And while his life may have been crosscurrent to the mainstream, his intelligence, interests, and abilities ranked him as exceptionally competent—there was little that he did not savvy.

Hart framed a one-room (ten by twelve) cabin and stuccoed over the wood because that made it rodent-proof and warmer. Later he added a two-story cabin, same size, with a balcony for his summer bed, and a third smaller building across from it, for winter sleeping, with a bunk on one side and fireplace on the other.

Every summer he tended his garden; canned, dried, and stored its production. He practiced with his crossbow and his Luger pistol. When the mood struck, he tried a little placer mining, a skill he had acquired at Idaho City when he first arrived in Idaho. "Five dollars a day was about average, but at least it was honest money—Hoover dollars. Besides, if you were a bachelor and got a job, you'd feel like there was some married man and his family who needed it more. Mining gold you were *making* money, not taking it away from somebody."

Occasionally river folk stayed overnight. His sister visited, as did his younger brother. In winter, however, it was always a solitary life. He had time for observation and notes:

> I've got six months, from November on, when this place is just like it's always been; nobody visits, and I get my mail two times a month.
>
> I pass the winters by doing something all the time. I'd get breakfast, watch otter, work on a gun in the shop. See mountain sheep come in for salt, take a few pictures. Cook supper. Read. That would take care of the whole day.
>
> When the river is frozen or on highwater, you wouldn't see anyone. If I wanted to see someone, I'd walk twenty or fifty miles.

> A shelf of ice lay against a huge granite boulder in Salmon River. Suddenly an otter appeared on the edge of the ice with a fifteen-inch squawfish in his mouth, and he stretched his neck and raised his fish high for about a second in a mighty-fisherman pose. Then he dropped on all fours, turned around, dived in strong, came up with a fish, and repeated his act identically, at least a half-dozen times. Well, this really looked like good fishing, except that the fish wasn't fighting, and it was always the same size. Then I saw what this grandstander was doing. He was dropping the same fish through a hole in the ice and

diving off in great style to retrieve it. That way one fish made a lot of fishing.

One evening just before dark, I saw an otter catch a couple of fair-sized fish. He ate little but laid them up on the ice as sort of a buffet for a party. As soon as he left, three magpies came and ate some. Early next morning, two ravens stopped and ate briefly. Then came a grand American eagle and ate all the remains, so all in all quite a party, with everyone taking turns and no rough stuff.

In very cold weather a cougar will kill a great deal of game because he can't eat it after it freezes, and it will make a warm kill on the same day.

If a fine animal like a deer or a mountain sheep pays you a visit at your living quarters, it perhaps wants salt. And yet animals get lonesome and keep coming back to see you because you do furnish them some entertainment, provided you are inside your fence. But the minute you step outside the gate the animals sense that it is not right.

Real names are so much better than any the imagination can produce. Nevertheless, in 1938 Sylvan Hart acquired his more popular, if less euphonious, nickname:

It was Don Oberbillig that named me 'Buckskin Bill,' when I showed up at Mackay Bar [a hunting and fishing resort about three miles downriver, accessible by back-country airstrip, or river, or by a tortuous dirt road] in a deerskin jacket. He was partly thinking of Buckskin Frank Leslie, who used to be around Tombstone and supposedly killed Johnny Siringo, the lone cowboy who made a career of knocking off outlaws. I was about the same height, build, and appearance. As for the Bill, if you're out in the West and not some kind of Bill, that's bad. Better to be Willy or Billy, the diminutive, than no Bill at all.

Salmon River country was wrapped in winter in December, 1941, when the Japanese bombed Pearl Harbor. Hart did not hear of it until spring. He flowed with the tide of the hour: packed his gear and hiked down to Mackay Bar, crossed the bridge over the river and climbed out of the canyon to Dixie, and then on to Grangeville, Idaho, where he sought to enlist at the recruiting office. He flunked the physical because of an enlarged heart. Moreover, at thirty-five he was considered too old to soldier.

Undeterred, Hart traveled to Wichita, Kansas, and went to work as a toolmaker in the Boeing factory.

At some point in 1942 the Army apparently reconsidered and inducted Hart. (Meanwhile the FBI was looking for him in Idaho under the misapprehension that he was a draft evader.) He was posted to Amchitka in the Aleutian Islands as part of the force intended to oust the Japanese there, but the Japanese withdrew before he saw combat.

Hart was then flown to Colorado, where he went through an electronics course (at night) for several months in connection with secret work on the Norden bombsight. Recruited as a toolmaker for the project, he worked in a machine shop in Peyote, Texas. When the war ended, and he was discharged, he was a buck sergeant—not a colonel.

Sylvan Hart, or Buckskin Bill, had it figured out: it does not matter where you die, but it matters where you live. He turned like a homesick steelhead back to the Salmon River and soon recaptured the pace of his life. "Back in the hills, I took up where I left off. I became a summer fire lookout for the Forest Service on Quartzite and Oregon Butte." Another lonesome job, one that allowed him to run his own show, with time left over to read. In the fall he worked at trail clearing for the Forest Service; later he was a fishing guide and elk-skinner for Mackay Bar.

Hart's free time, the winter months, were enjambed with projects. On the one hand, he was a trained toolmaker and consummate craftsman, who carved kitchen utensils and bowls from cherrywood, and hammered pots and even a samovar from salvaged copper. On the other hand, he might labor for weeks over a small, crude, whimsical stone carving.

His most famous and admired creations, unarguably, were his flintlocks: hand-bored, hand-rifled, handsome with carved mountain mahogany stocks, and each rifle at least a year in the making. He made pistols, as well. "Yes, I make my own bullets; that's simple, but I do make my own bullet molds, too." And he could shoot. At age seventy-two, with a .22 rimfire Marlin and open sights at 170 yards, he fired a three-shot group the size of a penny.

In the same sensible spirit in which he purchased some factory firearms, Hart owned a share of practical storebought clothes: long-sleeved shirts, pants with suspenders. He made, however, more dramatic ensembles of bearskin and buckskin, as well as fur hats and leather helmets appropriate for a conquistador or Viking. They suited him when he wanted to strike a theatrical pose, especially in his years of fame.

If food is the last pleasure of an old man, his fare was that of a much younger person. He relied on his garden with its corn, carrots, beans, beets, potatoes, and berries. A commotion of chickens and ducks furnished eggs. The land provided grouse, deer, elk, bear; the river, steelhead, salmon, trout. He had an outdoor bake oven for summer; in winter he often cooked a week ahead and thawed his provender as needed.

> One February day as I went out my gate to go fishing, my wild chicken ran right up against my feet, and just then I saw the coyote that was trying to get it. So I went back and got my .370 and killed the coyote, and I said, "that chicken ought to lay us an egg today for saving its hide." Went on down to Ludwig Rapid and caught a nine-pound steelhead, and when I got back I saw the chicken get off its nest after laying the first egg of the spring. So a good day: a coyote, a steelhead, and an egg. Furthermore, our confidence in the chicken was not

misplaced.

Hart's view of wage-work was original:

> If you were so hard up you went around asking for a
> job, you'd be a poor mountaineer. But I've always lived
> by taking a job nobody else wanted, like going to war or
> fighting fire.
> If someone asks you to work, all right, but you should
> not ask anyone. Making a living in a country like that
> [Salmon River] is not a problem.

Requiring little cash, he squirreled away most of his government
checks—some were eventually fifteen years old, and because of a
federal regulation regarding stale-dated checks, he lost the right to
cash any older than three years.

This insouciant attitude toward money once landed him in the
newspapers. Hart had not filed any tax returns because his earnings
never exceeded $500, especially when he did not cash the checks.
The Internal Revenue Service, scenting evasion, wrote threatening
letters. Finally Hart togged himself out in bearskin britches and
bearclaw necklace, shouldered his tent, sleeping bag, a sack of
jerked venison, picked up his .370-caliber rifle and traveled out to
McCall and on to Boise.

He strode into the IRS office, tendered his surrender, unspooled
his sleeping bag and brewed a pot of tea on his Primus stove. Higher
authority was summoned.

When the supervisor arrived, Hart poured tea all around, then
told of the threatening letters, explained his predicament, and
conceded he was ready to go to prison. He had even brought his own
pemmican. The officials were disarmed by his candor, of course,
and he was sent on his way, no longer to be troubled by the
taxman—a consummation devoutly to be wished.

Then in June, 1966, a visitor arrived by powerboat at Five Mile
Bar, a visitor who was to alter Hart's anonymity forever. Harold
Peterson was twenty-seven, crewcut, a self-proclaimed "radical

conservative, Jeffersonian liberal," a Harvard graduate not far into a dozen-year stint as a staffwriter for *Sports Illustrated*. (Usually he wrote about baseball or basketball.)

Although Chicago-born, Peterson regarded the city as "a fairly poor place to do anything, including getting born," and he looked forward to any assignment that took him West, a region he defined as "beginning where people in general begin to be delightful." He had exchanged letters with Hart before coming to Five Mile Bar "hoping to find the myth of total self-sufficiency not yet entirely obsolete. I found...that the reality far exceeded any fiction." He was, in fact, so impressed with what he saw and heard that in October his article, "The Last of the Mountain Men," embellished with seven photographs, appeared in *Sports Illustrated*. After thirty-four years of irregular solitude, Sylvan Hart's life and location were revealed to 1.4 million subscribers. Within three years, the ten-page story had been expanded into a book, followed by a revised edition, then by quality and mass-market paperback editions. Hart had been discovered.

(An equally unexpected twist would engulf Harold Peterson himself only a few years later. While at work on a Utopian modern novel dealing with sexuality and liberation, he ended his life and that of his wife when she became involved with another man.)

Back at the Bar, change was winging its way like a merganser upriver and down. The article engendered a deluge of letters, gifts, and books. Hart's mail finally leveled off at twenty letters a week— a constant for the rest of his life.

Further, in 1967 Hart's nephew Rodney Cox (his sister's son), who had visited several times earlier, arrived with his wife Chana from Windsor, Ontario, to build a house and raise their family. (Cox had discovered that the five acres had been patented as a millsite associated with the Painter mine a short distance upriver. When the Forest Service got the damp-eared notion that it should evict Hart from the Idaho Primitive Area, Cox purchased title from the third party and gave his uncle a deed to the four-tenths of an acre where his cabin stood.)

Over the next five years, an incongruous two-story house,

lemon-yellow, tumefied on the otherwise rustic site. A hydroelectric power plant with over 500 feet of pipe was implanted along the creek. And Chana gave birth to three children. (The oldest was initially home-schooled by correspondence from the Calvert School of Baltimore, Maryland.)

As the Coxes settled in, the flow of newspaper and magazine stories about Hart continued to grow; so did his stream of visitors. Backpackers, hikers, hippies in search of a guru marched in like army ants, camped on his place, and not infrequently abused his hospitality. By the early 1970s summer regattas of rafts and jet boats daily crossed the eddy to beach in front of his cabin and disgorge their passengers to view "Buckskin Bill"—the "Old Faithful" of Salmon River.

In the spring it was evident that Hart enjoyed this attention: animated and good-humored as an otter, he held forth in his best "Darn the settlements, I say" Oklahoma drawl. He was curious about his visitors, their hometowns and occupations; he regaled the tourists with anecdotes invariably colored by his humor and his limitless ability to beguile and amuse.

Aren't you afraid of the bears?

Naw. In a bad year where there is no food for bears, I have had to fight bears each night attired in a skivvy shirt and armed with a flashlight and a .44 magnum pistol. I would say it takes a quart of bear's blood to produce a pound of dried apricots. But don't feel too sorry for the bears. At night you can shoot, but at fifty yards you won't hit one; you'll just come close enough that he will get the idea that he is not wanted.

How cold does it get in the winter?

Not that bad. One time my brother Tommy and myself had fun fishing from the edge of the ice. A few days later it was much warmer, and from the top of the bluff downstream we saw the very same ice floe coming down that we had fished from, with our tracks on it, even the imprint of the fish we had caught. It was going at a fast clip, and we were creeping along the bluff, so I said, 'Since our tracks and the past are catching up with us, even passing and surpassing us, the situation is certainly irretrievable, and our little fishing trip is gone for good.'

Do you hunt?

Yeah. Course you gotta be a bit circumspect. One winter day Johnny Johnson was dressing out a deer at the Painter place. A couple of young guys came up and stood watching him. Johnny asked them what they were doing and learned they were counting game for the game department. So he said to them, 'Don't count *this* one.'

Another time I remember young Jensen was hunting out of season and met a man on the trail. He told the fellow he had just killed the biggest buck he had ever seen. Truly magnificent horns, like a rocking chair.

The man said, 'Do you know who I am?'

Jensen said, 'No.'

The man said, 'I'm the game warden of this county.'

Jensen said, 'Do you know who I am?'

The warden said, 'No.'

Jensen said, 'I'm the biggest liar in Idaho County.'

What if you get sick and need a doctor?

Well, it's like the farmer who was telling a rancher about his stomach ailment and his general run-down condition. He went on and on; finally the rancher said, 'I know just what will fire you up. Kill a sage hen, take the inner lining of the gizzard, make a tea of it and drink it.' Not long afterward, the farmer killed a sage hen and examined it, but no gizzard. Then he killed another, still no go. So he went over to the rancher's and said, 'Sage hen ain't got no gizzard.' The rancher replied, 'Imaginary treatment for an imaginary ailment.'

Whatever else the folks thought, few of them left Five Mile Bar disappointed or disillusioned.

But by early fall Hart had tired of playing the "dancing bear"; the parade of visitors had left him spent; he needed the winter to revive. After August, boatmen spared him if they could.

In the summers of 1974 and 1975 Rodney Cox, finance major, decided to charge river outfitters for "visitation" privileges at Five Mile Bar. Most outfitters were put off by this unwestern scheme, uncertain Hart would get the fees, but apparently he threw in with it.

Then in August, 1975, tragedy struck the Cox family: their oldest boy Jeremiah, age seven, was killed by a vehicle being used to haul firewood from upriver down onto the beach. He was riding on the back, fell, and was pinned between the wheel and the body of the vehicle. An Army medical helicopter flew in but it was too late. He had died instantly. Shortly thereafter the Cox family flew to Grangeville, leaving the Salmon River for a channel of their own. Jeremiah was buried in Portland.

The flow of summer visitors resumed. So did the interviews and articles. Fragments of Hart's philosophy were captured and quoted, many of them clear and sharp as the slap of a beavertail on the roof of a river:

> A young man wrote me that he was interested in the great and ultimate truths of life. I said that he was taking a very dangerous course—that the truth is sterile and produces nothing. There is no future in it. In his case he should start with a lie, like "I am the best little writer that ever scribbled." That way he might become one. The honest truth is that you are no writer at all and not likely to become one. So forget the truth and start building a lie into the truth, then you will be a solid success. The truth can even become a lie: You are the best rower, so you rest on your oars while someone else rows mightily and surpasses you. You see, you must fight the truth to keep it from killing you, whereas lies sustain you and help you grow.

Why would a man write, "Oh, how I hate to get up in the morning?" This just makes a difficult thing more difficult and doesn't help any. Marcus Aurelius told you how to get up, and there wasn't a lazy bone in his body. Contrary to general opinion, one of the most refreshing things you can do is to occasionally get up three or four hours earlier than usual, say at four o'clock. You should have a fireplace. Light a fire quietly, make yourself some coffee, and observe silence so you don't disturb some deadhead.

Now pretty soon your mind comes to life and takes over in a cheerful manner. As I said before, don't try to do anything. You can remember things you thought you had forgotten. You should be able to see the sunrise, which should cheer you up. Now don't expect too much from this little adventure, as the effect will wear off during the day, and you may need a nap in the middle of the afternoon.

The only way you can have any leisure time is to have no labor-saving devices. It is just as though a labor-saving device tempts fate to saddle you with days of extra work to make up for the little time you save. If you have just a little work to do, better do it by hand—then you are through.

About the finest little bird is the water ouzel. This bird is no tramp; it lives well on periwinkles, helgramites, etc. It is always cheerful. On the worst days it sings and hitches rides on little cakes of ice and has more harmless fun than a dozen people. No other birds compete with it, and it is a master of air and water. It never knows famine, and it always sets a good table with plenty of variety. This shows if you will pick a tough place to live, and work hard to make a living, you too can be strong, cheerful, and free.

If you look out your window and see a house, you're a poor man; if you look out and see a lot of houses, you're a very poor man; if you can't see any at all, you're all right.

I'm a great man for culture, but culture for the other guy—I don't want any for myself.

I am not in any hurry to become an author because my opinion of authors nowadays is that they are low down reptiles, and when I start to write a book, I want to be at least in the varmint class.

No point in overdoing religious ideas. Just have a good religious philosophy and let it go at that. I believe in God; you have to.

I lived in a cabin when I worked for the Forest Service, and an old religious man kicked the door open and said, 'How is it with your soul?' I said, 'Damn good, and get out of here until you learn a few manners, and don't be breaking into people's houses like this.'

When you die, you have to die by yourself anyway. But you should enjoy it up to the last minute.

In his "renowned" years, Hart traveled more frequently than he had in the past. He made trips to the Southwest, Iceland, and Russia; he also gave talks to schoolchildren, and often rendezvoused with fellow muzzleloaders at their summer regional matches. (He sent a picture of himself with a sixteen-inch bowie knife in his mouth and a .44-caliber Smith and Wesson six-shooter in each hand to the Boy Scout troop in Grangeville with the implied message "Be Prepared.")

In mid-June, 1978, Hart flew to Boise to throw the first pitch for the new baseball team, the Boise Buckskins, of the Class A Northwest League. Clothed in a coonskin hat, buckskin shirt and pants, and a bearclaw necklace, Hart signed autographs for young fans and told the local sports reporter that he had not thrown a baseball since 1918. Following the Buckskins' victory, the reporter's story the next day mentioned Hart, "looking like he'd just fallen out of a James Fenimore Cooper novel and depending on an arm that hadn't been tested in fifty years."

In April, 1980, a jet boat pilot from Mackay Bar visited Hart and found that he was not feeling well; the pilot promised to check on him the following day. Said Sylvan, "When you come back, I'll either be better or I'll be dead." Returning the next morning, the boatman found Hart sitting in his chair, dead apparently of a heart attack.

The funeral service took place at Nolands' Funeral Home in Grangeville, with Reverend Charles Martin from the First Baptist Church officiating. The casket was then flown to Mackay Bar and hauled up river by boat.

The burial took place at Five Mile Bar. Two dozen persons were present: Hart's three sisters, two of his nephews, friends from Grangeville and the Salmon River canyon. Hart was buried in his going-to-town clothes: plaid shirt, wool pants, and his favorite belt buckle. His pine coffin, flag-draped, was lowered into the grave that had been dug at the riverside of his garden. Rodney Cox delivered a eulogy, and Hart's three sisters planted an apricot tree and a lilac bush. Three friends fired a salute with Hart's own long rifles.

A month later nine weekend-mountaineers returned to mark the grave with a granite tombstone:

> Sylvan A. Hart
> "Buckskin Bill"
> May 10, 1906   April 29, 1980
> The Last of the Mountain Men

Hart left his comfortable estate to his nephew Rodney Cox. Cox offered to sell Five Mile Bar to the Forest Service; the Service eventually made an offer of $174,000—a figure at least $6,000 less than the one the owner had in mind. He subsequently listed the property, subdivided into eight lots priced from $20,000 to $181,000, with a real estate agent. Several lots were sold, but only one new building has been added at this time.

The Coxes donated a portion of Hart's effects to the Idaho Historical Society, and in December, 1980, two National Guard helicopters flew to the bar with state and guard personnel. The men loaded approximately 1,000 items—clothing, blacksmith tools, guns, knives, bowls, books, animal skulls—aboard the helicopters and flew the materials to Boise for the state collection. Some of the objects were exhibited at the museum.

Additionally, the Coxes donated a handsome sample of Hart's handcraft to St. Gertrude's Museum at Cottonwood, Idaho, in memory of their son Jeremiah. The pieces on display include a remarkable percussion rifle, a sheephorn powder horn, knives, sword, carved wooden spoons, bowls and boxes, and examples of his metalsmithing.

As for Five Mile Bar, Mr. Cox had substantial loans against the buildings on the property; he experienced financial difficulties, and the banks finally foreclosed. While caretakers look after the bar and greet summer visitors to the compound, the Forest Service still seeks to protect the site through purchase of a scenic easement.

That worthy effort—precluding development of the bench and gravesite where tributary and mainstream merge—brings to mind another remark Hart once made. "I never asked more out of life than a good creek, a good river." Appropriate that the man who lived by a creek and river lovely beyond any singing of them, should now rest within reach of the music of both.

41 SYLVAN AMBROSE HART.
42 INTERIOR VIEW OF HART'S QUARTERS WITH HIS HANDMADE KETTLES.
43 AERIAL VIEW OF HART'S HOLDING ON THE SALMON RIVER.

44 & 45 Examples of Hart's gunsmithing.
46 Last of the mountain men.

Life History of Sylvan
Ambrose Hart by himself.

Indian Territory in 1906
was definitely pioneer times.
Houses were cedar log, sod,
and not many frame house[...]
I was born in a dugout an
underground earth dwelling
May 10, 1906. The first animals
that impressed me were fat
toads. I really liked these insect
getters and where I went to a
place that had no toads I wondered if these people were
clean. When I was three years old
I helped my father build a
frame house, but I dont think

2- he thought I was a help. One
night I heard a commotion among
our neighbors fowling hounds.
I was sleeping just inside a
door when my little dog just out
side the screen was bitten by
a mad dog. Dogs, pigs, horses
and hounds had to be killed
when they went mad and it
was noon of next day before
someone killed the mad dog.
The telephone appeared soon
after and I dont think any
other mad dog ever destroyed
as many animals as that one.
I had a small creek to play
in with cutbanks some 15 feet
deep. A twine string a bent pin

47 PAGES IN HART'S OWN HAND.

LYDIA COYLE, **FREE PRESS FRANCES**

SOLITUDE HAS BUT ONE DISADVANTAGE; IT IS APT TO GIVE ONE TOO HIGH AN OPINION OF ONE'S SELF. IN THE WORLD WE ARE SURE TO BE REMINDED OF EVERY KNOWN OR SUPPOSED DEFECT WE MAY HAVE.—GEORGE BYRON

She was an old woman, typing alone at her desk by the window, pounding her unmalleable opinions into a weekly column as she had for forty years—a column that had become the mainspring for her life, a column that told her readers she was still there, overlooking the greeny depths of the River of No Return.

The log house was old, too. She belonged to it and it to her. Memories flowed within and without: Joe, and then Vern; the dogs Sister, Reuben, Gretchen; cats Mabel and Steamboat; the woodstove, rocking chairs, rifles, fishing pole; meadow and orchard (salted with deer and elk), haybarn and garden. She was married to this place, dying now. It was 1985 and no years left.

She kept on typing despite jolting changes over the past few years—even recorded them: the death of her third husband, Vern; the Salmon River flood; a severe fall; a broken leg; the Challis earthquake (7.3). Since Vern's death in 1974, she had lived alone at Campbells Ferry. Not that she did not have visitors. She did. Her sisters, river friends, Grangeville friends, Boise friends made a point of checking and cheering. And she let her readers—the "*Idaho County Free Press* family" up on Camas Prairie—know how she was faring.

Deep in December, she hammered out the last column—about a pair of ruffed grouse (she called them "ruffled") catching all but invisible insects on a leafless apple tree in her orchard. Two weeks later she was dead of cancer—herself "a tree made leafless by this wintry wind." Within days her dog died. A couple of years more, and Campbells Ferry was purchased by Trust for Public Lands, restrictive covenants attached to prevent subdivision, and then sold, the owners then opening the site to the public.

Although ambivalent about her status as an oldtimer, Frances Zaunmiller (she chose to go by her middle name and that of her second husband) at the time of her death had truthfully outlived all her contemporaries who had come to the river ahead of her. At times she made it sound as though she had been there as long as elk droppings in the ponderosas; at other times, she acknowledged her predecessors while some of them still lived. In 1965 she wrote, in the third person, as was her manner:

> And Frances, who is not an oldtimer but did come to the mountains before her hair turned white, remembers travel and living conditions in the early days, for it was still the early-day way of life when she came.
>
> She has watched the building of the bridge which replaced the ferryboat; a safe trail from that bridge to the end of the road; part of the meadow become a landing strip for small aircraft.
>
> Still she remembers enough of the old tales and old ways that it is easy for her to understand how of those who came first the men were soon separated from the boys.

By 1985, however, all her elders along the river benches—Pete Klinkhammer, Frank Lantz, even Sylvan Hart—had been drained away, like spring runoff down "the river of no return."

Lydia Frances Coyle was another transplant, like most Idahoans then and now. She was born in Bruceville, Texas, just south of Waco, in 1913. Central Texas. All room and no furnishings. Cotton country. Flat and stark as stretched canvas. In an early letter she recalled, "The only thing that keeps you from seeing all the way to China is the horizon. When I was a child, I loved it. But before I was even grown, people started clearing the land, plowed up the bluebonnets, dug out the sage and cactus. They cut the land up and fenced [it]."

Her father, J. A. Coyle, was an oil rig contractor who built drilling derricks, and the family that grew to seven children moved often: San Antonio, Three Rivers, Corpus Christi. Following high school, Frances worked as a switchboard operator in Beeville (sixty miles northwest of Corpus Christi) for Southern Bell. After an early marriage to Bob Gambel, and two stillborn children, she left Texas—"I finally got the courage to leave that wonderful farming country"—and never went back.

In 1940 this southern dude arrived, by way of Shoup, Idaho, in Chamberlain Basin, the outback of the Idaho Primitive Area, precursor to the River of No Return Wilderness. She was in the company of Bert Rhodes, reputedly a trick roper in his youth, and later a packer and guide. She was expected to housesit the Bill Stonebraker ranch. Oldtime ranch resident Harry Donohue became dude wrangler and tutor: he taught her to fish and to ride, how mountain hay was harvested and where huckleberries grew. Said she, "Now I am in a place I was born to be. All the good things I knew as a child are here, and more! Here there are trees. People who have lived in Idaho most of their lives have no idea how truly beautiful this country is."

Shortly, Rhodes, who had been living at the Moore place across the Salmon River from Campbells Ferry, was arrested for his part in poaching five Rocky Mountain bighorn sheep. In 1941, Frances, who had visited the place earlier, was hired as cook and house-keeper for Joe Zaunmiller's log house at the Ferry down on the river, ten miles northwest of the Stonebraker Ranch, and connected to it by trail.

Zaunmiller, originally from Walla Walla, Washington, came into the Salmon River country in 1926 and bought the Ed Harbison ranch on Big Mallard Creek, tributary to the Salmon. An exceptional horseman, he worked as a packer for the Payette and Nez Perce national forests. In 1933 he sold the Harbison place and acquired a half interest in Campbells Ferry, eighty acres on the south side of the river. He operated a cable ferry (wooden boat) at the site—the only dry crossing for almost fifty miles upstream and down. His reputation as a packer and guide grew with the years. After hunting season, in November, 1942, Joe and Frances were married at his younger brother's house in Walla Walla. It was the second marriage for both. He was fifty-one; she was twenty-nine.

As a packer, Joe was often out on the trails. Frances wrote, "Joe works for the Forest in the summer, so from May 1st to September 30th I am alone, except for the wild things. They have learned to trust me and my dog, and we have a lot of fun watching the deer and elk." She looked after the place, saw to its chores, and ran the ferry.

The Zaunmillers' log house was two stories, with handhewn beams, and a partial cellar entered from the downhill side of the house. The original Campbell house burned in 1906, and its replacement was built by the Aikens and Cooks the same year. The upstairs consisted of a large room and a small one, used for storage. The downstairs had two bedrooms, living room, and kitchen with woodstove. "The house is old and has its quirks, as many old houses do," she wrote. "It is a small house, of six rooms, though one is a combination storeroom, hobby corner and, in desperation, also will sleep one person. Yet the little house is elastic and can shelter many more people than seems possible."

In another column, writing about the lack of conveniences, she observed, "You can go to places on the river that have had the same owner for generations, and while they will be clean and comfortable, still they will show that the ones who live there found a way of living that suited them and settled to that, resisting any hint of change—and a lot of times a bit of change would make the way of living so much better.

"The Ferry is like that. For years Joe has wanted to put running water in the house, but she doesn't want it. Running water would make a lot less work, but Joe does not guarantee that the little water ditch [diverted from the creek] that talks its way past the kitchen door would not be taken away—so she will keep the ditch and listen to the water tell its tales of the places it has been; you should listen to it brag sometimes." The outhouse, called the "blue building," served a lifetime.

During the 1930s, the Civilian Conservation Corps scraped out a road from Dixie (a one-store hamlet) south down to the Salmon River at the Dalė Ranch (later Whitewater), four miles upriver from the Ferry. The road was the Zaunmillers' lifelink to mail and "civilization" at Dixie, and thirty miles north to Elk City (more elk than city), and another sixty miles to Grangeville (population 3,000). At the road-end, the Zaunmillers siphoned kerosene into five-gallon cans from a fifty-gallon drum and packed the lamp oil home.

They hayed their alfalfa meadow and hauled the hay to their barn—winter feed for horses, mules, and cows. They split pine and fir into firewood. Deer, elk, and bear provided winter meat, and Frances was fond of fishing. Ducks and hens furnished eggs. Although casual about weeds, Frances was a serious gardener, as one who leans on home-canned food for survival must be. She had to fend against weather, rodents, and hoofed ruminants. Among the produce grown: lettuce, spinach, kale, rhubarb, tomatoes and potatoes, carrots, turnips, parsnips, onions and garlic, squash, black-eyed peas, peppers, eggplant, asparagus, melons, strawberries, blueberries, blackberries, raspberries, boysenberries, grapes and currants. The orchard, too, provided variety: apples, peaches, plums, pears, and apricots, chestnuts, walnuts, and almonds (nuts winter-dried in the attic). Flowers mattered also: crocus, daffodils, violets, peonies, snapdragons, dahlias, daylilies, roses, lilacs, sunflowers.

In 1945 Frances began writing a column, for which she was eventually paid ten dollars a week, for the weekly *Idaho County Free Press*, published in Grangeville. (Initially, the column was sent out overland; after 1958 it was airmailed.) As already mentioned, she chose to write in the third person—often referring to herself as "the Mountaineer" or "the Woman" or "the little woman." Her pieces varied as much as the output of her garden—equal portions of gossip, opinion, river doings, observation, and introspection. Gathered in a bushel basket, they offer a remarkable record of changes and events along her short reach of the river.

Over the twenty years of her life with Joe at the Ferry, there were major transformations. In April, 1956, a suspension bridge was completed across the river, connecting Campbells Ferry with the Jim Moore place on the north shore, and by trail therefrom to the Dale Ranch and the road. The bridge was built largely by Frances' head butting; she lobbied Senator Dworshak, the U. S. Forest Service, and urban hunters. Her column proved a bully pulpit. Construction was a six-month project for an eleven-man crew; the completion was cause for a celebration. Frances crept out the night before and hung Christmas decorations from the towers and cables. The forest supervisor flew in for the festive dinner. Joe rode his appaloosa mare across the bridge, and Frances rode her back.

In 1958 weekly backcountry mail service began for canyon residents with airstrips. For the first time, the Ferry could send and receive packages without packing them overland or boating them upriver. Again, Frances campaigned hard for the service.

Within years, the Ferry had a propane refrigerator (cylinders could be hauled in to the Dale Ranch or flown in from McCall). Moreover, in 1960, when a stonemason flew in, a longheld dream of a fireplace was realized. "She learned that real fireplace men are rare varmints, difficult to locate, dated up like a debutante."

The same year, Joe Zaunmiller, whose lungs had been frost-burned, and whose legs were beginning to trouble him, sold the Ferry to John and Mary Crowe. The Crowes had graduated from the University of Idaho, and although John was a design engineer, they settled, after working on Shasta Dam, in northern California and worked a cattle ranch, but they maintained fond ties with their Idaho friends. The Crowes gave the Zaunmillers a life estate at the Ferry and built their own cabin a short walk uphill from the log house. (Joe had a small sawmill on the place.) They also brought in a Farmall tractor, in pieces, to help with the haying (John was a pilot).

Only two years later, Joe died at the Ferry of a heart attack. He was buried in Grangeville.

Allen Vernon Wisner, a longtime friend of the Zaunmillers, moved to the Crowe cabin at the Ferry, where he could be of help to Frances when she needed him. Wisner, born of an Indian mother in a tipi on the Sioux reservation, was raised in Nebraska and came to Grangeville in 1912. He had been a trapper, then a packer for the Forest Service, before retiring in 1960.

One and a half years after he moved to the Ferry, he and Frances were married at the Methodist church in Asotin, Washington. He was seventy; she was forty-nine. They returned to the Ferry and a busy, harmonious life.

They had seven good years; then Vern began to suffer from hardening of the arteries. He experienced blackouts with increasing frequency, and his vision was affected. Frances nursed him until two weeks before the end, March, 1974, when he was flown to the Veterans Hospital in Boise. She was with him when he died. He was buried in Grangeville.

Frances returned to the Ferry, as alone as she had ever been. She knew she could not drown her sorrows—they know how to swim. Work is the unfailing anodyne. She resumed her cycle of chores. Earlier, in response to the recurring question, "What do you do with your spare time?" she had written, "Spare time? Here in this canyon there is stock to be fed each day, wood to be split and brought to the house, dogs, cats, and chickens to feed and care for, water holes to be chopped through the ice so domestic and wild four-legged ones can drink.

"There are floors to be swept, meals to be cooked, and dishes to wash. Laundry day is especially busy, both wash and rinse water must be heated on stoves. There are books to read, letters to write, trails must be shoveled clean after each new snowfall. Before the mail plane can land, new snow on the landing strip must be snowshoe-packed. [The Ferry strip is a thirty-five degree slope facing the river.] The trail from dwelling to landing strip must be snowshoed firm too. Spare time? There is none."

Some winters thirty inches of snow could blanket the Ferry. Roofs had to be shoveled periodically. Domestic water was melted from snow, making laundry an impossible task, since an equal amount was needed for the rinse. Instead, clothes were saved in hampers until spring, when wash could be rain-rinsed and hung in the attic to dry.

Frances had a volunteer weather station and made daily recordings for the National Weather Service.

Diversions sometimes accompanied and interrupted her routines. The ground-line telephone linked the Red River ranger station with the Ferry and the Dale and Allison ranches and Yellowpine bar. Although the phone was for fire reports, folks visited on it early in the morning, and in return maintained the line. In later years, the line connected the Ferry only with the three ranches (small private inholdings, not really ranches). The radio-telephone, however, became the principal means of outside communication.

Frances had a sewing machine; she also knitted and crocheted—a queensize bedspread was a proud accomplishment.

Photography was a longtime interest. She was particularly delighted by the introduction of the 35mm single-lens reflex camera.

She had a shortwave radio and an AM one. She liked to listen to baseball games, and at night she could pick up stations in San Francisco, Los Angeles, and Vancouver.

She was enthusiastic about fishing, but in her last years had to give it up because she was too short of breath to hike back up from the river.

Prompted by an appointment with the dentist or eye doctor, she would fly out to Grangeville on occasion, sometimes staying to visit friends.

In a canyon replete with them, Frances Zaunmiller was a character. In fact, the unusual was so usual in this canyon as to inevitably raise speculation about whether these individuals would have stood out similarly had they chosen to live in the city—an unanswerable question.

As for her philosophy, she recorded it in an early column:

> She would tell you her belief that is as much a part of her being as the blood which flows through her body.
>
> It was explained to her when as a child she asked her grandfather, 'Why was I born?' Grandfather sat beside me and this is what he said: 'Every soul born on this earth is sent here to do a thing of good. That soul is left here

until its purpose is accomplished, or it has convinced the Gods that it will not [be]. Then it is removed. No one knows why he is here. Not always is he taken away as soon as his purpose is accomplished. Once in a while one is allowed to remain a while longer on earth—for the joy of living. And child, you are human, with the strength of everyday people, and their weaknesses too. You will do things not good. Each must be balanced by good. In the sight of your God every evil in your life must be balanced by good before you can accomplish your purpose.'

In another column she noted, "Just one little woman in a little house in a little meadow. The little things of people she can do (most of the time), but to the thunder and the wind she is a nothing."

In her opinions, Frances was certainly a match for wind and thunder—she harbored her fair share of dogmatic certitudes. Sometimes she offended people. When she inquired over the canyon radio, for example, about the price paid by the new owners of Shepp Ranch downriver and received the reply that it was none of her business, a coolness welled between the locations.

Her avowals of a right to privacy contrasted with her public columns and grants of interviews. Her feelings on privacy obviously vacillated: she could be sweeter than sage honey about it, or gruffer than a sour bear. When she saw a copy of a guidebook to the Salmon River that ignored her because she had threatened to sue if included, she was outraged.

In another instance, an editor for Time-Life stopped unannounced and later wrote of his encounter:

> Salmon River country is not what you'd call overcrowded. Here and there one finds an abandoned ranch or miner's cabin, but very rarely a place that is still inhabited. One day, walking back in from the river, we came to a small cabin surrounded by a little vegetable garden. A woman came to the cabin door. She had long gray hair and wore cowboy boots and jeans; she looked

as if she could block a pro lineman ten yards into his own backfield. The assumption is that a person living in such isolation would welcome any human contact, if only to hear another voice, and so we strode forward expecting the best.

'Get out of here,' she said, 'and don't come back.'

We shouldn't have been surprised, for the Salmon has traditionally been a place where misanthropes go to ground.

Frances was not a misanthrope. Often would-be visitors simply did not understand the lack of time salvaged from chores, or that she was caring for an invalid. Of mountain hospitality she wrote, "The coming of scores of tiny planes into the mountains and canyons has caused the old way of 'I am too busy to enjoy you,' to become 'by reservation or prior arrangement only, except in emergency.'" She wrote further, "Surely a thinking person should not expect one who had personal things she wants to do to play tourist-tidbit-hostess to every floater who makes the trip down the Salmon? Those who do quickly learn that she just will not play that stupid game." And when a newspaper article brought her to the attention of Johnny Carson's "Tonight" show, she declined an invitation to appear as a guest.

She did prefer visiting with women, and any male in the canyon knew he would meet with a more cordial reception if he was so accompanied. She got along with women like daisies in the same bouquet. Frances speaking (1956):

> It was early in hunting season when the last woman came to the Ferry. When one of the things [woman] is here, Frances really enjoys having her. Women are so rare at the Ferry that no other thing is more welcome. But when it is months and more months and the only woman is the one she sees in the mirror, there isn't a hunger to see one.
>
> She has learned to put *women* out of her mind—to look

at the catalogue and wonder what is it that wears dresses. Such a strange looking animal.

When a day comes that brings a woman, Frances loses her senses, starts to pour coffee and forgets the cups; she wants to stare but is afraid the poor creature will become frightened and go away. She wants to listen to that female voice but can't stop talking long enough to listen. After a few hours, the strangeness goes away, and then the new woman has a chance to get in a word.

It was her weekly column that raised Frances from nonentity to notoriety, a status she obviously preferred. Who would not? "News gathering is not difficult," she advised. "One just listens and is interested enough to remember and takes the time to write the account to you. Of course, it is easy for Frances, as she is so sure that everyone is just as interested in her forested mountains as she."

Yet her stated views were often inconsistent with her own lifeway, and while consistency has been called the hobgoblin of small minds, her views did make for a certain irony along the river. She was a foe of the Wilderness Act and of the Wild and Scenic Rivers Act. Both Acts, however, preserved most of the surrounding beauty she professed to admire; however, one must remember that she came from a state with no history of federal, public lands— reason enough her bluebonnets were plowed under. She was opposed to governmental regulations; at the same time she urged the federal government to remove beetle-killed trees, fight fires, deliver air mail, construct and maintain trails, build an expensive bridge spanning the river at her house—all subsidized endeavors— and both her husbands at the Ferry depended on federal employment. Of course, as she once said, "Frequent griping is one of the favorite pastimes in the mountains."

Frances also sought state help in destroying, as well as conserving, animal life near the Ferry (despite her disdain of conservationists). Although she often wrote about animal life and behavior around her meadow, particularly that of deer and elk, she had little patience or tolerance for the interference of nature: she killed fieldmice, bushytail woodrats, snakes, weasels, cottontails, raccoons, skunks, coyotes, and bear. And her crusty prejudices against eagles, wolves, and mountain lions—often rising to the level of harangue—displayed no understanding of the role predators have in a healthy food chain, nor any history of the deer herds in the Middle Fork Game Preserve that collapsed when they outstripped their habitat. She would have done well to read another loner, Edward Abbey, on mountain lions, "It is the lion's claw, the lion's tooth and need, that has given the deer its beauty and speed and grace."

In August, 1962, a sow grizzly and her cub came through the orchard and helped themselves to some fruit; she sought to have the conservation officer shoot them. When it came to deer and elk, however, she was instrumental a year later in securing passage of House Bill 213, outlawing the hunting and shooting of game animals and birds from motorboats or aircraft (including helicopters)—a practice prevalent at that time along the Salmon River.

Zaunmiller was at her best when she wrote about the landscape surrounding her place and her intimate relationship with it.

> So many nights Frances has bundled up warm, then gone out into the moonlit orchard to watch frost form on a board or fence post. She has watched an old board take on a sheen that seems unreal.
>
> Slowly but ever faster, until the eye cannot absorb all that is happening, and she must concentrate on just a few inches of the board, that sheen separates from complete coverage, and frost flakes grow outward. A constantly changing beauty. No two frost growths are alike, yet each is twin to all the others.
>
> A fascinating world of beauty is the Canyon of the Salmon during the nights of November when frosts begin to grow.

In another column, she observes the moonrise:

When waking from sleep, your Frances seems to always turn toward a window to see if the world is still in place. At a between-midnight-and-morning awakening, looking out her window she saw a glow begin to rise behind Big Trout Ridge.

It grew until the night was bright, stars dimmed in the brightness. And then two points of golden fire protruded above the ridge. Moon's horns. She watched the tips become fat and longer as the moon's body pushed from behind the horizon. Imagination said that one could hear the noise as the moon jerked free of the ridge. She wondered if any of the neighbors were awake and watching too.

Christmas, 1964, gave rise to such sentiments as these:

The great silence of the mountains is broken by the slither of one snowflake and then another, slipping from needle to branch and then to the ground. No church bells ring out, but there is a singing of the ridges as each decks its parts with the raiment of the approaching Mass of Christ.

Carolers? In the mountains and canyons a coyote sings and an eagle screams; a Canada jay eats from the elderberry tree beneath a kitchen window and talks his song to a watching woman. In a pine beyond the barn, a squirrel chatters his greeting to that woman as she spreads hay for the stock; and in the evening when all the chores are finished, she changes from her working garb into a dress of a woman and walks out to look at the meadows and mountain ridges which are her world.

'Tis no different than it was on that night nearly two thousand years ago, when the hills and ridges were snow-covered and hushed, and the very air did sing of a Glory.

Ten years later, the sentiments are the same:

Christmas in the Canyon of the Salmon is no different from Christmas in the rest of the world. Perhaps a little more quiet here. But no less holy. No less beautiful, even though the decorating is done in the Canyon by nature's artists, the frost and the snow.

Inside the house, it is quiet except for a woman singing the old carols. And reading the Old Story aloud. And thanking her Lord that there is Christmas both here and in all the world.

Vern's death in 1974 left a large hole in the fabric of life at the Ferry. She wrote, "to Frances *widow* is the ugliest word in any language. So many times this past week she has wondered how the new widow alone was able to get through those days."

By May, the loss was still sharp but it had softened at the edges. "Evening is the time to visit the riverbank. Not fishing, but just to walk among the boulders, looking at forget-me-not plants spreading over the sand. When the light fails so looking isn't easy anymore, and the little dog insists that supper is at the house up on the hill, then you straighten, watch evening come to the sand and boulders of the riverbank. And then it is time to return to the house to shut the chicken house, so night prowling varmints cannot get in; then gather the eggs and fill the cat dish with their special feed. The woodbox was filled before you went to the riverbank, so there are only the lamps to light before building a fire in the cookstove so supper for you and the little dog can be cooked. It is a nice world, this Canyon of the Salmon."

Seven years later, she still ached, however. "January (February, too) is my depressing time. Since Vern went away, it is now that I miss him most. Hunger to hear his voice and see his face. The quiet clatter as he makes the afternoon coffee, stomping on porch to knock snow off his shoes, the fun of our card games.

"It is just Vern I miss—in all his ways. Since there's no way that can be again, January and February I must endure, as I do."

As she celebrated her seventieth birthday, Frances turned pensive for a moment. "She knows that she is older than in those years past, but the feeling is of *older* rather than getting old. A pleasant feeling, to have weathered the bad years as well as enjoyed the good ones. And she has had many good years to cherish in memory. When she reached 20 she asked for another 20 years. At 30 the request was for another 30, and each request was granted. Now nearing 70 she does not want another 70 years, but 15 or 20 more would be fun to live through. She wonders, is afraid to ask, in 1993 will the river still run downhill?

It did, but it spooled past without her watch. Frances, who smoked and had been operated on for cancer twice earlier, despite resolute resistance succumbed to the disease in January, 1986. She was seventy-two. She was buried beside Vern Wisner in the Prairie View Cemetery in Grangeville.

48 FRANCES AND JOE ZAUNMILLER AT CAMPBELLS FERRY IN 1953.
49 & 50 ZAUNMILLER TENDING HER GARDEN BY HER HOUSE.

51 ZAUNMILLER AWAITING THE MAIL PLANE ON THE STRIP
AT CAMPBELLS FERRY.

RICHARD ZIMMERMAN, **DUGOUT DICK**

HE WAS ONLY SHY AT FIRST, AND AFTER THAT HE WAS FINE COMPANY,
AS THE LONELY OFTEN ARE.— ANON.

Going into Richard Zimmerman's quarters is much like going into a mineshaft, except that sunlight is no stranger there—it leaks through windows contrived from salvaged windshields. And thick-set rock walls, which should stifle every sound, simply dampen the murmur of highway and river drifting across the expansive equivalent of front yard.

Zimmerman, better known as Dugout Dick, lives in adit-rooms tucked flush into the base of a rockslide on the west side of the Salmon River, eighteen miles south of Salmon, Idaho. At first, in these handmade caves visitors feel a bit like wormbait, then gradually warm to their practicality and that of their maker. In an imagined dramatic monologue matching Dick's voice and a remembered spall of conversations, Idaho poet William Studebaker, who as a boy knew Zimmerman well, wrote,

> Dirt's the roof
> so when you die
> not everything's strange.
>
> I don't think I ever decided.
> I just started building out of rock.
> Not because there were so many
> but because they were
> arranged so bad.

Strange to say, it was really Zimmerman's mal-arranged stomach cavity that drove him to this talus slope along the Salmon River. Since childhood, he had been tormented by indigestion. "Yeah, all my life," he says ruefully, "from the time I was a little baby. Gave me pills I didn't want to take. My bowels wouldn't move." When he was inducted into the army in mid-1942 at Fort Douglas, Utah, he promptly volunteered for kitchen patrol because it offered him a shot at easing his dietary problems. Following basic training, to smooth Zimmerman's voyage from San Francisco to the South Pacific, his bootcamp buddies at Fort Hann, California, lugged grapefruit aboard his troop ship just before it embarked beneath the Golden Gate Bridge.

He sailed to the New Hebrides (now Vanuatu) between New Zealand and New Guinea and was stationed in the village of Efate on Port-Vila. He asked the first soldier he met there what fruit grew on the island and was promptly introduced to tangerines and mangoes, limes and coconuts. Fortunately, they suited his system. But soon fellow soldiers began making jokes—"Dick don't want no chow, he's out scrounging bananas with the monkeys." About three months later, Pvt. First Class Zimmerman, truck driver, was honorably discharged to work as a farmhand back in Idaho—a type of work he had known since he was buckle-high.

He earned his passage back to San Pedro, California, on a merchant marine ship, unloading fifty-gallon drums of gasoline by hand and keeping a starboard watch for enemy submarines. The food was good, however, and he was the grateful for all the V8 juice he could drink. "You can have as much of that stuff as you want," the cook told him, "nobody else likes it."

Zimmerman, oldest of five children, grew up on a 200-acre peppermint farm near the small town of Milford in northern Indiana—lake country and Amish country. His father was a German "apostate," ornery and mean; his mother a Dunkard (German-American Baptists opposed to military service and legal oaths). Their son went through the eighth grade with Amish children.

"I was kind of backward and shy as a kid," he says. "I got picked on quite a bit. I was a farm boy and didn't know how to protect myself. I wouldn't fight, so they'd pick on me."

In Indiana, Zimmerman's father distilled liquids other than peppermint oil and lost the farm. The family then moved to southern Michigan (between Benton Harbor and South Bend) to sharecrop a farm owned by the Lincoln Insurance Company. Eventually the boy rebelled against his tyrannical father, a constant taskmaster, and ran away from home—back to northern Indiana, where he found work on another farm. His mother, always sympathetic, sent along his clothes as soon as she learned his whereabouts.

In 1934, twenty-year-old Zimmerman left New Paris, Indiana, riding the Burlington Northern and Northern Pacific freight trains, pursuing the life of a hobo and drifter. "I had a girl leave me. She wanted a man who played basketball. That's when I decided to leave...." In the sandhills of Nebraska, Zimmerman found work on the Hall Ranch—a cow outfit that rode herd on seventy-two square miles—fencing and branding, bucking hay and punching cattle. There he earned his first ten-gallon hat and had to go home for a few months of swagger: "We were cowboys!"

Before long he headed west again, first to a ranch in eastern Montana to help an uncle range-lamb 500 ewes, then to the Big Hole Valley of Wisdom, Montana, where ranchers piled hay with Jackson forks and beaverslide stackers. When his wages were chopped because he was blamed for a boss's mistake with a malcontent John Deere tractor, he moved once more—this time to the Lemhi Valley of Idaho—in 1937.

Zimmerman cut firewood for folks, using a double-bitted axe to fell and limb the lodgepole; with a team of horses, he skidded the logs to a landing where they could be cut with a buzz saw and trucked fourteen miles to town. In spring, summer, and fall, he herded sheep—a solitary and biblical avocation—for several ranchers, including Ellen Yearian, the "sheep queen" of Idaho. At one point his sheepherding included a band of 2,200 ewes and lambs on the east fork of Hayden Creek.

Sometimes he wintered in a sheep wagon, sometimes in a log cabin, but he vowed if he ever built a house of his own it would be underground where it was warmer in the winter.

All the while, his stomach still troubled him. He drank goat's milk, and lemon and rhubarb juice, ordered vitamins by mail from Walnut Acres, and dreamed of papayas and mangoes, and of vegetables fresh from a garden his own.

Finally, in fall, 1947, he drove his old Buick south up the Salmon River highway to a wooden bridge that crossed the river just downstream from a landscape of obstacles—a bouldered slope owned by nothing but lichen and marmots. He crossed the bridge and pitched his tent on an alluvial apron smudged with tall sage and girded by cottonwood, juniper, and Douglas fir. The acreage, within earshot of the highway, is administered by the Bureau of Land Management; Zimmerman squatted on it, then filed mining claims to four twenty-acre parcels but was unable to patent them. He stocked the place with a few chickens and a half-dozen goats.

Over months that gradually waxed into years, he scraped out a half-mile of road between the slope and the river, upriver from the west end of the bridge. He worked with pick and shovel, iron bar and a team of horses. For want of hay, he had to break up his team.

Midsummer, while rooting out rocks with a pick, he struck an ice drift, hard as iron. He stacked woodpiles and torched them to thaw the rocks free. With the discovery, however, came the realization that ice stayed steadfast year-round within the rockslide—the consequence of snowmelt frozen and insulated beneath a shag of broken boulders.

He began prying rocks off the slide—some of them the size of respectable hay bales—and wrestled them into walls in the fan or scree of the slope. "I've liked caves for as long as I can remember," he says. "When I was little, I used to go down to the Yellow River and make little dugouts. I liked to play in them. It was cool and quiet there. I liked that. Here most of my building material is slide rocks I lag up with thinner slide rocks to keep out the varmints. I also use adobe when needed," he adds. "The outside front of my house is logs, but the other three sides are rock."

His main four-room abode consists of a sunroom-entryway, a living room, and a pantry. A small rear room has a refrigerator walled in and vented in back to tap the flow of cold air fed through the subterranean interstices among the talus boulders—ideal storage for meat, milk, yogurt, and cheese.

"One of my extra dugouts is almost frost-proof," he boasts. "Above twenty-two below, water won't freeze inside even if the place is unoccupied and unheated. I furnished my houses with homemade stoves. My smokestack didn't cost me a cent," he explains with satisfaction, "just an old ten-gallon milk can with the bottom cut out of it for a good fit with a six-inch stovepipe."

Built-in beds hang from the rock walls. A kerosene lamp is evident, but nothing requiring an electrical outlet: no radio, no television, no telephone. "My lumber doors are hung on wooden hinges I carved out with a chisel and knife. My floors are concrete poured over rocks and covered with linoleum [he bought cement in Salmon, shoveled sand and washed gravel from the river]." He winters snug as a caddisfly larva in its case.

With the passing years, Zimmerman added structures along his talus slope and out onto his flat until they number almost twenty. Sometimes he builds walls by stacking tires and tamping dirt inside them, then plasters the exterior with a mix of mud and straw. These shelters with their recycled windows cost him from twenty-five to one-hundred dollars. "You couldn't do this anymore," he remarks matter-of-factly. "Too many rules. Building codes, health codes, safety codes, zoning laws...they'd never let you build dugouts like this." Nevertheless, he rents them for two dollars a night or twenty-five dollars a month. "Oh, I got one for fifty dollars a month: got a porch, three bunks, a cookstove—quite a few conveniences."

Glancing at the roof, Dick explains, "Most of my buildings are roofed flat with peeled fir poles over eighteen-inch timbers. Topped with two or three feet of dirt and mud. I cover them with tarpaper and aluminum from an old house trailer, then lay carpet topped off with tires. My goat herd can bed down up there." (Goats overhead are what got him into trouble at age sixty-five. A nanny butted him off the roof, and the fall broke his hip, requiring a 160-mile trip to the hospital in Idaho Falls, where an orthopedic surgeon pinned the bone.)

After the first winter at his place, with a passable trail-road notched into the slope, Dick was able to concentrate on a garden. To keep out deer, he fenced about an acre of the rich soil near the river and planted trees: apples, plums, cherries, and apricots; also carrots, turnips, parsnips, beets, onions, asparagus, rhubarb, tomatoes, potatoes, peas, raspberries, and Jerusalem artichokes. The results were a productive and sumptuous cupboard. (What fruit and vegetables he did not can, he stored in a root cellar.) He hayed the flat with a team and mower; raked the hay and stacked it in a roughhewn barn.

His goat herd multiplied to thirty; he milked some, hiked after others, butchered a half-dozen each year, hung and aged the meat in his cooler-caves, and sold the carcasses for ten dollars each. "Goats," he says, "make milk, cheese, and stew meat."

Within a couple of years, he was devising a large side-spill waterwheel to irrigate the garden and replace his burdensome tote from the riverbank. The unruly river, however, was not long in reclaiming both waterwheel and garden. In fact, Dick weathered four consecutive years of spring floods. Surrendering to the current, he dug his own twelve-foot well, slate-lined. Then he built a windmill over it to irrigate his garden, and it serves still.

In 1956 highwater washed out his bridge—four local bridges were carried away in one week. Never one to let inconvenience disrupt his boundless determination and enterprise, Dick used a boat and a cable until, with the assistance of the Red Cross and nearby Twin Peaks mine, a railroad bridge salvaged from Boise was erected as a replacement.

In spring, he sold asparagus in town; in fall, potatoes and dried apples. Summers he found masonry jobs at Williams Lake Resort or Twin Peaks Ranch: septic tanks, steps, fireplaces, walls. In winter, he did assessment work for the Twin Peaks mine or labored at his own digs. Although no longer active as a mason, he still sells vegetables and fruit leather. And since he is now a vegetarian, his goat herd has been cropped to six.

Zimmerman and his stomach have reached an uneasy truce: homemade yogurt is his mainstay. "I learned how to make yogurt. I'm the one who got it started in this country," he says emphatically.

"Wasn't no yogurt in stores. Couldn't get any. Wasn't no health food stores, either, when I first come into this country. Was one in Pennsylvania. I used to send for powdered yeast at Walnut Acres." A pause.

A look of boyish glee washes across his creased and bearded face. "Well, I tried some. Works all right with me. I could use that. But I always runs out. I wanted to know how to make it, but they wouldn't tell me anything." He turns sober. "So I figured it out. I experimented until I figured out how to make yogurt. I went to Ogden to sell the formula to a company. The man says, 'Ain't much call for yogurt.'" Dick dismisses him with a grin and a wave of his large hand.

The balance of his diet is anything but intemperate: he avoids bread, preferring corn tortillas cooked in wine; drinks spud beer, carrot juice, and lemon juice; eats garlic and stinging nettles.

Anton Chekov wrote, "I find living alone boring and sad." In 1968 Zimmerman joined a lonely-hearts club. He began corresponding with a woman in Mexicali, Mexico. Two years later, when his pen pal sent him a telegram from Paso Robles, California, he went out to meet her, and they got hitched. Together they returned to his warren of rooms alongside the Salmon. En route, they stopped in Jackpot, Nevada, where his new wife ate hamburgers and played the slot machines—not a good omen. He recalls that she had no taste for goat meat or Rye Krisp, nor any inclination to work in the garden. "If you really loved me," she said, "you'd build a house across the river." With the approach of winter, she hitchhiked south. He sent her money at times, but now her photograph and whereabouts are gone like thistledown on a breeze.

His second love, Bonnie Trositt, he met in a bar in Idaho Falls. She came to the caves, but it did not work out. "She started drinking," he laments. "She wanted to be travelin' all the time, wouldn't settle down. She'd go back to Mom, then back to me. She wanted to go to town all the time. I got tired of that."

Bonnie met a violent end. When she was fired from her job on a potato sorter near Roberts, Idaho, her roommate, angry that Bonnie was not able to pay her share of the expenses, murdered her with a blow from a fireplace poker. She was buried in Blackfoot, Idaho, but Zimmerman says her ghost haunts his place. (A devout man, with a well-thumbed King James Bible, he believes in God, as well as dreams, visions, ghosts, and spirit travel.) Now for company he keeps a couple of small dogs—they work at spooking the rockchucks.

Among his other talents, Dugout Dick is a self-taught musician, playing the guitar and harmonica simultaneously, while dancing like a bear around a beehive. Some years he goes into Salmon to make music in the Fourth of July parade.

Occasionally, on a long summer evening, he will quit his chores early, perch on a chair by his front door, and sing songs of his own devising to the river:

Oh, Salmon River moon, I miss her so tonight.
Tell her to return, shine down with her light.
Oh, Salmon River moon, if I should hear her feet
When she comes close to me, my heart would skip a beat.
With my guitar I croon, Oh, Salmon River moon,
My sweet love melody, bring her back to me.
Oh, now the shadows fall on my windowsill.
Salmon River moon, I am waiting still.
Oh, Salmon River moon, down the trail I'll be there.
On a cool summer night, I'll know you still care.
Oh, Salmon River moon, there're tears in my eyes.
Does she wait for me still, just on the other side?
Now my love I assume, Oh, Salmon River moon,
You're coming back to me, I'm your destiny.
Now the moon's going down along the winding hill.
Salmon River moon, I am waiting still.

Dick has never flown in an airplane. His favored transportation—once his motorcycle was retired—is a toss-up between his ten-speed bicycle and a grizzled Datsun pickup. "I just have old-fashioned ways. The push-button age has almost passed me by."

Gradually, regional fame has bedaubed Dugout Dick. First it

was Idaho newspapers, then national television shows: "Real People," "Good Morning America"; and finally the *National Geographic* (Dec. 1992). He turned down an opportunity to appear on the "Tonight" show. "I told them that I didn't want to go to California, and that I ride Greyhounds, not airplanes. Besides, the show isn't in California. The show is here." He comments, "In the last few years, I've had so many visitors I decided to put up signs to advertise my layout— SALMON RIVER CAVE MAN—TV PERSONALITY—NATURAL ICE CAVES—and now I'm in the tourist trade in a small way." He charges a nominal admission fee.

Ron McFarland, an Idaho writer, visited Zimmerman in 1982 and later summed his changed and changing situation in an article for *Rocky Mountain Magazine* titled "The Art of the Eccentric:"

> What makes Dick Zimmerman particularly interesting is not his odd appetite or his decision to live the hermit's life, but his eccentric art, which is part of the art of being eccentric. His professed arts are husbandry, horticulture, and most important, architecture.
>
> Dick is not a fanatic opposed to modern conveniences, outraged by aluminum, angry at the automobile. He simply does without some things, and he uses what comes to hand.
>
> Reality is closing in on Dugout Dick, who is well into his sixties, on the mend from a broken hip, his eyes going bad, and his stomach no longer up to meat or goat cheese. U. S. Highway 93 is pretty busy across the river, at least during the summer, and new houses keep popping up along the banks. Access to his once very private world is easy. Yet Dick Zimmerman is a peculiar sort of fellow. A night spent in one of his huts will give you a pretty good notion of what life was like for miners and mountain men a hundred years ago, and an afternoon spent with him will give you a pretty good notion of what some individuals had to be like in order to live that way. In the long, dim months of winter, traffic across the river dwindles and

few tourists cross the bridge to visit Dick's ice caves, which are very inviting in July and August. There is an art to hand-building stone dugouts, and there is an art to living alone in hard country. Like most arts, these thrive on eccentricity, and Dugout Dick, who may be low on cash, is rich in that.

A rancher living across the river from Dugout Dick says he is a good neighbor: "He minds his own business, pays his own way, turns in sales tax on his vegetables."

As for his own ethic, Zimmerman says he believes in church but does not go; he tries instead to live by the Biblical admonishment found in Micah, Chapter 6, verse 8: "Old man, he has showed you what is good; walk humbly with thy God; love mercy; do justly."

52 ZIMMERMAN IN FRONT OF ONE OF HIS RENTAL UNITS.

53 ZIMMERMAN VISITING ON AN AUGUST AFTERNOON, 1993.
54 ZIMMERMAN SAMPLES SOME OF HIS DRIED FRUIT.
55 ZIMMERMAN THE MUSICIAN.

56 ZIMMERMAN'S QUARTERS DOWN ON THE FLAT BELOW HIS CAVE.

57 ZIMMERMAN'S GARDEN, LOOKING TOWARD THE RIVER AND THE HIGHWAY.

Helena Schmidt, **Wildhorse Cowgirl**

THE HAPPIEST OF ALL LIVES IS A BUSY SOLITUDE.—VOLTAIRE

Helena Moore Schmidt lives a fairly private life at the end of a very private road on Starveout Creek in the Snake River Breaks. She lives in the log house her parents built on the land they homesteaded, where in her mother's arms she arrived on horseback two weeks after she was was born, and she has never strayed from it farther than a brief visit to San Diego. Not many people like her will still be among us in a few years.

In the 1870s Elizabeth McDowell crossed the Snake River Plain in a covered wagon tugged by a span of mules. In the Boise Valley, she paused to teach school for the winter. There she met Daniel Taylor Cole; they married, and settled in the Salubria Valley on the Weiser River one hundred miles northwest of Boise.

Years later, one of their thirteen children, twenty-eight-year-old daughter Carmeta Cole, met cowboy Friend Moore at a dance in Salubria Valley. In 1907 they married.

At the time, Friend Moore was partners with his younger brother in a cattle operation in No Business Basin on the northwest slope of Cuddy Mountain—a 7,800-foot peak that indents the skyline just north of Cambridge, Idaho—but after the wedding, Friend sold his interest to his brother. Helena, the Moores' daughter, reports, "He said it was no place to take a woman, so they went off to his native country over on the coast [Everett, Washington], and he got a job in the mill down there—building a paper mill—but Mom didn't like that rainy climate, and she was homesick for Idaho, so they moved back up here."

After their return, Helena was born in March, 1910, in Weiser, Idaho. Ten days later, the family of three headed in a wagon for Starveout Creek west of No Business Basin, a journey of about eighty-five miles. They left their wagon at the west end of the road that shoulders its way alongside the Wildhorse River.

Every tool, every piece of furniture, every sack of food had to be packed four miles upslope to Starveout Ranch. "My Dad was a good packer," Helena confirms. The Moores bought preemption rights from Bigfoot John Gerbidge, who was occupying a dugout on the knob below their planned house site—a shelf of soil pinched between canyon and sky.

The Moores, living in a tent, had a summer to get their house up. Friend felled ponderosa pines in the Pot Hole, a hollow up behind their building site. He used a team of horses to drag the logs down, hewed and adzed the inside faces smooth, then with a chain and a rolling hitch he slid the logs up angled brace logs, and steeple-notched the corners with his axe. Carmeta drove the team of horses, and often joked that all she did was hold the lines up out of the dirt.

By fall, the house was twenty-two logs high (two stories), thirty feet long and twenty-four wide, caulked with clay. They shingled the roof with shakes split from pine bolts. Horses packed or dragged up from Wildhorse canyon what little lumber was used. The Moores closed off a kitchen and living room for the winter, and despite windows shuttered with flour sacks, made it livable. "Dad finished enough we could winter in the kitchen...got it sealed up enough they could live in it...."

Provisions—salt, sugar, flour, coffee—from the Brownlee store down on the Snake River were packed over the Summers Trail. A steep haul. Says Helena, "We didn't go to town very often. You either raised it or did without. We always raised a garden and our own potatoes and meat—chickens and pigs, smoked hams and bacon. Made our own butter and cottage cheese." Since the Moores kept a couple of dairy cows, when they rode down to Brownlee they packed along a pair of five-gallon cream cans to ship to Baker, Oregon.

As with all ranchers with children, eventually schooling surfaced as another problem to solve. Carmeta borrowed books from the Brownlee district and taught her daughter at the kitchen table. In 1918, when Helena had been home-schooled for three years, the Moores resolved it was time for a more formal arrangement. Carmeta moved with Helena down to a cabin on the Wildhorse, leaving Friend to look after the ranch during the week. Eight-year-old Helena was placed in the fourth grade. She walked two miles to lessons.

The hewed-log, one-room schoolhouse was on the far side of the Wildhorse River, and getting there required a balancing act across a fallen fir tree that spanned the river. "Falling into the river was a common occurrence; you just snugged-up to the woodstove in the center of the room until you got dry."

Shortly, a new schoolhouse was carpentered together on the nearside of Wildhorse, and seven children attended. After two years of Friend's weekday-baching, Helena completed her last three years of grammar school in Cambridge, on the other side of the mountain. She lived with her mother and grandmother on Rush Creek and walked half as far to school.

Since she was now ready for high school, "My folks quit the place to get me through school. Dad was a millwright and carpenter by trade. Dad went down there [LaGrande, Oregon] and got a job in the Stoddard Mill [sawmill]."

Following high school, Helena stayed home for a year, then decided to go to teachers' college. Friend Moore's sister lived in Bellingham, Washington, and Helena traveled there to enroll in Bellingham State Normal School. (Since 1977 it has been Western Washington University: normal schools were so named because they served to set a standard.) Her aunt and uncle would come over to Starveout in the fall and take Helena back with them. She completed her degree in two years there.

On returning to Starveout Ranch in 1930, the advent of the Great Depression, Helena realized her father had heart problems. To help the family, she took a teaching job at the Brownlee school.

The school was ten miles up Brownlee Creek from Snake River, and about a four-hour horseback ride from Starveout. A one-room structure, it perched on a knob just above the road at a site known as Joycelyn Gulch. The first year, there were ten children, and she taught grades one, four, and six through eight. Helena boarded with friends and relatives at the Ruth place, three miles below the school, and rode home on weekends to help with ranch work.

"We had some cattle, enough to get by with. Dad had kind of gotten rid of the cows after the heart attack. There's always things to do on a ranch; you have to live. At that time, you had to have horses; there was no other way to get places. You had to put up hay."

As for a social life, "We didn't have much. We had neighbors, of course, that we visited quite a lot; and we had dances at the Wildhorse schoolhouse, and we used to go to Bear [Idaho] for dances."

In spring, 1936, Helena went dancing in Bear, the copper-mining community in the mountains thirty miles north of Cambridge. That evening she met a tall, lean cowboy, Henry Schmidt, who was working for Albert Campbell's OX Ranch in the Snake River Breaks. Schmidt had run his folks ranch in Pine Valley, Oregon, then worked as a hand for the OX for a few years at fifty dollars a month, before going to work as a musical-instrument salesman in Nampa, Idaho. "No man can learn that which his heart has no shape to hold." Ranch boss Campbell pursued and persuaded, and eventually the cowboy was back in the OX harness.

An exceptional horseman, Schmidt was also a fiddler. He put his fiddle down several times that evening to dance with blue-eyed Helena, and before she left, he asked her to accompany him in a couple of weeks to a dance slated for The Cove on the Weiser River outside Cambridge. "They used to have some wild parties out there," Helena remembers with a smile.

Since there was no road to Starveout, she agreed to meet Schmidt at the McClemmons' house, which served as the Wildhorse post office. She had to ride her black mare down to their place, leading a packhorse that carried a dressbox. At the McClemmons', fearful of being "stood up," she stalled and fretted until she finally spotted Henry's headlights poking along the river. Then she hurriedly switched her riding clothes for a dancing dress, silk stockings, and suede shoes.

The pair were married within a year. They spent their honeymoon working out of OX cow camps near Bear. In the fall they trailed cattle southwest down out of the breaks, ferrying them across the Snake River and on to the Grover Ranch in Pine Valley, where the couple helped feed 800 head that winter.

Pine Valley winters can be colder than a meatlocker. The record is around fifty below. Feeding required forking loose hay from the top of the stack down onto a wooden sled. Once it was loaded, Helena drove the four-horse team in a generous circle while Henry and his helper forked the same load off both sides of the sled to the cattle that plodded and pushed along their track. Repetitious, demanding work.

At times, Helena was able to visit her parents briefly and help them at the ranch. Her father's heart condition continued to worsen.

In 1938 Henry and Helena left the OX Ranch for an endeavor of their own: they bought a ranch along the Wildhorse River immediately below the Starveout Ranch but over a thousand feet lower in elevation. "We just always called it the lower place. Arthur Campbell [cousin of Albert] lived there the first that I can remember." They lived in a small shack, with plans for a big house.

Hard work, as a rancher once said, does not make a very good story. They managed to get three cuttings of hay a year off the lower place; they acquired some additional acreage, and ran the places along with Starveout as one. It kept both families humming like a hive. They were always up before the dew was off the hay. Helena was rider, roper, teamster, hayhand, and cook. "You do everything on a ranch."

Friend Moore's heart condition worsened. "His heart got so bad, he went over to his sister's in Everett in order to doctor at the clinic, and passed away there."

The Schmidts went on ranching. Through the war years, many of Helena's women friends went back to teaching. However, she and Henry, who was almost forty at the time, continued to raise hay and beef, which were needed for the war effort. Carmeta moved around with them, helping with cooking and other chores as she could.

In fall, 1945, Dr. A. O. Jeffreys, native of Weiser, and his wife Maud drove their 1942 Cadillac down the Wildhorse to visit Carmeta, Helena, and Henry. Dr. Jeffrey's account of the visit, written in a letter to a friend and published in the Weiser *Signal*, provides some insights into the ranch life at that time:

> Helena and Henry had brought some boxes of pears on a hay rack as far as the blasted out road [Wildhorse], where they were being transferred to the old mail wagon, and the mailman would see that they were delivered to the storekeeper in Council. They loaded us with our luggage on the hay rack.
>
> On one narrow grade the hay rack occasionally struck protruding rocks on the upper side of the grade. Henry handled the gentle team with skill and released the rack from the stones.
>
> At the ranch [the lower place] they have horses, cows, pigs, cats, dogs, chickens, and goats. They all seem to get along very harmoniously. At dusk the goats begin to work their way up the almost precipitous side of the canyon to their sleeping place, which is a rocky shelf almost to the top of a perpendicular precipice. From their bedroom they have a good view up and down the canyon. Mrs. Moore, Helena, and Henry live in a little house about twelve feet wide and thirty feet long. It contains one single bed and one double bed. About dark the day we arrived, two men and their wives came to stay for the night. The men had fished all the way from the mouth of Wildhorse Creek, where it empties into the Snake River. They had caught lots of fine trout. The women were exhausted from their long hike. I wondered where we were all going to sleep. The Moores easily solved that

problem. Beds were made in the haystacks, and we all slept out in the open. Maud and I had the place of honor. Henry spread some hay on the hay rack and we slept there. It was wonderful. The air was so fresh, the stars so bright and beautiful. My, but we enjoyed it. We could see the goats on their rocky shelf hundreds of feet above us. Wildhorse Creek rushing over and around the big granite boulders made a sound louder than a murmur but not the volume of a roar, just the proper sound to lull us to sleep. The next day I saw the horses eating up our bed of hay.

While we lived with the Moores we enjoyed the most wonderful food that was ever served to humans: trout, chicken, fresh venison, watermelons, cantaloupes (cooled in the spring), tomatoes (the best), cucumbers, cauliflower, broccoli, onions, carrots, potatoes, blackberries, strawberries, peaches, many varieties of plums and prunes, pears, apples, apricots, walnuts, and canned fruit of all kinds. Lots of homemade butter and thick cream. We enjoyed churning the butter.

It was imperative that the Moores cut and put in the barn the alfalfa on the mountain ranch and also can some fruit and tomatoes. It took some packtrain to move us up to the upper ranch [Starveout]. There were five humans, nine horses, two cows, two dogs, and two cats. We rode down Wildhorse Canyon a few miles then turned up Starveout Canyon. The cows were ahead. They reached the ranch a long time before we did. The cats enjoy traveling. The Moores take them wherever they go. They like to ride on the top of the pack on the packhorse, but sometimes they slip back on the horse's hips and then when the cat's claws stick into the horse's skin he bucks off the cat and also the pack. If the cats fall off, they follow along in the trail and yowl until they are put on again. Usually they are carried in sacks tied to the horn of the saddle. A few minutes before we started, Mrs. Moore got a couple of sacks, called the cats, held the sacks open, and the cats walked in. After we had ridden for two or three miles, one cat meowed that he was in trouble. Mrs. Moore examined and found that he was standing on his head. When she turned him tail-down, he was perfectly contented. It was not over fifteen minutes after they let the cats out of the sacks at the mountain house that one of them proudly marched up with a fat mouse.

The commodious mountain ranch house is built on a small level place on the mountainside. It is surrounded by a nice green lawn and many beautiful flowers. Near the house is a good orchard with almost all kinds of fruit that will grow in that climate. There is a cool, clear spring at each ranch house. They have no wagon at the mountain ranch. The hay is pulled in on skids. They have a mowing machine, hay rake, and derrick fork. Everything is brought up here on packhorses. When they brought the mowing machine up, the horse that was carrying the heaviest part fell over the cliff and was killed. I think it is marvelous that they have been able to bring up—on the backs of horses, over a trail built along the side of a canyon where one false step would mean death to man or horse— machinery, furniture, lumber, and all the other things and appurtenances it takes to equip and operate a ranch. In this spacious ranch house they have two big stoves, cream separator, washing machine run by gasoline engine, several bedsteads, linoleum and rugs on the floors, many large easy chairs, davenports, settees, sewing machine, extension dining table, full length mirror, bookcases, radio, and many other things too numerous to mention.

Many ranches are down in the canyons but they could not be seen. Living here one might in fancy feel there was no other human being on earth, if it were not for the mail planes which fly over each day between Lewiston and Boise.

One afternoon Helena decided to go down into Wildhorse Canyon to the post office and get the mail. She took along a packhorse to get some supplies. She got back at 9:45 p.m. It was very dark. About dusk Henry called the cows from the pasture. Coyotes along Starveout Canyon answered him. I asked Helena if she was afraid when she heard the coyotes howl as she came up the trail in pitch darkness. She has been riding up that trail since she was two years old, and she has implicit faith and trust in her old horse Traveler. She said she is never afraid. She never carries a gun [pistol] and has never fired one.

Henry is a versatile young man. He is a good cowboy, carpenter, ranchman, excellent blacksmith, farmer, good cook, mechanic, and can even play the violin. His wife Helena is just as versatile as he.

She works right along with her husband in the field, on the ranch and out on the range with the cattle. She can play the piano, is a college graduate, and is an excellent housekeeper.

We canned fruit and tomatoes while Henry and Helena cut and stored the hay for the winter.

The day before we arrived in Wildhorse Canyon, as Henry was walking through the alfalfa field he stubbed his toe on a deer and killed it, or something like that, at any rate we were obliged to eat the venison. They have no refrigerator or ice but they managed to keep that meat fresh for ten days. Just as the sun goes down they tie a rope around the carcass, throw the rope over the limb of a tree and pull it up so no wild animals can reach it. Just as the sun comes up in the morning they take it down, wrap it up in quilts with canvas on the outside and put it on the damp ground in the shade by the spring. During the week we were there the meat remained fresh and delicious.

While we were at the mountain ranch, one morning we discovered that several chickens had been killed. After an investigation we found that they had been killed by bobcats. Henry set traps and caught two of the big felines.

A short time before we visited the Moores, the dogs

bounded up from the grape arbor onto the front veranda. They were trembling and whimpering. Mrs. Moore, being alone, locked the door and stayed in the house all evening. In the morning she called the dogs but they had disappeared. Several weeks later they found that one had gone down the canyon to one neighbor and the other up the canyon to another neighbor. There being no telephones or roads, the neighbors could not notify them for some time. Mrs. Moore went out to the grape arbor the next morning and found the tracks of a big mountain lion.

After we finished the work at the mountain ranch house, we reorganized our packtrain, rode down to where our car was parked [and started back home]. We cut our visit a little short as the fall storms were coming on and we did not want to be snowed in and forced to spend the winter in Wildhorse Canyon.

We marveled at Henry Schmidt's versatility, enjoyed his frank western friendliness and common sense. Helena's unlimited energy, good nature, and open-hearted cordiality amazed us. Carmeta Cole Moore astonished us with her skill at cooking and serving meals and doing various household duties. Hotcakes for breakfast almost every morning, hot biscuits twice a day, and many other tasty and delicious foods were prepared with such dexterity and ease.

P.S. After we returned to Los Angeles, Henry wrote us that while they were taking us down into Wildhorse Canyon to our auto a female bear with her two cubs visited the ranch, broke into the storehouse, and ate all the pears we had picked, several cans of tallow, and other food that was stored away for the winter. She stayed around the ranch until all the fruit was picked!

In 1947, the same year Carmeta died of stomach cancer, the Schmidts bought No Business Basin from the OX Ranch—400 acres adjoining Starveout on the east but separated by a high ridge. Now they had fencing, hay, and cattle to look after on 1,800 acres, much of it steeper than a cow's ear. The only certainties of ranching, as one writer has put it, are work and hard luck, both of which arrive regularly and by the bucketful.

With or without water, the upper places provided one cutting of hay—thirty to fifty tons at Starveout—and the lower fields, irrigated, were usually good for three. Until 1963, they always mowed, raked, and stacked with horses and buck rakes and Jackson forks, although later at Starveout they tried a Jayhawk stacker for a spell and decided to use it on all three places. "We learned to take it apart, haul it on a wagon, and put it together again in a half day."

July harvest in No Business Basin was an annual event. The steep slopes that tilted toward Wildhorse required expert, determined hayhands. Neighboring ranchers would leave their places to hire on as the crew. The harvest was piled in a minor constellation of loose stacks, and the total could run to 350 tons, depending on the year. On average, the Schmidts expected to begin feeding from the stacks at Christmastime.

July of 1960 was hotter than an autoclave, the hottest and driest July in Idaho in over thirty years. By mid-month, most days had recorded well above ninety degrees; Boise and Caldwell had endured days of 111 degrees. Thunderstorms sparked six fires on the Wallowa-Whitman National Forest on the Oregon side of Hells Canyon; on the Idaho side of the canyon, Eckles Creek and Johnson Bar each had fires burning out of control for days. By July 23, Idaho's Governor Smylie authorized use of the National Guard as firefighters, and President Eisenhower declared Idaho a disaster area. The sky in the Snake River Breaks was hazed with heat and smoke.

One evening in late July in No Business Basin, after Henry had told some trespassing fishermen, who had repeatedly left pasture gates open, to leave, the Schmidts were shaken awake by their hayhand's shout of "Fire!" They scrambled out of bed, threw on clothes, saddled their horses, grabbed shovels, and rode a mile down the fields to meet the advancing flames coming through the stubble. The three of them spent the night scraping out fire line on the uphill side of the fire, fighting to save their new haystacks, their house and barn.

A Forest Service crew arrived in early afternoon, July 27, as did a converted B-25 bomber, under contract to the Bureau of Land Management. At Gowen Field in Boise, tanks in the bomber's fuselage had been filled with five tons of borate slurry; then the plane had been dispatched to strafe the Wildhorse fire in No Business Basin.

The Schmidts watched from horseback on a sheltering ridge as the plane droned into view. After two passes over the fire, the plane itself caught fire and as it attempted to land in the field exploded on impact. The pilot, co-pilot, and a training pilot were killed instantly. Suddenly, new fires ignited by the explosion threatened the house and barn. Firefighters ran to save the buildings so recently secured. Henry and Helena spurred their horses down off the ridge and over to the barn, where six work horses were corralled. Helena held the fractious horses, while Henry hurried off to join the fire crew.

Faster than it can be told, they set up a portable pump in the irrigation ditch and wet down the house and barn. A second plane lumbered into view and dropped smokejumpers, some of whom intentionally landed on the haystacks. These reinforcements, coupled with a favorable windshift, saved the structures and all but one haystack. Within three days, the rest of the fire was contained. (The Schmidts always carried the worthy suspicion that the fire was set by the departing fishermen.)

The following spring, Henry said let there be road: he began building one from Wildhorse River up to Starveout Ranch. "He made a brave start, but it was too much for his TD-9." So they hired a Catskinner from Fruitvale, Idaho, with a D-7 Caterpillar. By fall, the skinner had reached a rocky outcrop within view of the ranch, but then the ground froze. On New Year's Day, Henry employed the last of his dynamite on the rock, then finished the road with his own crawler. Inconvenience was no longer as thoroughly a part of their lives as packhorses, kerosene lamps, and distant doctors.

At this point, the Schmidts stopped long enough to take stock.

Henry was sixty-three, and Starveout, having been neglected in favor of No Business Basin, was in need of fulltime attention. They decided to sell all their acreage except the Moores' original 110-acre homestead.

Concentrating their efforts on Starveout did not significantly reduce their chores—just the distance traveled to perform them. They were still firmly harnessed to routines. Most of the fencelines had to be renewed. New pipelines were laid from the springs. Henry replaced the steep-peaked barn—the old one had been swatted by a windstorm. They worked without visible hurry but never pausing. They put an aluminum roof on the house, and when it ripped off in a windstorm, put on a heavier one. They caulked the logs with lime mortar over wire mesh. They bulldozed a basement and built a utility room above it.

The Schmidts had five crowded years at Starveout, scarcely stopping long enough to enjoy their view across the troughed ridges of the Wildhorse and Snake rivers all the way to the blue-hued Cornucopias.

Then one night, after he had labored on the barn, Henry suffered a stroke. Helena cranked one long ring to the telephone exchange operator on Hornet Creek and asked for help. The operator's husband drove his Scout International to the Starveout Ranch, placed Henry on the floor inside the vehicle, and then drove him, along with Helena, to the hospital in Council. No one lives forever, no one lives long enough. Four days later, Henry died. He was buried in the community cemetery.

Helena returned to Starveout Ranch, like a boat coming ashore. "Well, it's home," she says quietly. The loss of her husband of thirty years—a rancher widely admired from Pine Creek in Idaho to Pine Valley in Oregon—knocked a huge hole in her spirits. It was a time of tearless sighs. The cycles of the ranch, however, meant that she had only time to align herself with the way things are.

"There were just things you had to do. I was alone for a year. It was hard at first, hard in a way. But not in the sense that I needed things done for me. I cut my own wood and dragged it in with a team. I had my milk cows and my garden."

The following year, Holworth Nixon, who owned the nearby Dukes Creek ranch, gave Helena a neighbor's attention and hired a man to look out for her. For six years, Tom Wiggins helped with chores.

In 1979, Helena met Ralph and Dodie Brown, who had moved from California and were living on the Smithy place in No Business Basin. Ralph was a carpenter. Helena made a contract with them to build a cabin at Starveout, where they could live and assist her when needed; in exchange, she agreed to deed them the homestead upon her death. The agreement stands.

Living alone, Helena had more time to garden. "I enjoy my garden. We always had a garden and a milk cow." For most of three seasons, flowers flare: crocus, daffodil, narcissus, peony, carnation, impatiens, yellow sorrel, daisy, marigold, iris, phlox, gladiolus, geranium, rose, daylily, hollyhock, snapdragon, bachelor button. The more functional garden furnishes carrots, beets, radishes, asparagus, cabbage, chard, spinach, cucumbers, tomatoes, corn, pumpkins, strawberries, and raspberries.

The orchard is fruitful, as well. "Henry needed my help more than left me time for canning. There was just the two of us, and we bought canned things. We always canned fruit, had plenty of that, but it's more work to can vegetables. We put up just enough to do us through the winter," she adds. "We always raised lots of fruit. We used to have good apricots, but our tree is too old now I guess. Neighbors have apricots. We have pears and peaches and plums and apples—Jonathans, Snow, Yellow Bananas, dark red Black Bens for cider." A wooden press in the tall grass beneath an apple tree silently vouches for the abundance.

The flowers entice hummingbirds, which Helena notes with pleasure. Swallows twist in and out from under the eaves; robins, her cat notes with matching pleasure, nest in the grapevines. Goldfinches, house wrens, and lazuli buntings flit across the yard. Beyond the yard, a red-tailed hawk traces the thermal contours of Mahogany Mountain, and occasionally a golden eagle gyres like a tiny toy above Notch Butte.

Helena still keeps a couple of horses and four cows—all dry for the first time in years. "Never been without a milk cow, that's no way to be. The bull must have been no good." In the coop behind the house, she feeds a flock of Plymouth Rock pullets busy feeding themselves in the field—open-range chickens.

Inside the house, with its wide-angle view of river canyons and eastern Oregon mountains hazed with the dust of distance, a visitor feels precariously perched, like a loose boulder at the angle of repose. A wall clock pendulum ticktocks audibly. Every flat space seems to sprout a vase of flowers. Even the wall: a framed print of Vincent Van Gogh's "White Roses." Helena says, "I've always been an active outdoors girl. Always had to make myself do housework."

When the garden is given over to winter, she goes for a daily walk. Ruff, her border collie, goes too. "I try to go as far as I can—sometimes an hour." Helena knits and crochets in winter, and works on quilts. She plays a lot of solitaire: "I can lose myself that way, and it don't strain the eyes." She listens to music. She reads *Good Housekeeping, Better Homes and Gardens, National Geographic, Range* magazine. "If I wake up at night, I read; that's when I do most of my reading. I read quite a bit...whatever I get. I've got books loaned to me, and I've been reading on them. James Michener's *Alaska*—it takes quite a while to read through one of his."

Helena at fourscore-plus years sits at ease and thumbs through her memories. Ruff, eyes watchful, muzzle resting on his forepaws, lies on the woven rug at her feet. ("I generally have to tie him up when people come. He's very protective.")

She explains that Starveout got its name in the early 1890s, when the Emerys went partners with the Meyers and agreed to spend the winter feeding their jointly owned cattle, while the Meyers packed in provisions periodically. The Emerys sledded bunchgrass, cut on the upper meadow, down to the cattle feeding in the bottom of the canyon, but so infrequently did the groceries arrive from the Meyers that they had to call it quits.

Helena recalls, "Deer wasn't as plentiful as they are now, and there aren't that many now. I remember hunting with my Dad. We really needed the meat, and more often than not, we didn't get anything. He was a good shot, too. Now we butcher a beef some-times."

She continues, "No elk to mention then, and they're still scarce on this side of the mountain. Not many bear then. Pretty plentiful now. Once I was riding Misty back from Brownlee and we met two bears on the trail. She just looked at them." Then expanding: "There's always coyotes and bobcats. Never saw a lion. Used to be lots of grouse—you could always find a grouse between here and the old chicken house—now they're almost extinct up here." She saw the salmon come annually and then finally disappear forever from the Wildhorse River; she even remembers the last salmon trying to spawn on Starveout Creek after the Oxbow Dam diversion on the Snake River got underway in 1958.

Asked about grazing conditions, she volunteers, "Native bunchgrass feed got pretty well killed off, and the cheatgrass took its place. Kind of took the country by storm. People said it would ruin the country, but it's been a blessing as early feed."

With a bit of nudging, Helena tells of the two emergencies that required a tortuous trip for a doctor.

"I was just a kid when I fell off a horse and broke my arm. Must have been four or five years old. I went over to Nixons' [two hours] and about thirty miles to Dr. Whitman in Cambridge. [A two-day, sixty-mile trip.] I rode Roxy, she was a regular horse, not a pony."

A pause. "When Mom broke her leg it was in the evening. Somehow a horse knocked her down, and she fell on a little round rock down below the house. I rode all night with Toots Rogers to Billie Hanson's place on Hornet Creek [about twenty miles] and called Dr. Thurston in Council. Hansen loaned Doc a horse, and he rode in here, and he brought that dining room table in here where it was light, put all three boards in it, and lay Mama down on it and set her leg. We loaned Dr. Thurston a pillow to put in his saddle for the return trip." Such was life in the hames and handpump days, before the road, before Vermeer round balers and center-pivot irrigation.

Although the schoolhouses down on Wildhorse are gone now, the teacherage still stands. The last school closed in 1946, and the

Schmidts used some of its lumber in their utility room. The Wildhorse mail run ended the same year; now Helena has to go to Council for it. Consequently, she does not subscribe to any daily newspaper.

What about a telephone? "We had a tree-line phone before; it went through a central on Hornet Creek. We used the radio some. They [Cambridge Telephone] laid the new phone line in mid-summer [1978], buried the line. They hired a family to lay the cable. Wife drove a D-8, daughter drove a D-6, the man was behind, running that thing that buried the cable. One evening along about mid-summer—long days, of course—they came a huffing up the road. It was quite an event!" She adds, "It didn't use to get lonesome for me, but it has been since I've been widowed. It's nice to be able to talk to someone now and then."

At present, a generator provides electricity for some chores (washing clothes) and to recharge batteries every three days. "Browns instigated that." Helena does not use the generator (except for batteries) for lights or kitchen appliances. "It's easier to use an eggbeater than start a generator." She hauls in propane tanks for her lights, refrigerator, and small kitchen range. "One person don't do a whole lot of cooking."

Gasoline for the generator is also trucked in the fall. Helena drives to Cambridge with her Chevrolet pickup and five fifty-gallon drums. She returns with a ton of gasoline on board and Ralph pumps it into a holding tank at the ranch. Once winter arrives, she parks the two-wheel-drive truck in the shed, where it takes its place alongside her tractor, Subaru, fuel barrels, ladders, sickle bars, lanterns, chokers, hoses, pipes, and a hundred other indispensables.

Asked if she still rides horseback, she answers matter-of-factly, "Not since I had this last hip done [1989]. After I had the first one replaced," she explains, "I could ride pretty good. But it's harder for me to get on anymore. I have to get up higher than the horse, so I don't bother anymore." Then as afterthought, she adds, "It's not as necessary as it used to be."

This change brings to mind another anecdote. "One time I needed a bigger collar for one of my workhorses. So I went into

John's leather goods in town and asked him. He said, 'Why, do you wanna put a mirror in it?' 'No,' I said, 'I want to put a mare in it.'

The Browns aside, no neighbors are nearer now than seven miles by road. Gazing out her window, where for fifty miles no other building punctures the view, and the late light drapes the receding ridges in a floral lavender, she observes, "Used to be quite a few people lived up and down Wildhorse—each one of those ranches had a family on it. We counted seventeen neighbors between No Business and Starveout." She tucks a hand under her chin, pensively. "Now there's just Quillams and Emerys, only ones that's left. It's kind of worked backwards here."

"It's changed, all right," she goes on. "We didn't used to have tourists. The hunters do give us a bad time when the season's open... we don't want a bunch coming in on us."

She says her philosophy of life is summed by the Golden Rule. "Do unto others as you would have them do unto you. I don't know of anything better than that."

At times other than winter, Helena visits friends in Halfway, Oregon—a three-hour journey by way of Kleinschmidt Grade to the Snake River—and friends in Boise, although she prefers not to drive in the city.

The changes in Helena's lifetime are reflected on the mountain itself. Cuddy Mountain includes the largest roadless area in southwestern Idaho, with a range of forests from cottonwood to ponderosa pine and Douglas fir, and from aspen to spruce and subalpine fir. Ground cover runs from balsamroot to calypso orchids and trillium, from sage to syringa and elderberry. Elk and mountain goat are still found in some drainages. Yet visitors to the west slope near Grade and Dukes creeks can now hear the cough of chainsaws, a sound heard for years on the northern slopes. The mountain is changing. "We want to get the pumpkins," a Forest Service district ranger explains. Logging creeps up the drainages like gangrene up a leg.

Helena Schmidt, however, is holding her own. Told there is a pine with a girth of fourteen feet behind her house, she retorts, "Don't tell the Forest Service." The frequent question, "How often do you go to town?" brings a firm, "Not any oftener than I have to."

"Well, it's home," she repeats. "Ruff don't like it when I go to town. It's home here. I have my garden and my rosebushes and my dog. My cats. They're my family." A distilled silence. Then with gentle emphasis, she declares, "I hope I don't ever have to live in town."

58 HELENA MOORE SCHMIDT AT STARVEOUT RANCH.

59 HELENA ON HER PLACE WITH HER DOG, RUFF.
60 HELENA MOORE SCHMIDT IN HER FRONT YARD IN 1993.

61 FRIEND A. MOORE AND HIS DAUGHTER, HELENA.

62 SECTION OF THE ROAD TO SCHMIDT'S HOMESTEAD.

Claude Dallas, Outback Outlaw

WE ARE ALL OF US SENTENCED TO SOLITARY CONFINEMENT
INSIDE OUR OWN SKINS, FOR LIFE.—TENNESSEE WILLIAMS

Time pulls apart. On a graveled shelf of sage and bitterbrush in the bottom of a basalt gorge on the South Fork of the Owyhee River, two men wearing pistols face each other with taut expectancy. "You can go easy or you can go hard," says the lawman. "It doesn't make any difference to me." Silence runs between them like a fuse. Suddenly the younger man's hand jerks his .357 Magnum from its holster—sound floods the canyon, resounds off the somber, saged slopes. Two rounds slam into the lawman's chest, the next drops his partner standing a few feet away. Three more bullets punch their fallen bodies.

Time becomes more distinct: it is January, 1981. Conservation officers Bill Pogue and Conley Elms, Idaho Fish and Game Department wardens, were down on the South Fork to arrest part-time trapper and full-time poacher Claude Dallas. Illegal deer carcasses and bobcat hides studded his camp.

All three men loved the Owyhee desert and mountains, but two of them, Pogue and Elms, were fervent protectors of the public's wildlife; men who took the body politic's money and returned fair value. Dallas, however, took the state's wildlife—whatever and whenever—and gave nothing in return. Pogue had written on a scenic photograph given to a friend, "If there is a future for wild things, then it is the burden of those who have reached further than me to save them for the rest of us. It will be done by those whose convictions were forged in campfires." Dallas, too, had convictions, but they were forged in a bonfire of confused romanticism. He had not been in the West or Idaho long enough to grow up with the country. Saddled with a whopping insecurity—he wore a pistol even when welding a stock rack or driving a tractor—and packing a contempt for rules, he finally killed like a rogue bear unable to tell human from animal.

Claude Dallas was born in mid-March, 1950: the year Orlon was introduced, and the first Xerox-copy machine came out; the year authors Riesman and Glazer attracted wide attention with their book, *The Lonely Crowd,* analyzing inner-directed character types; and A. B. Guthrie won the Pulitzer Prize for his novel, *The Way West,* about mountain men being elbowed aside by emigrants.

Dallas, second of seven children by a second marriage, was born a Southerner of a Southern father for whom he was named, in Winchester, Virginia, near the northern end of the Shenandoah Valley, just west of the Blue Ridge Mountains. In the eighteenth and nineteenth centuries, wagons and stagecoaches lumbered through Winchester's muddy streets carrying adventurers westward. The town was a center of military activities during the War between the States; a requisitioning area for the Confederates, it changed hands many times.

Claude Dallas, Sr., moved the family to Akron, Ohio, where briefly he worked for Firestone Tire and Rubber Company, before moving again, to northern Michigan, about ninety miles from Sault Ste. Marie.

In Michigan the Dallas family ran a dairy farm with 120 Brown Swiss cows. The boys, together with a couple of farm hands, did the morning milking, then rode the bus to a two-room schoolhouse. Claude had one fight there, with a boy three years older, costing Claude a black eye, a broken nose, and apparently his self-confidence.

Meanwhile back at the farm, to help bring in the cows he was given his first horse. At eight, he tried trapping mink along the nearby creek; at nine, he was given a 16-gauge shotgun. At eleven, he was allowed to hunt deer; at sixteen, he was given a .30-06 for his birthday, a reward for not smoking.

Dallas' father, a Catholic convert, was a strict disciplinarian with the six boys. They had to be perfect. "No goddamn backtalk. I tell you to do something, you better move!" Dallas' mother describes her son as "strongheaded like his daddy." In the summer, the boys put up the single cutting of alfalfa. In the fall and winter, they put up deer—their father showed them how to poach with jacklights. "We put up thirty to fifty deer a year for meat." They sold the antlers by the point to less successful, if more honest, hunters. Out in their hayfields, they knocked off all the migrating Canada geese they could nail.

In 1962, the family moved again, to Mount Gilead (population 2,500) in south-central Ohio, where young Dallas went to high school, while his father worked on bridge construction for the state.

It is generally agreed that Dallas, missing Michigan, was never very happy in Ohio. Academically he was sixty-fifth in a class of eighty. He was, according to a classmate, "the most silent guy in class." He never had a date. When long hair was popular—it was the dawn of the Beatles, Bob Dylan, Joan Baez, and the Grateful Dead; "Hair" was playing off-Broadway—he favored a crewcut. He wore flannel shirts, blue jeans, and work boots, and he was the only senior photographed in a bow tie. After school hours, Dallas worked for a farmer down the road; at home he continued to trap small animals. (One hundred years earlier, and fewer than one hundred miles away in western Ohio, Annie Oakley, a teenager, was feeding her impoverished Quaker family by shooting the heads off running squirrels.)

Gradually, Dallas' longing for Michigan gave way to an infatuation with the West. He steeped himself in Ohio-born Zane Grey, whose novels such as *Riders of the Purple Sage* and *Knights of the Range* and *Code of the West,* written fifty years earlier, were peopled with dryland farmers and valiant cowboys in the mythic space of the tourist West. Dallas fancied Louis L'Amour, a novelist whose 101 westerns in style and story-formula were derived from Grey and a West that never existed. Would-be cowboy Dallas was fond of Owen Wister's *The Virginian*, whose populist hero was from his native state, a detail not lost on the young reader. He devoured Jack London's Alaskan fiction. On television he watched "Bonanza," "Gunsmoke," and "Rawhide." In movie theaters over the next couple of years Dallas managed to see "Guns of the Magnificent Seven," "Winchester .73," "The Undefeated," "The Wild Bunch," and "Butch Cassidy and the Sundance Kid."

In 1967, a few months after graduation in June, Dallas took his savings, and a 1941 International pickup signed over by his father, and left Ohio, going first through the South, then, after the truck gave out, hitching west across Texas, and arrived in California for a visit with his sister.

Dallas wintered outside San Jose, a sprawling, ill-defined city just south of San Francisco, feeding cows at a dairy farm, a chore he knew all too well.

In the spring, he hitchhiked southeast toward Visalia, the gatepost to Sequoia-Kings Canyon National Park, and camped one night in an orange grove. Slow to rise in the morning, he encountered the owner, who a few years earlier had owned a ranch in Oregon's Alvord Desert, and his description was enough to make Dallas abandon thoughts of a journey to Alaska, and hive north to eastern Oregon instead.

In another and real world, the United States had lost its 10,000th plane over Vietnam, and the Tet offensive had taken everyone by surprise. Eugene McCarthy was making a bid for the presidency. Students for a Democratic Society were calling for the mobilization of a half-million protestors at the national Democratic convention in Chicago.

Snagging rides when he could, walking when he had to, Dallas reached the Alvord—where southeastern Oregon butts up against Nevada on the south and Idaho on the east. He headed up the road to the Alvord Ranch, a 53,000-acre spread located on the sage and rabbitbrush flats, flanked and watered by the lonely, largely treeless, basaltic rimrock of Steens Mountain (9,700 ft.).

There he talked his way into a fencing job on the upper range for the spring and summer, working out of the line cabin on the upper pasture. With his first paychecks, he bought a commemorative Winchester .73 rifle (.30-30 with a hexagonal barrel), and took to wearing a pistol the way boatmen used to wear pliers, and with as many ready excuses for its use. He practiced, first on ground squirrels, then on deer. Hoyt Wilson, the foreman and owner's son, said, "He couldn't hit the broad side of a barn because his eyes weren't very good." Before long, however, wearing wire-rimmed glasses, his marksmanship improved, and eventually he acquired the reputation of being good enough to shoot the red off a blackbird's wing.

The high-desert Alvord suited Dallas right down to the ground—he was enamored of the mythology and ideology of the West, and here was reality matching itself to the dreamer's dream. Dallas in Wonderland.

He stayed on through the winter to feed hay to the Alvord Herefords. By spring, having distinguished himself from mere drifter or saddletramp, he asked to be kept on as a buckaroo. Wilson agreed.

Dallas had his problems with horses, not being born to them like most cowboys, and by more than than one account he could be rough on stock. The foreman gave him a suitably broken saddlehorse and an older packhorse. Dallas' crewcut had grown to a ponytail; he affected an old-fashioned, round-brimmed, Tom Mix Stetson, black as his old bow tie; he also preferred an old-fashioned spade bit for his horse—called a "bear trap" by those using a more humane bit. The other cowboys noted with approval, however, that he took care of himself and his rigging.

By the spring of 1970, Dallas decided it was time to pull the plug; he said he was heading for Canada. Without Dallas saying it, the fine point prodding him was his draft board: he was a draft dodger fearful of getting caught. He bought a pair of buckskins from the Wilsons, "Buck" and "Dan,"—as in the ballad, "I ride an old Paint; I lead an old Dan"—but unable to make a clean break, he hung around the Steens range for a couple of months, living on poached venison and camping with the other Alvord buckaroos, then finally rode south and found work for a season on the Camel Creek Ranch in central Nevada. (He never wrote or telephoned the Wilsons at the

Alvord Ranch until four years later, when he needed to borrow money.)

In the fall, he rode up to Paradise Hill Bar, owned by George Nielsen, among a collection of houses north of Winnemucca, at the southern end of Paradise Valley, Nevada. For the next ten years, the aging Nielsen became Dallas' outlet for poached meat and fur.

Paradise Valley, once called Paradise City, is another of those settlements whose elevation (4,300 ft.) is a hundred times its population, in a valley by the same name and eighteen miles from Paradise Hill (sometimes called Paradise Junction). Settled in the 1860s as an agricultural base for the mining camps at Unionville and Star City, Paradise Valley survived long after the camps had eaten their own bowels. A guidebook written fifty years ago by someone who had never had his feet on the ground, referring to the valley itself, said, "No one who has ever seen it denies its right to the praise implied." The valley, hemmed in on three sides by mountains, was a natural sanctuary. Dallas needed the place a lot more than it needed him, and he tethered to it.

Every life has its periods of no particular significance. Dallas got a job on the seven-man crew of the nearby Quarter Circle A Ranch, part of the two-million-acre Nevada Garvey spread. Its 9,000 cows demanded winter feeding, spring calving, and summer herding. During the next three years, he did ranch work with various outfits, piece work and contract work; and he trapped in central Nevada. Summers usually in a tent, winters holed up in a trailer.

He developed a reverence for the western paintings of Charlie Russell and made a trip to the C. W. Russell Museum in Great Falls, Montana. His regard for Russell was natural enough, since the painter had been a dropout from a New Jersey military school, came west to Montana, trapped for a couple of years, cowboyed for a spell, and then with an impromptu watercolor of a dolorous steer titled "Waiting for a Chinook," began his celebrated career.

At times Dallas went hiking for several days by himself in the Owyhee Desert, forty miles northeast of Paradise Valley. In his unencumbered time he worked on his apparel or his tack. As always, he practiced his draw and his shooting, schooling himself to use either hand. Evenings he might reload cartridges, or fortify himself with Louis L'Amour, choosing anything from *Hondo* to *Heller with a Gun*.

Unknown to Dallas, however, his past was dogging him. In July, 1973, he was indicted by a federal grand jury in Columbus, Ohio, for failure to report for induction back in September, 1970. The FBI tracked his family to its new quarters in New York State, then followed son Dallas as far as Oregon. Finally in October, 1973, a pair of FBI agents from Reno and a Winnemucca deputy sheriff rousted him while he was napping in the bunkhouse of a buckaroo camp in Elko County, Nevada. They drove him, in belly handcuffs, to Battle Mountain, booked him in the Lander County jail, then hauled him to Ohio for trial.

In January, a day before his jury trial, charges were dropped by the U. S. Attorney because of a technicality: the Mount Gilead draft board could prove that Dallas had received his first notice but not his second. Besides, by now all combat troops had been withdrawn from Vietnam.

Dallas returned to Nevada and called Constance Wilson at the Alvord to borrow $900 for lawyer's fees. In May he rode north about 250 miles from Fallon, Nevada, and worked cattle on Steens Mountain to repay the debt owed the Wilsons. In a short conversation with Hoyt Wilson about his arrest, he said, "I just don't want anybody to mess with me. That's why I came west in the first place." At summer's end, he headed south again to Paradise Hill.

It has been a long time since raising cattle was a sure way to manure the money tree. Over the next five years, Dallas worked cows when he could, but fulltime range work grew scarcer as beef prices dropped and BLM requirements for range improvements increased. Much of the work was seasonal at best; now it became ever more temporary. By 1975 Dallas was finished as a buckaroo. He worked on a well-drilling rig, drove harvest trucks, performed day labor, poached, and trapped. The last of the uncurried West was getting combed out. Increasingly, cattle were trucked rather than trailed to and from summer pasture. Whatever the other work, though, he always wore his pistol like a claw hammer holstered at his side, and when the work eased, he filled his hours practicing his quick-draw, his aim, and his reload. Deceived or disappointed in his vision of the West, and living on the rim between illusion and reality, Dallas seemed determined to salvage some corner of the myth.

A trailer and a half-converted schoolbus in Nielsen's court behind his bar became Dallas' headquarters. Nielsen, an ex-Californian and reputedly a one-time cattle buyer, lived with his wife, Liz, in a white house adjoining their bar on Highway 95. (His wife worked as the head nurse at Humboldt General Hospital in Winnemucca.) Nielsen and Dallas spent nights visiting in the bar— they talked guns, horses, and government, while playing cards. The pair grew closer, bound together by their expressed hatred of authority and pleased with the new Sagebrush Rebellion, a cheatgrassroots movement of agricultural corporations—one is at liberty to believe or disbelieve—subsidized on public lands and eager to see those lands escheat to private hands. Nielsen became a stepfather figure, always approving. They were pulled together, too, by the spoils of poaching. The bobcat fur market, spurred by unforeseen causes, was on the rise, and Dallas planned to ride it as far as it went.

The major reason for the rise was a long way from the Owyhees: in 1975 the Convention on International Trade in Endangered Species (CITES) was implemented by eighty-five countries. It was designed to promote conservation of endangered species, while allowing commerce in species that could withstand the pressure of trade. Spotted cats—jaguar, leopard, cheetah, tiger—received legal protection. Member countries required import and export permits for that wildlife trade; however, the convention did not apply to hunting or poaching within a country. (In the United States the Endangered Species Act sets out domestic requirements to implement CITES—and that act listed ocelets and margays as endangered.)

Furthermore, consumer-awareness campaigns and protests by advocates for animals discouraged affluent shoppers from buying coats made from spotted cats. Furriers who deal with spotted-cat fur need great numbers of those pelts to match patterns for each garment or accessory. They suddenly pounced on the one spotted fur still available: bobcat. The market boomed, and consequently the American bobcat became one of the more highly sought and heavily traded animal skins. In 1980, European nations alone (mostly France and Germany) imported over 450,000 skins. The price of a bobcat pelt jumped from $21 to $283, with Idaho trappers reporting an average of $170-$190.

For Dallas, public animals on public land appeared more profitable than ruminant chattels ever had. He laid out long lines, mostly in Nevada, occasionally in southeastern Oregon or southwestern Idaho. He wanted bobcat, but he also took fox, coyote, and mountain lions. Trapping lions was no more legal than baiting traps with animal parts, or using exposed bait, two additional violations he commonly practiced. Despite the federal Wild Horse Act, Dallas also was known to shoot mustangs for meat and bait. He refused to use the spacers on trap jaws required to let raptors escape, nor did he tag his traps as the law stated. In short, he was a trash trapper, working the Santa Rosas, the Bloody Run Hills, the Snowstorms, Tuscarosas, the Monitors, and Cortez mountains.

At Paradise Hill, Nielsen was known to fence the meat and fur for forty percent of the take. Two mountain lion hides without validation seals were found in his house, and the poaching hotline often rang with tips and complaints about Dallas' doings.

In 1976 Dale Elliot, Nevada Fish and Game officer, surprised Dallas in his winter camp on Savory Creek and wrote him a citation for an illegally baited trapline. Dallas posted a one-hundred-dollar cash bond, appeared in Eureka before the justice of the peace, forfeited his bond, and got his traps back. But he could no more change his ways than a bobcat can change its spots. Dallas was a man who believed that most of his troubles resulted simply from getting caught.

Two years later, Dallas had moved his trapline to the Bloody Run Hills southwest of Paradise Hill. In December, Gene Weller, fisheries biologist and warden from Winnemucca, was hiking in the Hills with an eye on enforcement and found a rabbit hanging over a trap—a violation. The trap had no spacer or tag. He pulled the trap and left his business card in the rabbit's ear. Then he followed the line out and pulled five more baited traps.

The next morning he returned and spotted Nielsen's red Jeep ahead of him. He pulled off, climbed a knoll and watched the Jeep stop at the mouth of the canyon. He could see the trapper's round-brimmed Texas hat as he set off to inspect his sets. Weller drove his truck up alongside the Jeep and waited for its driver to return. Well after dark, when the trapper failed to return, Weller removed the Savage rifle and Ruger Blackhawk .357 pistol from the seat of the Jeep and headed back to Winnemucca.

Three days later, Dallas showed up, asking to get his guns back. With icy indifference, he lied about the traps. Weller returned the guns, and Dallas resumed his unregenerate slaughter.

During the summer of 1979, he spent some of his fur money on a long-dreamed trip to the North. With his younger brother Stuart and a friend, he traveled to Canada, avoiding customs at the border in order to take in illegal firearms, and went on to Great Slave Lake in Northwest Territories, where the trio canoed north on the Mackenzie River for almost a thousand miles. (The river, although large in volume, is not difficult.) Along the way, happy as a worm in an apple, Dallas poached a Dall sheep, severed its head and, holding it, posed for photographs, thus graduating from tri-state gamehog to an international one. Nielsen wired money to get them home from Whitehorse.

By January Dallas had his trapline staked in Star Valley in the southwest corner of Idaho. The price of bobcat fur was at an all-time high—$284 on average—well worth the effort, especially if one cheated. According to more knowledgeable trappers, one reason Dallas refused to play by the rules was that he was not an accomplished trapper—he had a lot to learn, and he was too proud to ask—high-desert trapping being a good deal different from fecund Midwestern trapping. He ran eighty sets altogether, some of them in Idaho, the rest in Nevada, where the season was three weeks longer. That winter he told another trapper that his take was fourteen cats.

In late spring Dallas decided to load his green Mad River canoe and investigate the South Fork of the Owyhee, a river that drains the Bull Mountains of northern Nevada, cutting canyons through ancient volcanic deposits. At the right time of year, it is an ideal three-day canoe trip—fifty-six miles when one launches at the YP Ranch, as he did. The river in this reach requires intermediate skill: "Open canoes should expect to do a certain amount of judicious scouting...and may have to line or portage a few spots, depending on the flow."

About fifteen miles into his float, three miles north across the border into Idaho and thirteen miles east of Oregon, Dallas stopped and beached his canoe for the night on the west side of the river in a spot known as Bull Camp. A marginal road from Paradise Valley ravels along the rim to an overlook above the camp. He liked the feel of the hedged basin and filed the location away as a prospect for the winter. Two days later, he pulled his canoe out of the river at Crutchers Crossing and trucked back to Paradise.

He did some farm work for a Paradise Valley rancher, then left for northern California, working with his brother Stuart, peeling bark for a logging company through the summer. By September he was back in Paradise Valley. He caught the tail end of the spud harvest at Smith Farms; he "ripped some ground" until early November for a potato grower on the west side of Sand Pass Road, south of Paradise Hill. He then moved his trailer back to the court at Paradise Hill.

In late fall, with an open winter and the price of bobcat fur holding at only twenty dollars a pelt lower than last season, Dallas decided to pluck what he could out of the rimrocks above Bull Camp for a few weeks. He was considering drifting up to Alaska in the spring; poaching would help pay his passage.

Isn't that what we're all hunting for? A green valley somewhere?—Louis L'Amour.

December 3, 1980. Dallas set out with a three-vehicle caravan: a vintage, squat bus; a four-wheel-drive pickup; and a Chevy

Suburban pulling a horse trailer with a pair of rented mules in it. George Nielsen and his son were along, as were Craig Carver and Jim Stevens. The jolting ride, just over a hundred miles, required six hours.

After a wrong turn and a late arrival, the next morning the men stacked several hundred pounds of gear and food at the overlook: canvas tents, sheepherder stove, five gallons of kerosene, lanterns, traps, guns, food. Snow was beginning to feather down, and Carver and young Nielsen each made a backpack trip with supplies down to the flat about fifty yards from the river. Then they pulled out, leaving Dallas and his visitors (four over the next three weeks) to work his provisions downslope. The place fit him like a snake's skin does just before shedding.

Always operating on his own season, Dallas promptly knocked down two bucks and a doe and hung them from tent poles in camp. True to form, he also cut pieces to bait the traps he set out in the rimrocks half a mile from the river a month before the three-week season opened.

On New Year's Eve, Dallas had a visitor from the nearby 45 Ranch—a cowboy on horseback, Eddie Carlin, who felt Dallas was infringing on his trapping area and winter range. He was annoyed by the discovery that his cattle had been pushed out of the basin and gates closed behind them. Dallas would not budge, and Carlin, as he left, mentioned that the Idaho Fish and Game might show up. "I'll be ready for them," Dallas replied.

A few days later, a pair of experienced long-line trappers moved in on the Carlin range and baited their sets with sagehen parts. Not wanting to be blamed for the illegal sets and concerned for his own season, Carlin felt compelled to call a warden in Boise.

Bill Pogue, age fifty, was a senior conservation officer, having been with the Idaho department since 1965, and with the Nevada Fish and Game years before Claude Dallas knew how to spell cow. He had even been, reluctantly, the police chief of Winnemucca for a year. Until recently, the Owyhee Desert and game management Unit 42 had been his district. When he received Carlin's call, he agreed to come because the conservation officer assigned to the

Owyhee could not go. The officer's younger brother, however, Wilson Conley Elms, age thirty-five, was available as backup. At 10:30 p.m. the men left Boise on the five-hour drive to the 45 Ranch. On reaching the rim above the ranch, they slept in their Dodge Powerwagon until dawn, then ate breakfast inside the house with the Carlins. After thanks, Pogue and Elms left the 45 Ranch, uprooted the sagehen-baited sets, located that trapper and cited him for three violations. Back on the road, they encountered the Carlins again, and in the course of their conversation about the illegal sets, Carlin's wife inadvertently revealed that Dallas was in Bull Camp running a poaching operation. Pogue and Elms then poked slowly south toward Dallas' camp.

At the same time, Jim Stevens, who had been in on the camp set-up trip with Dallas a month earlier, was on his way north for a short visit and a spell of arrowhead hunting. His 1977 blue and white Blazer carried mail for Dallas, as well as groceries, fruit, brownies, and pudding. It was almost noon when he arrived at the overlook. With the .357 Magnum Nielsen had loaned him for the prearranged signal, he fired two shots, waited a few minutes and fired two more. Dallas was to respond by bringing a mule up to the rim for the supplies.

After a half-hour wait, eager and impatient, Stevens started down the trail. A short distance on his way, he met Dallas, dressed in yellow fireman's coat, coming up with a pack on his back. They visited briefly, then Dallas said he would go on up for a load while Stevens went on down to the river. Once Stevens arrived at the snug camp, he dropped his load beside the river-facing tent, and then walked a way upriver, watching for arrowheads, found one, and scuffed at likely shards.

He was lost in an archaic era when he heard a shout from the direction of the white tent. He glanced back and saw Dallas with two uniformed men. From their demeanor, he sensed there was a problem.

A lawman is not a restraint, but a freedom, a liberator. He restrains only those who would break the laws, and provides freedom for the rest of us to work, to laugh, to sing, to play in peace.—Louis L'Amour

When Stevens reached the tent, he realized from their uniforms that the men were Idaho Fish and Game wardens. At the request of the older man, he handed over his signal pistol. Pogue removed the cartridges, dropped them in Stevens' pocket and returned the gun.

Stevens introduced himself; the wardens gave their names. The conversation drained away as the parties eyed the game violations in view: two closed-season deer with, as everyone knew, more violations closeted within the tent. Pogue gestured toward the deer. Dallas said he was so far from town that he had to hang up meat. A mountain man lived on jerked vension and pemmican; Dallas was living on closed-season meat and pistachio pudding. And his quills were up like a porcupine's.

The world isn't built around people who do what they want to do...what they want regardless of who gets hurt. It is built by people who do what they should do.—Louis L'Amour

Pogue asked Dallas to bring the bobcat hides out of his tent. When Dallas stalled with a question about search warrants, Elms entered the tent and came out with the pelts in his arms.

Stevens had distanced himself a few feet from the triangular confrontation and stood looking at the river, hoping the dispute would end with citations and a cash bond rather than an arrest that would end his outing. If Pogue was gruff, Dallas at this point lacked qualities essential to a trespassing-host on public land.

When somebody tries to make it with a gun, he has already admitted he hasn't the guts to make it the honest way. Whether he realizes it or not, life has already whipped him. From there on, it's all downhill.—Louis L'Amour

Stevens heard Dallas say, "Are you going to take me in?" Suddenly the bellow of a Magnum deafened him beyond hearing.

Stevens whirled and saw Dallas firing from a crouch, both hands wrapped around his pistol grip, police style. He heard Pogue grunt, "Oh, no!" as he staggered backward.

Dallas spun to shoot Elms, then back to Pogue, motions perfected by his endless rehearsals. With his gun empty, both men lying on the ground, Dallas stepped inside his tent, grabbed .22 long-rifle cartridges from a box, loaded his Marlin rifle. He stepped back outside, walked to Elms lying face down, shot him behind the ear, then stepped over to Pogue and shot him face-up in the same spot.

When a man uses a gun he'd better have a good reason, even if he does have a good lawyer.—Louis L'Amour

Stevens stared in disbelief. The canyon was quiet as a crypt. "Why, Claude?" he asked. "Why? Why?"

"I swore I'd never be arrested again," Dallas said stiffly. "They were going to handcuff me." (Pogue had lost his handcuffs earlier.)

Stevens was stunned. Dallas spoke again, "I'm sorry I got you involved in this. I gotta get rid of these bodies and you've gotta help me."

Stevens was certain he would be gunned down next. Dallas read his mind. "I know what you're thinking. But nobody has the right to come into my camp and violate my rights. In my mind it's justifiable homicide." Stevens had no thought to argue. "We've got to hide the bodies," Dallas informed him. "We'll haul them out. You cover them in case a plane flies over, while I get the mules." Dallas went down and waded the river while Stevens scattered sage over Pogue and Elms. He noticed Pogue's pistol, a Model 66 Smith and Wesson, a few inches from his outstretched hand.

The smaller mule was picketed across the South Fork, but the larger one decided to display its independence. Dallas, unable to catch it, hollered for Stevens to bring some grain. Stevens considered shooting Dallas, or running for it, then dismissed both options. With a pan of oats, he waded the stone-strewn riffles. They led the smaller mule back to the campsite.

"We gotta get these guys outta here," Dallas reiterated. He hobbled the mule, rigged a packsaddle, and together they loaded Pogue's body and lashed it down. Dallas retrieved Pogue's pistol and remarked grimly, "This gun is going into the ground with this guy." Then he started for the rim, leaving Stevens to pack his own gear and hike up behind.

When Stevens had reached a bench just below the rim, he met Dallas returning downhill on foot. He ordered Stevens to drop his belongings and return with him to "get the other guy."

At the tent Dallas rigged a sawbuck saddle for the little mule, removed Elms' pistol from its shoulder holster, and together they tried to load the warden, who weighed a firm 265 pounds. The mule turned fractious, and Elm' bloody body fell heavily to the ground. When Stevens acted as though he were about to vomit, Dallas told him to go off into the brush where it would not be noticed. As Stevens regained his composure, Dallas suggested quartering the body, then when Stevens refused outright, conceded that he was not up for it either.

Once the body was loaded, Dallas sent Stevens ahead with the mule on a lead rope, while he stayed to burn some of the evidence and bloody ground, and heave the deer carcasses into the river.

Stevens had not proceeded 200 hundred yards before Elms' body shifted and rolled the mule on its side. Stevens loosened its cinch. Smoke roiled from the campsite, and Dallas appeared carrying a pack, the bobcat hides, his pistols, shotgun, and two rifles. "As long as you can carry it, there's no such thing as too much firepower."

Unable to reload Elms' body, Dallas gave Stevens his pack and sent him on up the trail. Meanwhile, he roped Elms' legs, dallied the other end to the forks of the packsaddle, and dragged the body face-down to the river—quicker than quartering.

When Dallas caught up with Stevens, he said, "I dumped the big guy in the river. This is murder one for me. I didn't weight the body. They'll find it in the morning." As darkness gained the rim, they climbed together up the trail. Dallas kept thinking he heard motors.

On top, the tailgate was open on Stevens' Blazer, and Pogue's body lay face up on the ground next to it. Dallas had cleared a space inside and urged Stevens to help him load the body, as though it were a hunting trophy he was packing back to show Nielsen. The dead man's boots protruded from the back window. They wrapped them with an orange tarp. Dallas poured kerosene over the place where Pogue had lain, set it afire, then slid in next to Stevens and told him to drive to Paradise Bar.

They drove slowly through the desert dark, following the frayed road while Dallas whittled one alibi after another. He had trouble getting a set of facts that would screw on straight. Then he began discussing where he would or should hide Pogue's body. Stevens said he did not want to know the plans; with no end of hiding places along the way, he thought it took sage for brains to haul a body all the way to Paradise Hill. Though fearful for his life, he was not yet a victim of modern callousness. He could not help being horrified by the grotesque: next to him sat a man who had wanted so badly to haul *both* bodies back that he suggested quartering the heavier one! Dallas, for his part, was jumpy, frequently spotting false lights, and once bolting out of the rig to run off into the dark. Shortly before they reached Paradise Hill, around ten-thirty, they agreed on a cover story.

Dallas commanded Stevens to park in back of the bar, then climbed out and knocked on the door. George Nielsen answered. "I dusted two Fish and Game," Dallas informed him matter-of-factly. "They came into my camp. We got one in the Blazer. I put the other guy in the river. I need your pickup to bury the body."

Nielsen let them in. When his wife, Liz, joined them from the front room and learned of the murders, she was quick to say they did not want any trouble but told Stevens to burn his clothes in the living room woodstove, then take a thorough shower. While George fueled the family pickup, Liz burned Stevens' clothes. Once Stevens reappeared from the shower, Dallas warned him to clean out the Blazer, destroying all evidence of fingerprints and bloodstains. Dallas had them help transfer Pogue's corpse to the pickup, borrowed a pick and shovel, then left. It was midnight.

Nielsen and Stevens had a drink in the bar, then Stevens headed for his potato farm, halfway to Winnemucca and fifteen minutes away. At his doublewide he showered again before he went to bed.

In the morning he was up early, before his wife and children, planning to flush out the Blazer. He opened the back of his rig and saw Pogue's blood and Nielsen's pistol. He climbed in and headed back to Paradise Hill to return the pistol and box of shells.

When he handed the evidence to Nielsen, the bar owner admitted that he and his wife had not been able to sleep. Before Stevens' turned for home, he told Nielsen he would try to stick by the story.

At his house, Stevens scrubbed out his Blazer. Then he went inside and blurted out the story to his wife, who already sensed something was wrong. They decided to do the right thing. They drove to the hospital in Winnemucca and informed Liz Nielsen. Liz, in agreement, called George, so that they could all confess together. While they waited for George to arrive, she told them how Dallas after two or three hours had come back with the pickup. She had put together a bag of food for him before he asked George to drive him south about fifteen miles and drop him off on the Sand Pass Road at the edge of the Bloody Run. Those hills that had no known origin for their name had one now.

Early that afternoon, the Owyhee County prosecutor received a report from Winnemucca, 230 miles south by road, that two Idaho conservation officers had been shot at a place called Bull Camp. He called Sheriff Tim Nettleton of Owyhee County at his office in Murphy (population fifty), Idaho.

Nettleton at forty was ten years older than Dallas, but he was a fourth-generation Idaho cowboy who filed for sheriff when his family's Box-T Ranch went belly-up. He won the election by one vote out of two thousand. Six feet, four inches, 180 pounds, and quick to laugh, he was also savvy, shrewd, patient, and unabashedly rough-hewn western.

His job came with hardships firmly attached. Owyhee is the second-largest county in Idaho, over seven thousand square miles for eight thousand residents—thinner of people than cows—and Nettleton piloted his own plane to cope with its distances. While much of the Owyhee gives evidence that there was once a better time to be a cow, its canyons and bottomlands look much as they did on the day of creation. And out in all this wide-brim Idaho, Nettleton straightened out wrecks, refereed saloon brawls, and wrestled with rustlers.

The sheriff had known Bill Pogue for ten years, liked and admired him. As soon as Nettleton spoke to the Humboldt County sheriff and verified the killings and their location, he telephoned a rancher in Grandview with a plane, called his deputy sheriff and a policeman in nearby Homedale, and they were airborne by 4:30 p.m. An hour later the single-engine Cessna 210 was flying along the rim of the South Fork of the Owyhee. They spotted the Powerwagon parked above Dallas' camp. As darkness thickened to night, they continued on to the Winnemucca airport.

There they met with Humboldt County deputies and later with Jim Stevens. Nettleton spent the night in a motel. (Exactly one hundred years earlier, Wyatt Earp had been named a special deputy policeman in Tombstone.)

The next morning Nettleton drove north to McDermitt, Nevada, and hired a helicopter pilot to fly him to Bull Camp. He had only fuel enough to get them to the 45 Ranch; a news helicopter from Salt Lake City hauled Nettleton the rest of the way.

Elms' body was recovered from the river a quarter mile below camp, and evidence was collected by crime lab specialists; however, because of the lack of a search warrant, the tent was not entered. Then at dark, seventeen lawmen and investigators were flown by National Guard helicopter back to McDermitt. (The next day, Elms' body was flown to St. Alphonsus Hospital in Boise for an autopsy.)

What rain is to grass, a killing is to newspapers. Word of the murders had reached the media. Third District Magistrate Charles Jurries signed a warrant charging Dallas with two counts of first-degree murder. Since Dallas had crossed the state line into Nevada, the FBI also issued a fugitive warrant. The agency had his mugshot and fingerprints from his draft-evasion arrest. Nettleton's telephone was flooded with calls from would-be informers and helpers, as well as with sightings in several states.

As eighty-some searchers from nearly a dozen local, state, and federal agencies—looking for Pogue as well as Dallas—spilled out onto the desert, caution and apprehension ran high. Dallas had more than a two-day start, but he could be holed-up in any nearby cave or abandoned shack.

On Friday, January 9, four days after the murders, an FBI Special Weapons and Tactics (SWAT) team, slow out of the chute, was searching the Bloody Run Hills with a Bell helicopter and two fixed-wing aircraft. They spotted nothing more exceptional than animals.

Lawmen measured the gas remaining in Nielsen's pickup and plotted a circle, with a radius of thirty miles from Paradise Hill, within which they were confident Pogue's body would be found.

Actually, Dallas himself had covered fewer than fifty miles—about twelve miles a night—out into the Black Rock Desert, part of the big playa of the Great Basin, an area that drains in upon itself. Even a tumbleweed makes better time. But Dallas was living his dream. As Nevada rancher Benny Damele, for whom Dallas had once worked, commented, "I think the son of a bitch just wants to be chased."

Although there was no snow on the ground, the days were colder than a crowbar. An itinerant cowboy spotted Dallas' campfire out among the shadscale and saltgrass one night and reported it, but no one had time to investigate.

Searchers from the FBI, Nevada Fish and Game, and Idaho Fish and Game beat the sagebush, checking caves, deserted cabins, played-out mines. Nothing. After twelve days, Nevada authorities called off their search. In Myrtle Beach, South Carolina, where Dallas' parents now lived, FBI agents asked questions, trying to assemble a profile from parents, relatives, and family friends, who had no interest in being helpful.

The public view, while divided, was not by any means divided evenly: most saw Dallas as a loner, dependent on friends for supplies and money, acting out a twisted, run amok fantasy; a minority rushed to romanticize the notorious—a desperado living off the land, wronged by oppressive authority. An *Idaho Statesman* reporter wrote, "Some of Dallas' acquaintances are openly rooting for him to escape."

The power of mythology once again swamped reality; countering it was like trying to make water run upstream. As westerner and writer Bill Kittredge, who grew up on an eastern Oregon ranch, has put it, "There's a darker problem with the Western. It's a story inhabited by a mythology about power and the social utility of violence, an American version of an ancient dream of warrior righteousness. And because of that, it's a story many of us find threatening. We don't want to live in a society fascinated by fantasies of killer wish-fulfillment."

On Saturday afternoon, January 17, a memorial service for Pogue and Elms was held in Boise's Memorial Park near Fish and Game Department headquarters. The families of the two men, and more than 400 persons from the IDFG and other fish and wildlife organizations and law enforcement agencies, attended. Pogue was eulogized as an exemplary conservation officer; Elms, as a man whose love for fishing was second only to his love for his work. After a closing prayer, two Boy Scouts from a Boise troop played taps on trumpets, one echoing the other.

Back in Murphy, a time zone away from Winnemucca and from fantasy, Sheriff Nettleton settled in for the long, persistent, methodical pursuit. Paradise Valley and the Owyhee Desert gave off rumors the way a wildfire gives off heat. He sifted the evidence and filled in the picture of the type of man they were looking for. What he saw gave him the same regard for Dallas that a buckaroo has for a sheepherder's dog.

When Dallas' split-line of sixty traps was followed-out in the rimrocks above Bull Camp, all the sets contained exposed bait cut from rabbits or deer. Two bobcats were found, one dead, the other starving; two golden eagles also were found dead, and a pair of raccoons. The traps lacked spacers and tags.

A search of Dallas' old schoolbus and travel trailer in Paradise Hill revealed deer hides, a mountain lion pelt, a Confederate flag, seven rifles, ten handguns, cartridge reloaders, several speedloaders, a case of .30-caliber bullets, a bulletproof vest, a gas mask, an Israeli army tanker's helmet, and a small library on firearms and combat shooting. Among the books found: a field manual for *Submachine Gun Caliber .45, M3 and M3A1; No Second Place Winner*, about quick-draw; *Firearms Silencers*, dealing with silencers for various weapons; and *Kill or Get Killed,* about riot control and close combat, which included the sentence, "Fast gun handling can be a fascinating game as well as the grim difference between living and going down."

On a chilly weekend in mid-February, seventy volunteers working in concentric circles out from Paradise Hill, made a second thorough search for Pogue's body. They raked the desert on foot, horseback, dirt bike, and Jeep. No clues were unearthed.

Since January 27, Dallas, whose peregrinations can never be completely understood unless he chooses to unknot them, had been in Sioux Falls, South Dakota, at work under an assumed name for the Sioux Steel plant, lifting and cleaning steel gates off a conveyor belt and assembling their hinges—a job whose irony surely could not have been wholly lost on him. When a fellow worker fumbled his end of a gate, caught Dallas with a blow under his chin, and spouted a quick apology, Dallas replied, "Being sorry don't mean shit!" and went on with his work.

A second testy reaction to a mild prank made Dallas' co-workers label him quick-tempered, like a skunk with its tail up.

There is a saying among my people that the deer may forget the snare, but the snare does not forget the deer.—Louis L'Amour

Nettleton ran his national manhunt and media campaign out of his little office in Murphy. Even with a wounded budget and the most limited resources, he logged every tip and checked every lead. The reward for information leading to the arrest of Claude Dallas had grown to $20,000. The Idaho Fish and Game Department made a contribution; so did California Fish and Game employees; the Audubon Society contributed, as did the national Trappers Association, and the Idaho Trappers Association. A four-page article appeared in the July issue of *Outdoor Life*. The worker who had apologized to Dallas at the steel plant recognized his picture in the magazine and notified local authorities who called Nettleton, but in early April Dallas had moved on. (An elated Nettleton kept the report secret, hoping the killer might use the same alias at another job.) A two-page spread appeared in the October *American Rifleman*: "Brutal Slayings Spark Nationwide Manhunt." Dallas had been a subscriber to the magazine; now he was the most wanted man in the West. Nettleton intended to turn his wanted poster into the national wallpaper. There was a trap in the path and the path was getting narrower.

Dallas moved by bus to Texas, where two of his brothers lived, then west to northern California.

Nettleton continued to work the case, spending at least half his time on it. Harry Capaul, officer for the Idaho Bureau of Investigation, was equally persistant. The two lawmen cooperated and collaborated. Despite the lack of leads and the tapering of others' interest, their determination never ebbed. They understood Dallas: a 3-S killer—shoot, shovel, and shutup. By Dallas' own admission to George Nielsen, however, he had done a sloppy job. They knew the killer was too much the loner to call attention to himself; and he seldom let down any personal gates. He did not drink to excess or womanize. Yet sooner or later he would foul up again. A man almost always picks the trails that best suit his horse, thought Nettleton, and the trails that best suit Dallas are in Paradise Valley and out in the Owyhees.

Dallas was next sighted off-trail, however, in June near Fort Bragg in northern California, apparently taking refuge with his brother Stuart, a woodworker. The elderly informant who reported seeing Dallas recognized him from his earlier stint in the woods. The sighting worked its way back to the FBI and Nettleton a month or more too late.

In mid-November Hoyt Wilson at the Alvord Ranch received a brief backdoor visit from Dallas, wearing camouflage and carrying a sawed-off shotgun. After a few minutes of conversation, the two shook hands and Dallas decamped. He did call later to complain that his brother had sneaked back into Bull Camp to salvage some of Claude's gear, "but the cops took it all." Dallas the *naif*.

The first anniversary of the murders brought renewed media attention, including a detective magazine article. Nettleton was gratified but not satisfied.

Spring, 1982. Pogue's body still missing, and Dallas on the run for sixteen months. Nettleton's range-fed telegraph was picking up some faint signals. In mid-April, for the first time in months, he suggested a meeting with FBI agents from Boise and Reno. They all met at the Thunderbird Motel in Winnemucca. As it turned out, the FBI had detected similar signals. Nettleton drove back to Murphy encouraged and impatient.

Four days later, at 5:00 a.m. on Sunday, April 18, he received a telephone call from the Boise FBI agent. Dallas had been located near Paradise Hill, and Nettleton was wanted at the Thunderbird immediately. He rounded up his deputy, the Homedale police chief, and state IBI agent Capaul, and sped south beneath a denim-blue sky. Oh, what a beautiful morning, he cheered to himself. They arrived in Winnemucca at 9:30 a.m—239 miles in three hours.

The FBI was assembling and briefing SWAT teams from Butte and Las Vegas, as well as agents from San Francisco and Reno—thirty-three lawmen altogether, including Nettleton's group, Humboldt County sheriff and deputy, and a few Nevada state investigators. The investigators were assigned to keep Dallas' location under surveillance, positioned on a bluff nearly a mile away with a 25X spotting scope and a two-way radio.

An informant asserted Dallas was staying at Craig Carver's trailer just northeast of Paradise Hill, on a dusty sagepatch known locally as Poverty Flats. Carver, thirty-six, was a tall, lean, ex-Marine lance corporal, who had at least four firefight commendations for his combat duty in Vietnam. A native of Los Angeles, he had been around Paradise Valley for ten years. Quiet but well-liked. Like Dallas, he was a loner. He drove an old Ford pickup, building corrals and fences for ranchers, but he insisted on working with hand tools and alone. Home was a wood-heated trailer with a nearby outhouse. He had been in on the original Bull Camp caravan, and he had packed a load of gear down to Dallas' camp. Now Dallas was his dependent for shelter and supplies.

At noon, at the request of the FBI, Nettleton and state investigator Capaul flew a Cessna from the Winnemucca airport north at high altitude over Poverty Flats and made Polaroid reconnaissance photographs. They returned from the flight for more briefings at the Thunderbird. The plan was to take Dallas alive if at all possible because he held the secret to Pogue's remains.

It was 4:00 p.m., however, before lawmen began to take up positions out in the desert. The Humboldt County deputy sheriff and the Idaho trooper were stationed on 101 Ranch Road between the trailer and the Little Humboldt River.

It was 5:00 p.m. before the Las Vegas SWAT teams arrived by car a mile from Poverty Flats and moved to flank the trailer. Nettleton was stationed behind them in full view.

A Cessna 206 flew cover and communications—at a three-mile altitude little more conspicuous than a turkey vulture.

It was nearly 6:00 p.m, with the sun going down over the Bloody Run, setting the sky on fire, when out of its dying rays a black Bell "Huey" helicopter stormed at 140 knots, hovered just long enough to drop the Butte SWAT team of four men behind Carver's trailer, then flared away in reverse, fired its siren, and executed a series of high-speed circles at a quarter-mile distance. The pilot's voice blared over the speaker. "This is the FBI. Claude Dallas, come out with your hands up." (Carver, no stranger to the sound of Hueys, was already face down under a pickup at the far end of his lot.)

Dallas came out all right—through a trailer window, just as he had seen in all those movies. He grabbed a rifle, jumped into Carver's Ford pickup and drove toward the access road. When he saw FBI cars moving to cut him off, he turned and drove through the barbed-wire back fence and out into stirrup-high greasewood and rabbitbrush.

The Cessna pilot reported blue flashes of gunfire from the truck, and the Huey moved in over the powerlines, trying to herd the runaway. Dallas drove toward the river; the deputy sheriff and Idaho trooper moved from their post to intercept him as the SWAT teams dashed forward in irregular three-step darts. Dallas aimed east for the Owyhees, jolting and bouncing through the sage until a second barbed-wire fence sliced the truck's battery cable loose.

A dirt cloud enveloped the truck. The door flew open, Dallas jumped out, ran, then fell. The helicopter retreated to Carver's trailer, picked up one team and dropped it 200 yards from the abandoned truck. The other teams leapfrogged forward. Light was beginning to fail.

As one SWAT team leader crawled forward on his hands and knees, about six yards past the truck, he heard a voice plead, "Don't shoot. I'm over here." He turned and spotted Dallas lying on his back, holding his hands in the air. "Don't move!" the agent shouted. "I'm not gonna do anything," came the subdued reply.

The other lawmen moved up on signal. Dallas had a loaded .30-30 lying next to him. He was dressed in combat fatigues, long-sleeved shirt, and tennis shoes. The shirt had a speedloader in its pocket.

The assault had lasted twenty-two minutes; the truck chase two minutes (almost two miles). The truck door had nine bullet holes in it, and two loaded revolvers lay on the front seat. While one agent read Dallas his rights, another slapped handcuffs on him. The helicopter landed, the murderer was lifted aboard, then he was whirled off to Winnemucca.

As the law enforcement vehicles headed back to Winnemucca, the last one hit its siren as it passed Paradise Hill Bar, a special howdy for the regulars. (To the month, it had been one hundred years since Jesse James was shot down for the reward money posted by the Governor of Missouri.)

At Humboldt General Hospital (Liz Nielsen was off duty that night), Dallas was treated for a superficial heel wound, apparently the result of a steel fragment flaked off by a bullet striking the truck. He was housed in the county jail, before being moved to the Washoe County jail in Reno. He remained uncommunicative there, speaking only to his lawyer, Michael Donnelly, who had been hired on retainer over the telephone by Dallas' parents shortly after the killings.

Back at Poverty Flats, Nettleton had taken Carver into custody and transported him, too, to the county jail in Winnemucca.

For lack of proof that Carver knew he was harboring a fugitive, the fence-builder was released the next day. Accompanied by Nettleton, he returned to his trailer, where a search turned up the latest Dallas armory: a .22 rifle, a .30-30 lever-action, a 12-gauge shotgun, four handguns, reloading equipment, boxes of ammunition, four sacks of traps, sleeping bag, cooking gear, portable radio, a tube of hair coloring, and two books: *The Criminal Use of False Identification*, and *The Paper Trip: A New You Through New I.D.* Nettleton returned to Murphy; he would pick up the evidence in Nevada a week later. (At trial, the county prosecutor was barred from introducing the books as evidence of a state of mind.)

Because state murder charges take precedence over a federal fugitive charge, Idaho filed extradition proceedings against Dallas. Owyhee County Prosecutor Clayton Andersen delivered the request to the Idaho attorney general, and a courier took the papers to Reno. Federal authorities dropped their interstate-flight charge so that it would not have to be tried first (in Reno), thus clearing the way for Idaho procedures. Dallas, held without bail, waived extradition.

At dawn, six days after the capture, Nettleton with a borrowed Winnebago motorhome arrived in Reno. He was accompanied by four armed deputies and an escort car.

At 6:00 a.m. Saturday morning, in orange prison garb, shackled and handcuffed, Dallas was brought out in a wheelchair and transferred to the motorhome. The drive to Murphy was speedy and uneventful. Dallas was lodged in the stoutest of Nettleton's four cells.

Monday morning, at the order of Third Magistrate Judge Marvin Cherin, the prisoner was moved sixty miles north to the modern Canyon County jail (five guards instead of one) in Caldwell, where he was housed in the maximum security cellblock on the third floor. The move was common: the last four murders in Owyhee County had been tried in Caldwell, avoiding a three-hour daily shuttle for lawyers and litigants, and thereby providing sufficient eating and sleeping accommodations for jurors.

On arraignment, Dallas was charged with two counts of first degree murder; three felony counts of using a firearm during the commission of a crime; and misdemeanor counts of resisting arrest and obstruction of justice (concealing and destroying evidence). Dallas pleaded innocent to all counts, contending his actions were based on self-defense and therefore the shootings were justifiable homicide.

Public and press were barred from the arraignment, as well as from the preliminary hearing in May, which lasted two days, and where the state and Owyhee County furnished sufficient evidence to bind Dallas over for trial. During the summer, except for a notice of a denied motion, a change of venue request, and an attempt to delay the trial date, the case of Claude Dallas disappeared from the local newspapers. In July, however, a story in the *Idaho Statesman* reported that the $20,000 reward had been paid to the informant, who had taken delivery in California.

Herb Holman, vice-president of a Reno bank, and his wife Geneva, employed by Nevada Bell, on learning that lawyer fees for the killer would run at least $20,000, started the Claude Dallas Defense Fund. They had met Dallas six years earlier at the Paradise Hill Bar, while on a chukar-hunting trip. Having befriended him, Geneva Holman now apparently examined telephone records in an attempt to learn who had informed the FBI of Dallas' hideout.

Dallas' parents drove their black Chrysler to Reno and joined the Holmans in their motorhome for a drive to visit Claude in the jail in Caldwell. The thirty-minute reunion was divided by Herculite glass and a telephone. Dallas' parents did not return for the trial.

In mid-August Donnelly filed a motion for a change of venue, and in early September, Administrative Judge Edward Lodge approved the motion, ordering the trial moved to Canyon County because of extensive prejudicial pretrial publicity. (Owyhee County still had to pay the costs.)

A week later, Lodge issued a gag order, applied to all attorneys, officers, employees of the court, law enforcement officers, and persons subpoenaed to testify. Persons having knowledge of the case were not to give the public any "purported extrajudicial statement about the defendant, possible evidence, or testimony."

It was mid-September when the trial got underway. Prosecutor Clayton Andersen, thirty-two, had with assistant counsel a single murder trial under his belt (a conviction for a stabbing in Marsing, Idaho). A graduate of the University of Idaho College of Law, in 1981 he had campaigned for the part-time elective office, and after winning it, worked out of a house in Murphy. With his predecessor, he had been in on the collection of evidence at Bull Camp. The state assigned Michael Kennedy, thirty-four, a veteran deputy attorney general and former county prosecutor, as co-prosecutor to assist Andersen, but by established procedure, his was the subordinate role.

Michael Donnelly, thirty-six, a graduate of the University of Missouri Law School, had been in charge of Canyon County Legal Aid before going to work for the Boise law firm, Skinner, Fawcett, Donnelly, & Mauk. Although it was his first murder case, he was regarded as "aggressive and thorough."

His partner, William Mauk, thirty-five, a native Idahoan, was generally regarded as more astute and every bit as thorough. An M.A. from Columbia University and a graduate of Antioch School of Law, he had served as law clerk to Idaho Supreme Court Justice Allen Shepherd for a year. At the time of the trial Mauk was general counsel for the Shoshone-Paiute tribes.

Presiding Judge Edward Lodge of the Third District Court was a graduate of The College of Idaho and University of Idaho College of Law. In 1965, at thirty-one, he had been appointed to the District Court in Idaho, the youngest judge ever named to that court. He had been a trial attorney—"I've always loved the trial court, that's my stall"—and for two years, probate judge in Canyon County. Lodge, who tried more murder cases than any other Idaho judge, was widely regarded within the state legal community as one of the better district judges. Idaho Senator Jim McClure called him "a fair jurist of the highest caliber." For what was to be his longest trial, Lodge ran his court in a business-like manner, impartial as death.

The strategy of the defense team had two thrusts: discredit Jim

Stevens, the eyewitness to the homicides, by impeaching his testimony; slander Bill Pogue, who could not testify on his own behalf. Conveniently, Pogue's body was still missing, as was his gun, which Dallas had vowed was "going into the ground with this guy." Donnelly and Mauk did not want to know where the body was, and thereby excused themselves from concealing evidence during the discovery process.

The trial opened with eight armed deputies standing in the courtroom, five of them near the defendant. A delegation from the Idaho Fish and Game, Pogue's brother and sister, and two of Dallas' brothers were among the hundred spectators. Widows Dee Pogue and Sheryl Elms, chosen as the first witnesses for the state, were permitted to sit in the audience, but they were restrained by judicial order from sitting alongside each other, or with the Fish and Game delegation, nor were they to display any emotion or talk with the press. The media soon tagged a group of female supporters, who rooted for the defendant and wrote him notes, "the Dallas Cheerleaders."

The prosecution wanted a predominantly male jury. Luck of the draw furnished a predominantly female venire (jury list), many of them Dallas' age. Each side exhausted its ten peremptory challenges, and the judge excused fifteen jurors for cause. By Friday, September 17, the jury of two men and ten women was impaneled. It ranged from a twenty-five-year-old schoolteacher to a sixty-seven-year-old farmer from Nampa, Idaho. The trial lasted a month, and its double-spaced, typed transcript runs 3,000 pages. A drastically edited version of the events goes more or less like this.

The prosecution made its case to the jury during the first two weeks of the trial. Nearly one hundred pieces of physical evidence were introduced, and forty witnesses testified. The strategy of "overkill" was a tactical error on the part of the prosecution— overwhelming details raised numerous and confusing questions in an otherwise airtight case.

As first witnesses, Dee Pogue and Sheryl Elms described the calls that had taken their husbands south to the Owyhee. Eddie Carlin related the late arrival of the wardens at his 45 Ranch. Lawmen and criminologists described their findings at the scene of the crime. (Lodge allowed photographs of Elms' body, but refused to admit a photograph of the bullet wound behind Elms' ear.)

On the fourth day, George Nielsen took the stand for the prosecution. He recounted the midnight session at his house at Paradise Hill after the homicides. All he offered in Dallas' defense was that he had said, "I did a sloppy job, but they deserved it. They had it coming." Nielsen concluded by saying he had not seen Dallas since he dropped him off at Sand Pass Road. Since nothing in his testimony justified the killings, Nielsen had helped the prosecution.

On day five, Stevens appeared, dressed in a suit, to testify for the prosecution. Claude Dallas, at the table across from the witness stand, avoided all eye contact with Stevens, who had given six testimonies within the last twenty months. He had been tape recorded at Bull Camp and filmed with a video camera while narrating events on the rim above the camp.

Bill Mauk, who handled the cross-examination of Stevens, had combed the transcripts for inconsistencies the same way searchers had combed the Bloody Run for Pogue's body. He questioned Stevens for almost eight hours, laying the foundation for reasonable doubt.

Stevens' testimony spanned a Friday and Monday. After the rust of two years, minor inconsistencies awaited inflation by the defense.

On redirect examination, deputy prosecutor Kennedy, through his questions, tried to clarify the sequence of events at the time of the shootings. Stevens said, "I don't know how you can say three things happened all at the same time. I stated everything was simultaneous. I don't know what came first. When you tell people something, you've got to tell them one at a time, you know. And I'm sure sometimes I said I heard a 'No, no!' and then I heard a shot. I saw movement. I might have turned it around again. But bear in mind, all of this happened so fast that I don't know what happened first."

He described Pogue's conversation with Dallas as "firm and short, to the point...stern and forceful...it wasn't loud or anything."

Stevens recalled what followed once Dallas emptied his .357

Magnum. "I couldn't believe what was happening. Claude ran into the tent [stopping to untie the flaps], and he got a rifle, and he went out with the rifle, and I saw him going up to Elms, and he shot both officers in the head, but I turned around, I couldn't watch."

As Stevens' testimony unfolded, Dallas' chilling efforts to conceal and destroy evidence and to fog-up alibis were exposed. Stevens recalled words of premeditation: "Claude said, 'I woulda took 'em up there [on the rim], but they woulda killed me.'" He told of Dallas ripping off the emblems and service stripes from Pogue's uniform with the venomous comment, "I can't imagine anybody working that many years with the Fish and Game."

Testimony from the FBI about blue flashes from the truck in which Dallas tried to flee was not convincing, and an agent's admission that neither pistol on the truck seat had been fired was a setback.

The prosecution's case sustained another hit when a pathologist from Pocatello, Idaho, stated that the first shot to hit Elms struck him in the back under his right shoulder, which spun him around for the second bullet in the abdomen. The defense disparaged his credibility, getting him to admit that his opinion was based on diagrams drawn by Stevens.

A second pathologist, from Boise, testifying for the defense on the basis of photographs and the autopsy report, contradicted the first, swearing that he was "ninety-seven percent sure" the first shot was an entrance wound to the chest.

The state team fumbled again with the revelation that a senior Idaho criminologist in the forensic lab at the Idaho Health and Welfare Department had concluded Elms had been killed by Stevens' gun. Subsequently, criminologists in California had been consulted and testified that the three bullets recovered at the scene were not fired by Stevens' gun. The Idaho criminologist reversed his opinion.

The problem in the testimony, never clarified by the media, was that apparently Dallas had a third pistol, obtained in a trade with a Nevada highway patrolman, on his person: a short-barrel Smith and Wesson .357 Magnum concealed in a holster at the small of his back. The bullets recovered at the scene matched that model gun and not the Ruger Security Six in his hip holster.

On October 6, three weeks into the trial, Claude Dallas took the stand. He described Bull Camp. "It's just a big basin on the South Fork of the Owyhee River. It's an area where the rim opens up from a fairly narrow canyon. I figured the location was in Idaho."

Asked about the three deer (parts of the third were found by investigators) he knowingly killed out of season, he replied, "I didn't think anyone would give me any problems with the venison due to the conditions I was living under." Idaho outfitters, however, routinely provision camps far more remote for longer periods and for more persons. The claim that Dallas was somehow entitled to special or exceptional treatment had no merit.

When asked why his frequent visitors—four in three weeks—could not bring him meat, he answered, "I could have made arrangements, but even if I had wanted to, I couldn't have afforded it." This from a man who spent thousands of dollars on his gun collection, and who said money did not have anything to do with his being in Bull Camp.

Questioned about the meaning of his "I'll-be-ready" response to Carlin's warning of a possible visit from Fish and Game officers, Dallas said, "I meant I wasn't going to have any fur in camp, you know, if they came in before the season. I was going to have my meat hid away from camp. I was thinking of pulling out early." In that event, he had no need for 300 pounds of venison.

Dallas then told of his unexpected encounter with the two wardens when he came up over the rim to fetch supplies from Stevens' Blazer. Pogue introduced himself and said he had heard about the poaching. Dallas tried to excuse himself, asserting his remote prerogatives. Pogue was curt. "It seems like he was on the fight," said Dallas. "I've never been approached like that. Pogue's hand kept going to his gun every time I moved. When I went to the rig, they split up and flanked me...I just told him that I thought he was a little bit out of line."

The officers accompanied Dallas down the trail to his camp. About fifty yards from the tent, Dallas said, Pogue asked him to hand over, butt first, the .22 pistol he carried in a shoulder holster under his coat. That surrender left Dallas with a .357 Magnum on his right hip in a Safari-Land, open-topped holster still concealed beneath his coat—at least according to the defendant.

Gradually his testimony closed around the confrontation. Stevens had returned to the tent and introduced himself to the wardens. In his narrative Dallas positioned the characters: "six feet in front of the tent...Conley Elms on my left and a little in front, Bill Pogue five or six feet in front of me, Jim Stevens three feet to my right."

Donnelly then heightened the drama by requesting a ten-minute recess.

The narrative resumed. Dallas said the discussion about the venison went on for five to ten minutes. Stevens moved fifteen feet off to the right, facing the river "like he wasn't taking any part in what was going on." Dallas reiterated, "Pogue's hand was always in the vicinity of his gun or gunbelt"—no more significant for a law officer than having his hand in the vicinity of his pocket.

Dallas insisted that Pogue needed a search warrant to inspect his tent—a preposterous allegation given Carlin's account, the two game violations in view, and the law of probable cause.

Once the cat hides were out in the open, Pogue stated that he was going to confiscate them, and Dallas said, "You don't know that I didn't get those cats in Nevada." Then he told the jury, "Supposedly, when you bring a cat across the line it has to be tagged, and that came up. And we went back and forth on that...." As usual, Dallas was long on excuses and short on facts. Not one of his traps was within three miles of Nevada.

Pogue, aware of Dallas' reputation as a nonresident gamehog, decided with four violations in view an arrest was justified. Dallas argued that he could not leave his camp and stock. An arrest meant a trip to Murphy, Idaho, to post bond, and a return to camp the next day. Fish and Game would have arranged to grain the stock, but even if they had not, mules forage well on their own. (In the end, Dallas ran off and left them anyway.)

The direct examination finally centered on the shooting. Asked Pogue's response to his plea for an undisturbed poaching residency, Dallas answered, "He said you can go easy or you can go hard."

Donnelly: "What did you understand him to mean by that?"
Dallas: "Well, hard, that's only one way. That's dead."

No single statement in Dallas' testimony more clearly reveals how he rearranged things to his mind's desire: a conclusion based on a premise that needed proof as badly as the conclusion. The same day, en route to Dallas' camp, Pogue had cited the trapper near Carlins' place with the remark, "You either sign these tickets or go to jail. You make up your mind which way you want to go." Moreover, in the Idaho Fish and Game Department's eighty-year history, not one of its officers had ever shot a suspect. As Dallas was aware, Pogue and Elms did not know that he was still armed. Going hard meant carrying the handcuffed poacher to the rim, and Elms was big enough to do that if Dallas would not cooperate. It required a broad and deeply paranoid leap of the imagination to equate "hard" with a death threat. Even so, as one juror observed, "If an armed officer of the law [a full peace officer by Idaho code] says you can go easy or you can go hard, why not just go easy?"

> Dallas: Well, after that was said, you know, he said to me, he said that to me, and he said he could carry me out. And that's when Pogue, he was drawing his gun.
> Donnelly: Did he go for his gun at that point?
> Dallas: He did.
> Donnelly: Then what happened?
> Dallas: Well, I just reacted to it. I went for mine.
> Donnelly: Then what happened?
> Dallas: Well, we fired.
> Donnelly: Did he fire at all at you?
> Dallas: He fired one round. I fired. His gun went off, you know. And I fired again. And I spun Conley Elms. He was going for his gun. I fired one round at Elms, and Pogue was going down and bringing the gun to bear on me. It was up over the lower part of my body. I just threw two more shots at Pogue. And Elms crouched and I threw one at Elms. And I just ran back and into my tent and grabbed my twenty-two and shot both men in the head.

They were on the ground. Elms was face down and Pogue
was on his back.

Donnelly: Were they alive?

Dallas: I don't think so. They weren't moving....

Donnelly: Why did you shoot them in the head?

Dallas: Well, I was a little bit out of my head at that
stage. I was afraid.

Dallas' allegation that Pogue drew his gun and fired had no
more substance than most of his other assertions. One has to ask,
if Pogue had drawn and fired, why Dallas was so immediately intent
on disposing of the gun that would prove his protestation of self-
defense? Even more apposite, why was he unable to remember
where he buried the weapon? When Andersen asked about its location, Dallas answered, "I couldn't tell you within four or five
miles. I was heading across one of the flats and valleys when I buried
it. It was at night."

Later, Donnelly told the jury, "After burying Bill Pogue, Dallas
went off across the desert. Somewhere in that expanse is the weapon
that could prove our case—and God, I wish I could find it for you."
A jury that would swallow that would swallow goldfish.

Following the killings, a "frightened" Dallas went on to direct
the erasure of evidence and the disposal of his victims. On the stand
he revealed that he had thought a storm would cover things up. "It
was ugly. The whole thing looked ugly and hopeless. I didn't want
these bodies in my camp. I told him [Stevens] I don't want these
things found in my camp." On the witness stand, he neither
mentioned the "murder one" remark, nor the suggestion to quarter
Elms.

After two years in which to get his story straight, and considerable coaching on the theory of the "reasonable man," his crime was
now "justifiable homicide" because "I gave them no reason to
approach me in that manner...the whole thing was unreasonable...I
could see no reason for them disarming me. I tried to reason with
Pogue on the citation. It was just, Christ, it was all of that."

In the afternoon, on cross examination of Dallas, Andersen

asked the defendant if he could mark Pogue's gravesite on a map. The courtroom grew quiet as a classroom after a hard question. Dallas smiled and said, "I'd be happy to. Would you like me to mark the location of Bill Pogue's body?" He stepped over to a large map and X'd a site just off Sand Pass Road. After all those months, Dallas opened up in order to appear cooperative to the jury, and not out of any belated sympathy for Pogue's family.

Nettleton relayed the information to the Humboldt County sheriff, who, with his deputy, drove his pickup to the site, three-tenths of a mile north of Sand Pass Road, eight miles west of U.S. Highway 95. They found the coyote den in which Pogue's body had been stuffed. His skull and scattered remains were recovered.

Dallas' testimony continued for over six hours.

While Pogue's skeleton was being exhumed at Sand Pass Road, Judge Lodge decided to let the defense dig up other bones as well. At the start of the trial, he had ruled out all testimony regarding Pogue's character: "The law is clear that specific acts of violence by deceased individuals are inadmissible, particularly when the defendant was unaware of previous acts." Now he reversed his earlier ruling, explaining, "I think now that the defendant has testified and put into evidence the issue of self-defense, the victim's prior conduct as to aggressive and violent behavior is now an issue." The testimony was to be limited to Pogue's reputation for "turbulence, dangerousness, violence, or quarrlesomeness."

The defense attorneys had Pogue's personnel file. They summoned nineteen witnesses to testify that as game officers, Pogue and Elms had a pattern of aggressive behavior. Not all of Dallas' Nevada friends were willing to speak ill of Pogue, however. And a Boise electrician, who claimed to have been bullied by Pogue, was entirely discredited when the Department proved Pogue had not been in the area the day the witness was cited. Two other witnesses were similarly mistaken.

The prosecution produced rebuttal witnesses, of course. Most had been cited by Pogue or Elms during the performance of their duties. One remembered Pogue as firm but fair. Another called Elms "a big sweetheart." None of them found the officers overbearing or abusive.

A portrait of Pogue emerged: a Marine veteran who served with distinction in Korea; an overwhelmed and underpaid game warden, who took great pleasure in the wild landscape and the animals in it; a man who worked more hours without pay than any other conservation officer in Idaho; one who used his own funds for gasoline when his monthly allotment was gone. His first eight years with the Fish and Game had been spent in Garden Valley, north of Boise, in a Department house with a woodstove on a hillside above the South Fork of the Payette. A self-taught artist, he labored evenings over his ink dot-and-line drawings of cowboys, Indians, mountain men, birds, and mammals. (With impaired sight in one eye, he used a magnifying glass, and could only work for a few hours at a time.) Pogue applied the law equally to all: he could be brusque ("command presence") with those who scoffed, or with repeat offenders, but he was gentler than some people wanted to believe.

Elms, born in Beaver Marsh (population twenty), Oregon, grew up in a ranchhouse with no indoor plumbing. A former logger, he graduated from Oregon State University with a degree in wildlife management. He had been an Idaho conservation officer since September, 1977; his wife had been a schoolteacher in Twin Falls, Idaho.

On Columbus Day weekend, Dallas wrote his father in South Carolina, confiding his confidence in the tenor of the trial. "Have caught a wink or two from the jury, so we'll see. I intend to get out of this one way or another." Concluding, he wrote, "It's going to take me a while to get rolling again even if I beat this as I'll have to move out of this area or else I'll have to pop another one of these bastards."

Finally, on October 13, after closing arguments of several hours, the case was handed to the jury.

Judge Lodge's instructions to the jury covered fifty pages and required forty minutes to deliver. He gave them four options on the principal charges of killing Pogue and Elms: first degree murder; second degree murder; voluntary manslaughter; justifiable homicide.

The jury was lodged at the Sundowner Motel in downtown Caldwell. It deliberated forty-five hours over seven days.

On Sunday, the fifth day, the judge ordered a day off, and the ten female jurors were escorted to a movie, "The Man from Snowy River," about an Australian drover-cowboy. One of the jurors later commented, "The hero was the type of person who reminded us all so much of Claude. We all sat there seeing Claude, seeing the beauty of the mountains, and why a man like Claude would choose to become a mountain man." Hardly a four-star selection for a sequestered jury.

On day six, Lodge dismissed one woman for bringing unspecified outside information (knowledge of Dallas' draft evasion) into the jury room. The prosecutor asked for a mistrial. Lodge denied the motion and replaced the woman (a holdout for first-degree murder) with an alternate. The reconstructed jury, deliberating anew, reviewed the case for only five hours before reaching a verdict the next morning.

Told to convict Dallas only of the highest degree of which they had no "reasonable" doubt as to his guilt, they found him guilty on two counts of voluntary manslaughter, two charges of using a firearm in commission of a felony, and the misdemeanor count of concealing evidence. They acquitted him of the charge of resisting arrest. Voluntary manslaughter was the least serious of the three offenses of intentional murder. In Lodge's instructions to the jurors he said, "to be considered manslaughter rather than murder, a killing must occur while the person who kills acts under the direct and immediate influence of sudden quarrel or heat of passion."

As they left the courtroom, Donnelly and Mauk were greeted by applause from Dallas' supporters. The attorneys said Dallas was dejected by the verdict, that he wanted a not-guilty verdict on all counts. They said they would file an appeal.

Prosecutor Andersen called the verdicts a tremendous injustice. He added, "I think he lied on the witness stand. The Claude Dallas who was in the courtroom, and the Claude Dallas at the shooting scene are two different individuals. This is a verdict the jury will have to live with." On momentary reflection, he added, "There isn't anything the state could have done in the case that we could have done better."

Dallas was returned to his Canyon County jail cell.

In November, over the objections of the county prosecutor, who insisted that Dallas had no family, residence, employment, or community ties to Idaho, Judge Lodge set bail at $50,000 for each manslaughter conviction. He pointed out that he was obligated by constitutional law and state statutes to set bail in a case that did not involve capital punishment, but he restricted Dallas to Idaho, Oregon, and Nevada.

Constance Wilson Ickes, former owner of the Alvord Ranch where Dallas had once worked, had moved to Caldwell and married a local veterinarian. She put up the $100,000 property bond to get the convicted killer out of jail while he awaited sentencing.

Out on bail, Dallas visited friends in Paradise Valley. He also journeyed to Steens Mountain and, without license or permit, poached a mountain sheep. Even some of his most indulgent supporters were finally embarrassed by such behavior—evidence of a deeper problem. As Loren Eiseley wrote, "The solitude of the person in the body is the final divorcement of man from nature."

On January 4, 1983, nearly two years to the day since his murders, Dallas appeared in the Canyon County courthouse for sentencing. He faced a maximum of fifty years. Prior to sentencing, thirteen witnesses testified. The county prosecutor asked for a forty-year determinate sentence and a ten-year indeterminate sentence. The defense attorneys asked for probation.

Judge Lodge had spent considerable time reviewing the trial transcript and a pre-sentence investigative report. He spoke to Dallas for almost an hour, telling the defendant that his actions and his statements to Jim Stevens following the killings indicated the shootings were premeditated, totally unjustified, and morally reprehensible. As Lodge spoke, Dallas watched him intensely, sitting back in his chair, his hands clasped across his stomach.

"I can conscientiously and sincerely tell you that I do not believe the issue of self-defense arose at Bull Camp," the judge said. Moreover, he said he could not accept Dallas' claim that he fired his gun only after Pogue had drawn his own gun and fired first. "To me it's contrary to common sense to believe that peace officers of Mr. Pogue and Mr. Elms' experience would ever attempt to shoot anyone over a misdemeanor."

"My judgment," he continued, "is that you drew that gun because you didn't want to be taken in. You drew and fired that gun at Mr. Pogue. You could do that because they did not know you were armed."

Even worse, he said, Dallas did not give Elms a chance either to drop his hand or to drop his gun—if he ever drew it.

Lodge said Stevens' testimony concerning statements by Dallas and his actions immediately following the shootings showed the defendant acted rationally and had no remorse for the killings. "Practically all of those acts at the scene at that time, particularly going and getting the twenty-two and coming back out, were offensive, not defensive acts."

He continued, "Human life is too precious, too valuable, and we cannot let you or anyone believe they can kill someone and then get a second chance. When you kill someone who represents a public office you'll be dealt with more harshly. They need extra protection because they deal with life-threatening situations every day," Lodge concluded.

When Dallas was asked if he had anything to say, he told the judge, "I do regret what happened in Bull Camp, but I feel I reacted the only way I could under the circumstances." As the poet George Byron wrote, "One lies more to oneself than to anyone else."

Lodge then sentenced Dallas to three ten-year prison terms: one for killing Pogue, a second for killing Elms, and a third for using a firearm in the commission of both crimes. He handed down an additional six months for the charge of concealing evidence. This indeterminate thirty-year sentence meant Dallas would have to serve at least one-third of each ten-year term before he could be considered for parole, and he would have to be paroled from the first sentence before he could begin serving time on the second. Upon hearing the sentence, the killer expressed little emotion. Sheriff's deputies led him back to the county jail.

Sheriff Tim Nettleton called the sentence "as good as we could hope for," and praised the judge for his statements about the shootings. "It pleased me to have the judge put this in perspective," he remarked. "I'm well pleased today."

That night someone who cared as much about animals as Dallas did shot Judge Lodge's German Shepherd and threw it on his front lawn.

Two years to the day after the murders, Sheriff Nettleton drove Dallas to the Idaho State Penitentiary, five miles south of Boise, to serve his sentence. It was not to be an uneventful residency. (Exactly one hundred years earlier, a young Theodore Roosevelt, wearing round eyeglasses, came west to a sagebrush outpost in the Dakota Badlands, riding, talking, and blazing away at game. He stayed to become a rancher, and won the respect of the cowmen.)

Jail suited Dallas like a flankstrap suits a bronc. He got a job in the automotive body shop of the prison industries. After a few months in the penitentiary, however, he was disciplined for having contraband in his cell. Prison authorities alleged that lock-picking tools and wirecutters were found during a search of his private, medium-security cell. Dallas claimed that the items were planted as an entrapment scheme, and perhaps they were. He failed a lie detector test about the incident, however. He was given twenty days in detention and lost his body-repair job. After detention, he was transferred to the prison bakery.

In mid-October, the same year, Dallas and another prisoner were discovered missing from their cells during a routine head count. Guards found the pair fifteen minutes later in a garden area in the center of the prison's compound. Since an intercom speaker in the area was not working, the men may not have known about the security check. They denied knowing what time it was.

Dallas was given a hearing, then the classification committee for the prison ordered him moved from medium security to close custody with fewer privileges. He spent ten days in disciplinary detention and remained in close custody for almost a year. Attorney Mauk filed a complaint in the U. S. District Court on Dallas' behalf.

As soon as Dallas' medium custody (one step higher than

minimum) was reinstated in winter 1984-1985, he was placed back in the yard and got a job with Pendyne, the prison's food service. Later he was assigned the task of hauling garbage. He kept himself healthy, tended a vegetable garden, joined the Captive Artists Guild and made ceramic pieces.

In November, 1986, the Idaho Supreme Court, on a three to two vote, upheld Dallas' convictions and sentence, finding no evidence to substantiate his claim that killing Elms and Pogue was self-defense.

Easter Sunday evening, March 30, 1986, a deputy warden at the penitentiary announced that Claude Dallas had escaped. He had been found missing at 10:00 p.m. during a count of inmates in the 10-House cellblock, Cell 67.

Prison authorities stated that Dallas was returning from a 4:00 to 7:30 p.m. visit with Geneva Holman of Reno, in the visiting area in the administration building, when he used boltcutters to open a triangular hole through two chainlink fences enclosing the building. The area was not visible from the nearby guard tower.

His prison-issue baseball cap and eyeglasses were found in the nearby parking lot for visitors. Tire marks gave evidence that he was given a ride.

Geneva Holman, who had visited Dallas on Friday and Saturday as well, was driving a silver Mercedes. The Humboldt County, Nevada, sheriff's office received a tip that a silver Mercedes had dropped Dallas off at George Nielsen's Paradise Bar late Sunday night. At 6:30 p.m. (PST) the Reno police department received a tip that Dallas was in a trailer at Paradise Hill, but the police did not want to search it at night.

Monday morning, with a baseball cap for scent, bloodhounds found Dallas' scent on a stool at Nielsen's bar and in an unmade bed in an empty trailerhouse nearby, but then they lost the scent at Highway 95—an indication that he had gotten into a car. True to form, Dallas had gone to Nielsens' for approval. At 2:00 a.m. Holman's car was impounded in Reno for a fingerprint check, but none belonging to Dallas were found.

Warden Arvon Arave reported that when last seen on the prison ballfield, Dallas was wearing blue denim clothing. Law enforcement agencies in Idaho and all the surrounding states were quickly notified of his escape. Three thousand wanted posters were distributed. Six weeks later, FBI Director William Webster informed the media that Dallas had been added to the agency's "Ten Most Wanted Fugitives" list, and the Bureau posted a $10,000 reward. By June-end, an additional reward fund in Idaho had reached $8,700.

Enter the redemptive woman. The killer-celebrity always taps at least one public fantasy: solving problems through some spectacular act of violence, without resort to lawyers. In variations on this western theme, the myth-justified gunman often attracts a redemptive heroine, usually a schoolmarm, who must learn to live with the "good" violence that is inherent in "true manliness." She cannot abide his outlawry, understanding that it will "get into his blood" and cause him to degenerate into an animal. She seeks his surrender to justice or a pardon; if he agrees, she will wait out his sentence and marry him. In mid-June, interest in Dallas was suddenly rekindled by news reports from the San Francisco Bay Area after Margaret Lundy, believed to be traveling with Dallas, was spotted on a street in Newark, California, about thirty miles southeast of San Francisco, and not far from where Dallas had wintered in 1969. No arrest warrants were issued for Lundy, but the FBI had reasons to believe she was with Dallas.

Lundy, a native of Boise, graduated in 1966 from Boise's Capital High School, then took a B.A. in international affairs at the University of Southern California. She was active in Idaho Republican politics, and in 1973 went to work for then-Representative Steve Symms in his Washington, D. C., office as a secretary and analyst, staying four years. In 1980 she worked as a legislative analyst for C. L. "Butch" Otter, who at that time was an executive with the J. R. Simplot Co. Two years later, she worked as a secretary at the campaign headquarters of Representative Larry Craig. She began visiting Dallas in prison at that time.

Two days before Dallas escaped, Lundy quit her job at Ray Chem Co. in Palo Alto, California. San Francisco media, monitoring police radio frequencies, picked up a transmission from a Boise

FBI agent concerning the sighting of Lundy in Newark. In Newark the FBI impounded a 1978 Fiat coupe with Idaho plates believed to have been used by the couple. The ensuing publicity caused both of them to flee the area. It was the last trace of Dallas for eight months, at least four of which he spent in Mexico.

On the afternoon of Sunday, March 8, 1987, the feathers on his lark were sadly ruffled when Claude Dallas was shoved face-down on an asphalt parking lot by FBI agents with shotguns. Dallas was leaving a Stop-N-Go convenience store in Riverside, California. The town, with a population of 200,000, is a ranchland community fifty miles east of Los Angeles. At the time of his arrest while carrying a small bag of groceries, Dallas was wearing jeans and a T-shirt and was unarmed. On hearing the news of the arrest, Sheriff Nettleton said, "It's been a good day, a great day."

Reconstructing Dallas' movements, the FBI reported that at noon he had checked into the Skylark Motel on University Avenue, two blocks from the market, using the alias Al Shrank. Because he insisted that was his name, and his appearance was altered—short hair, shaved beard, moustache, contact lenses—the FBI ran a fingerprint check to verify Dallas' identity. Once his identity was confirmed, he was placed under tight security in the Riverside County Jail.

The following day, Dallas was arraigned, as before, on a federal fugitive charge. An escape charge from the Idaho State Penitentiary was filed in the Fourth District Court in Ada County (Boise), and extradition papers were readied yet again.

Dallas made a brief appearance before a U. S. magistrate in San Bernardino, where he was informed that the federal fugitive charge—"unlawful flight to avoid confinement"— would be dropped, and that he would be held without bail, pending the arrival of the Idaho legal papers. Dallas wiped his eyes as he told the public defender that he would like to see his father, Claude Dallas, Sr. His father never arrived.

Dallas was arraigned in Riverside Municipal Court on the Ada County charge of escape. William Mauk waited in his office for a call from his client, but it never came.

As the corral dust settled, and details of Dallas' capture became available, mythology suffered a serious flesh wound. Claude shrank. He had moved to Riverside a few weeks before his arrest. He was dependent on a California horsetrainer and calf roper whom he had met and wrangled with seven years earlier in Paradise Hill. (The man had been a character witness at Dallas' trial.) Dallas had been seen at the friend's rented house in Riverside, while trying to find construction work.

Employees at the Stop-N-Go, where Dallas was arrested, said he had been coming there for two weeks to buy food and half pints of vodka. He carried on such extended conversations with the clerks that the manager, Ernie Soto, considered throwing him out. "He seemed crazy. He was always talking, talking, talking."

The manager also said that Dallas (the draft dodger) claimed to be a Vietnam veteran of eight years, and that after twenty years in the military, he now worked for the government part time. Soto recalled that Dallas voiced his disgust with shoplifters: "They should take those people and throw them in jail for the rest of their lives."

Another clerk remembered that Dallas said he went to church every Sunday and always contributed five dollars. The same clerk recounted that a few days earlier Dallas had bought a California lottery ticket, and after he scratched off the cover film, learned that he had won one hundred dollars. "He was literally jumping up and down with delight. He was screaming 'I won! I won! Congratulations to me!'"

The FBI indicated that over his eleven months as a fugitive, Dallas had traveled a spiderweb from South Dakota to northern California, Oregon, Nevada, and Mexico, subsisting on handouts from friends.

Once Dallas waived extradition, Riverside authorities released him to the custody of an Ada County undersheriff and a detective. With the prisoner in handcuffs and footshackles, they flew him in a single-engine Cessna 206 to Tonopah, Nevada, where he spent the night in the local jail. (Dallas discovered that he had left his contact lens solutions in the airplane; the undersheriff bought some for him at the local drugstore.)

They all flew to Boise the next morning. En route, instead of talking, talking, talking, Dallas only spoke when spoken to. The undersheriff asked him if he had seen the CBS TV movie ("Manhunt for Claude Dallas") on his killings, or had read the two books about the murders. "He hadn't seen the movie and had only scanned the books, but wasn't very complimentary about them. He said the books were full of hearsay and half-truths [a reply that belied his cursory claim]."

When the conversation in the plane turned to trapping, "He said there are a lot of places in the East where there was better trapping than Idaho and Nevada put together." (Poachers may be rarer in the East.)

At the airport, Dallas, in orange jumpsuit, was escorted off the airplane and driven back to the Idaho State Penitentiary. He was arraigned there by video on the escape charge, then boarded and housed, courtesy of the state legislature, in a maximum security cell with cement walls. Again, $22,000 in reward money was paid to an informant whose assistance led to the arrest.

Enter a second redemptive woman. In early April, Laura Miller, thirty-five, a Boise resident and talented freelance director of live theater, announced that she was setting up a fund to pay legal expenses for Claude Dallas. Her task proved easier than raising money for live melodrama. She placed advertisements for donations from people who believed that the convicted killer was "the victim of a travesty of justice," and she said she wanted to reverse the legal "miscarriage."

At the time of Dallas' murder trial, Miller had been living in Twin Falls, Idaho, and watched the television reports and read newspaper accounts. At a hearing on April 27, 1987, she met Dallas for the first time. A theater friend, commenting on Miller, gently offered, "She's not a crazy. She's very idealistic, very romantic. She truly believes this folk-hero business."

Putting her money where her heart was, Miller loaned $5,400 of her own savings to the drive, and by mid-June the fund reached $14,000. Before and after the trial on the escape charge, she had one refrain: "I'm prepared to do whatever it takes to get him out of jail legally." Every Friday she visited Dallas for an hour and fifteen minutes.

In June a preliminary hearing on the escape charge was held at the penitentiary, and Dallas was bound over for trial. Mauk, given the press of other personal and professional commitments, declined to represent Dallas, and Lance Churchill, his new attorney paid from Miller's defense fund, had his client plead innocent before Fourth District Judge George Carey, and requested a five-day jury trial. Churchill said Dallas' defense would be based on conditions and treatment the inmate experienced while serving his sentence.

In preparation for the trial, Churchill employed Howard Varnisky, a psychiatric-socialworker from California, to assist in jury selection. Varnisky emphasized that the defense needed only a "preponderance" of evidence to make its points, while the state had to prove its case "beyond a reasonable doubt." He wrote a twelve-page, detailed questionnaire, believed necessary to offset extensive publicity, for all sixty-three prospective jurors to fill out before the selection process. Judge Carey and the prosecuting attorney adapted portions of it—the first time such a device had been used in Idaho.

At the *voir dire*, prospective jurors provided considerable humor. "I don't understand why this is going to court," one commented, "I mean, he broke out of jail." The last juror seated caused additional laughter when he admitted, "Yeah, I read about his alleged escape in the *Statesman* and saw his alleged recapture on TV."

Varnisky said he "wasn't trying to stack the jury with more women than men...but statistically, women are more understanding and liberal in evaluating a criminal defense. Women are also a little more prone to acquit."

Lance Churchill, defense attorney, and Jim Carlson, deputy prosecutor of Ada County, settled upon a jury of four men and eight women.

The trial got underway Monday, August 31, at 8:30 a.m. at the Ada County law enforcement center on Barrister Drive in Boise. Only eight to ten spectators, including Laura Miller, and Dallas' mother, who had flown in from South Carolina, were present.

The prosecution's case appeared, so to speak, open and shut. To succeed, it had to show that Dallas had been convicted of a felony; that he was confined to prison; that while there he escaped; that he acted with the requisite criminal intent; that the escape occurred in Ada County. If the jury found that the state proved those elements, then in order to satisfy the defense of duress or necessity, the defense had to prove by a "preponderance of the evidence" that Dallas faced a specific threat of death or bodily injury, and that threat was imminent; that he had no time to report the threat and had compiled a series of futile complaints with the authorities; that he had no time to seek court relief; that he had made an attempt to notify Idaho prison authorities after reaching a place of safety.

This time the county prosecutor presented the state's case in less than an hour, calling five witnesses who testified about the escape and capture.

Testifying for the defense on day four, Dallas was once more long on excuses and short on facts. Again, he feared for his life: "[From the first day] I was worried about getting set up. I didn't like the way things started off. I was afraid." (Keep in mind that for the first time since age nine, Dallas was without a gun.) "I felt that if they had a chance to get me," he complained, "they were going to do it all right." He heard that prison guards, "were using my picture for a target on the shooting range." Just before he escaped, Dallas said the prison administration "convinced me that, given the opportunity, they would kill me."

Asked why he did not return to the prison, he replied in his most aggrieved air, "I needed some assurance that I wouldn't be killed off." Yet he never refused extradition from California. He also claimed that he had intended to return to Idaho after he had raised enough money to fight his conviction and escape charges—say, $15,000 or so.

Dallas, after being ordered to do so by the court, recounted portions of his months on the loose. He claimed that he walked out of Idaho, but being a practiced liar, he could scarcely expect to be believed; furthermore, he could not afford to reveal names without risk of harboring-charges being filed against the named. He revealed that he had lived and worked in the San Francisco Bay Area; following media reports of his whereabouts, he said he returned to Nevada; then in mid-October left for Mexico for four months to have cosmetic surgery done on his face, at a cost of $3,000—money that well could have gone to his putative defense fund.

(A Boise plastic surgeon reviewed photographs of Dallas after his testimony and said the nose and chin jobs were acceptable, but that the chin appeared to have a silicone implant—"a completely unsafe and unethical procedure only done in Mexico"—and that Dallas should avoid any extra trauma "like getting hit on the chin.")

Dallas asserted he reentered the U. S. in early February and traveled to Eugene, Oregon, where he was fitted for contact lenses. "I didn't like the feel of that place," he said of the college town; he moved south to Los Angeles.

On the same day that Dallas testified, Judge Carey told the defense attorney, Churchill, during a recess and outside the presence of the jury, that so far there was no showing of an "imminent death threat" that would justify Dallas' escape. "I will tell the jury that vague threats do not constitute the type of defense for escape."

Carey did allow, over objections by the state, testimony for the defense by several inmates who said they overheard correctional officers at the penitentiary say that in the event of a riot, they wanted to kill Dallas. But Carey also cautioned that type of evidence would not be enough to acquit.

On Friday at 2:40 p.m., after listening to testimony and arguments for nearly three days, the jury received the case. They took a two-hour dinner break, and after five and one-half hours of deliberation, at 10:30 p.m., announced their unanimity. Three of the female jurors were crying, and two were sobbing.

Judge Carey read the verdict and informed Dallas that he had been acquitted of the felony charge. The convict was then promptly returned to a maximum security cell at the Idaho State Penitentiary.

The next day the jury foreman in an interview said, "No one felt absolutely comfortable with the decision. I tell you, it was very, very bad. Everyone in the jury felt bad and mad." Asked if Dallas had communicated his fear for his life to prison officials, the foreman replied, "That was kind of hazy." Did he notify them once he was out? "No, but the law didn't say how long he had to do so."

Another juror asserted that the state never proved Dallas' guilt beyond a reasonable doubt.

Varinsky, the jury specialist, said he and Churchill never expected to win the case. "Acquittal was a wonderful surprise. We felt the optimum outcome was a hung jury."

Local opinion was largely one of shocked surprise, even bemused disbelief. The *Idaho Statesman*, in an editorial titled "Astonishing Dallas Verdict Dead Wrong," weighed in:

> Rarely does this newspaper question a decision rendered by a jury. But then rarely has a decision escaped the bounds of both common and legal sense as the one that acquitted Claude Dallas of escape.
>
> The average person will have difficulty understanding how an inmate can snip his way out of the Idaho State Penitentiary, elude law enforcement efforts for eleven months, and then be acquitted of escape. We do.
>
> Such flimsy grounds hands every inmate a license to flee. The decision mocks the system that took so much time and effort to bring Mr. Dallas to justice.

The newspaper's editorial page swelled with letters. One reader wrote, "Based on the recent acquittal of Claude Dallas for felony escape, no one of us in Idaho should ever again make reference to those out-of-state 'bleeding-heart liberals.'"

Bob Sherwood, an outdoors writer based in Idaho Falls, wrote, "Let us hope the public will see him as he really is and stop fashioning idols out of jawbone and Johnson grass."

Back in the penitentiary, Dallas was not allowed to mingle with other prisoners. He remained in a maximum-security isolation cell.

Two weeks after the trial, at 10:00 p.m. on September 19, Dallas, accompanied by two prison guards and an assistant for the Department of Corrections, was flown in secret, with a refueling stop in Wyoming, to Nebraska, where he arrived at 5:00 a.m. He was taken in a van to the maximum security prison at Lincoln.

That afternoon in Idaho the corrections director said that to be rid of a high-risk prisoner he had planned to move Dallas whether or not he was acquitted of the escape charge. "It's a very typical thing. We do it all the time." In return, Idaho would house a prisoner from Nebraska.

Attorney Churchill telephoned Dallas and reported that "He said he liked Nebraska a lot better. He's got a lot more freedom there than he did here." (An odd remark, since Dallas was being held in isolation until a decision could be made on the appropriate type of confinement.)

Laura Miller, who had talked with Dallas before he left, said, "He had mixed feelings about it."

In March, 1988, Idaho agreed to an exchange of prisoners with New Mexico. Dallas was taken on a commercial flight from Lincoln, ankles and wrists shackled, between two officers, to Albuquerque, New Mexico, where he was met by authorities and hauled to the maximum security penitentiary in Santa Fe.

The transfer was made at the request of the Nebraska director of corrections. "We just needed the space [for a Nebraska prisoner]." In prison in Lincoln, indoorsman Dallas had filed a grievance, asking to be released from maximum security. The warden reported that the convict spent much of his time on legal work on his own behalf, along with assistance from an inmate law clerk, whose help he had requested. The warden said the fact that Laura Miller had moved to Lincoln had nothing to do with the transfer. In New Mexico, as in Nebraska, Dallas was allowed outside his cell one hour a day. His mother, who visited him there, said that he was reading biographies (had just finished one about Gordon Liddy, the Watergate conspirator) and was studying Spanish.

In April, 1988, the Idaho Pardons and Parole Commission, meeting in Boise, gave Dallas a twenty-minute hearing to consider whether or not he should be paroled from his first sentence term to begin serving his second. By telephone from New Mexico, Dallas followed the proceedings and conversed with the commissioners.

Chairman Del Ray Holm asked Dallas how he felt about Pogue and Elms. "I can't say as I feel a great deal of anything," Dallas answered. "I believe I had no other choice." Asked why he had shot both men in the head after they had already been shot in the chest, he replied, "They were mercy shots." Another board member asked Dallas if he had any other statements for the board to consider. Dallas responded, "I find it hard to believe you haven't already made your decision. I really don't have a great deal else to say, other than it wouldn't take me long to pack my things if you give me the ticket."

Based on the severity of the crime and the length of time served, the Commission voted to deny him parole, but in part Dallas' unrepentant attitude was an obvious influence. After the conversation ended, the chairman observed, "He didn't show much remorse, did he?"

In mid-July, 1989, because the New Mexican exchange prisoner was returned by Idaho, Dallas had to find a new home. He was moved to the Lansing State Correctional Facility, a prison over one hundred years old, at Lansing, Kansas, thirty miles northwest of Kansas City. Dallas was unhappy about this transfer. He called Lance Churchill, who reported, "He was upset; he has a lawsuit pending." The suit claimed Dallas was the victim of a conspiracy led by Idaho corrections authorities to keep him in maximum security. Those authorities stated that Kansas had been chosen because there was a "backlog" of prisoner-exchange time owed Idaho by Kansas.

Dallas remains imprisoned in Kansas, and to out-of-state inquiries, the correctional department refuses to even confirm his presence there. Reportedly, he struck a guard and received six months of solitary confinement, followed by three months more when he refused strip searches. His life is a leghold trap, with spacers. He is behind walls in maximum-security custody—the highest, short of twenty-four hour lockdown—but he is allowed activities and recreation. In Idaho, the pardons and parole commission states that the prisoner is still serving time on his first sentence, which was merged with the felony-firearms conviction into a one-to-twenty-year sentence, and he will not be considered for parole from that sentence before A.D. 2000. At that time, even under the most favorable decision, he would still have to serve time on his second sentence.

As for the other lives that figured in the Dallas case:

Jim Stevens and his family moved to Paul, Idaho, where he runs a retail garden center. (His parents and in-laws lived there, and he had graduated from Idaho State University in Pocatello.)

George Nielsen suffered a paralytic stroke and died in 1990. The Paradise Hill Bar closed. Liz Nielsen retired from her nursing job at Humboldt General but continues to live in Paradise Hill.

Geneva Holman retired from her job with Nevada Bell.

Constance Wilson Ickes died in August, 1992.

The Carlins left the 45 Ranch.

Margaret Lundy returned to Idaho.

Craig Carver traded his trailer for one slightly younger, married, and remains at Poverty Flats at this writing.

Clayton Andersen left Owyhee County for the Valley County prosecutor's office, and then left that for a law practice in Coeur d'Alene, Idaho.

Michael Kennedy, special prosecutor, was appointed Judge of the Magistrate Division, Jefferson County, and resides in Rigby, Idaho.

In mid-April, 1983, Michael Donnelly, defense attorney, formally withdrew from active law practice and was hospitalized at St. Alphonsus Hospital in Boise for psychiatric care and treatment. In April, 1984, he was brought before the Idaho Supreme Court by the Idaho Bar Association on four counts of unprofessional conduct and was suspended from practice. Many of his misrepresentations to four clients, including the falsification of letters, medical reports, and filing dates occurred while he was involved with the Dallas trial. In his affirmative defense he alleged an excessive workload, marital difficulties, and emotional problems. In April, 1990, while he was under conditional reinstatement and probation, formal charges were filed seeking Donnelly's disbarment. Instead, he resigned. In his resignation, he admitted that he failed to act with reasonable diligence in handling client matters, that he lied to clients, and that he engaged in unauthorized practice of the law. He was fined $750 for contempt of court, and informed that he would face a presumption of "unfit to practice law" should he ever again apply for admission to the Idaho State Bar.

Bill Mauk, defense attorney, remains a member of Skinner, Fawcett, & Mauk in Boise. In 1986 he was elected president of the Idaho Trial Lawyers Association. In 1988 he was appointed a member of the board of directors of the Western Trial Lawyers Association.

Edward Lodge, in November, 1989, was confirmed by the U. S. Senate as a federal district court judge—a lifetime term—and was sworn in three weeks later at the Federal Building in Boise.

At this writing, Sheriff Nettleton still patrols Owyhee County by Camaro and Cessna. In 1992, running as a Democrat in a Republican stronghold, he was reelected with sixty percent of the vote. He has been granted two additional patrolmen and a new thirty-bunk jail.

Nettleton took Dee Pogue and three of her children for an airplane flight over the Sawtooth Range, northeast of Boise, where they sprinkled Bill's ashes. It was another of his favorite places, one less tarnished than the Owyhees had become. To honor Pogue, the U. S. Forest Service renamed a trail on the Middle Fork of the Boise River.

Wilson Conley Elms' ashes were scattered by his wife, Sheryl, on the South Fork of the Boise River. It was his favorite stream: in his gray, weatherbeaten Stetson, accompanied by "Old Blue," his Labrador retriever, he liked to fish the reach below Anderson Ranch Dam, casting his own hand-tied flies. Mrs. Elms continues to raise their adopted daughter, Allia, who will soon be a teenager.

The Fish and Game Department increased its training for officers (mandatory police academy), and changed its optional policy regarding officers in the field wearing a gun, to a mandatory one. Instead of buying their own weapon, officers are now issued a Glock .40 caliber semi-automatic.

Moreover, the state altered its procedure for prosecuting first-degree murder charges. When named special prosecutor on a case, deputy attorney generals are now assigned the lead role. (Michael Kennedy said that had he been in charge, he would have abbreviated the state's case in order to shorten the time Dallas was exposed to the jury.)

Near the existing prison, at a cost of $8 million, Idaho completed a new maximum security prison, with a central vantage point for guards. New security measures were adopted at both prisons. Razor wire replaced cyclone fences. And fifteen evergreens near the front entrance to the older prison—trees that did not block a view of Dallas—were cut down, triggering a prison employee to pen:

> Oh, pine trees gone
> Which stood so straight
> Inside the fence
> By our front gate.
> It's such a shame,
> A great pity,
> You weren't classified
> As maximum security.

In January, 1993, the Ninth U. S. Circuit Court of Appeals rejected an appeal by Dallas to overturn his manslaughter conviction. The three judges ruled unanimously that the testimony by Stevens and Dallas supported the jury's conclusion that Dallas did not shoot the conservation officers in self-defense. It marked the end of his appeals.

Dallas has never granted an interview. As though sheltering a matchflame from the wind, he draws in upon himself. The years tick past. "What day of the month I do not know, which day of the week I am not sure, far less what hour of the night." Perhaps, lying in his cell, he hears at times in his head the inaudible sigh of the South Fork running irresistibly downstream, and the thought of life flowing past without him pains him in the same unwarranted way he pained two families that awful afternoon, when he unloaded his temper down in Bull Basin and ended his search for a western solitude with a solitude more real and more profound than that of any cave or canyon in the remotest quarter of the Owyhees.

63 DALLAS WITH THE SPOILS OF POACHING.

64 DALLAS' CAMP ON THE SOUTH FORK OF THE OWYHEE RIVER. HIS TENT IS THE
WHITE DOT NEXT TO THE RIVER IN CENTER OF THE PHOTOGRAPH.

65 DALLAS' TENT AT BULL CAMP WITH ONE FLAP PULLED BACK, SHOWING HIS BED
AND STOVE.

66 & 67 DALLAS AFTER HIS CAPTURE IN 1987.

68 THE MARKET IN RIVERSIDE, CALIFORNIA, WHERE THE SO-CALLED
MOUNTAIN MAN WAS SHOPPING WHEN HE WAS CAPTURED AFTER HIS
ESCAPE FROM THE IDAHO PENITENTIARY.

James Angleton, **The Poet**

Solitude gives birth to the original in us, to beauty unfamiliar and perilous—to poetry. But also, it gives birth to the opposite: to the perverse, the illicit, the absurd.—Thomas Mann

Beneath the intricate, ramose shadows of a patriarchal silver maple in a corner plot of the Morris Hill Cemetery in Boise, Idaho, lies a plain gray, inconspicuous, granite gravestone, flush with the mown grass, and marked only with three lines: James J. Angleton / Boise 1917 / Washington D C 1987.

Six feet to its right, a prominent vertical tombstone is shared by James Hugh Angleton and Carmen Moreno Angleton, and that is the better place to begin.

James Hugh Angleton, father of James J. Angleton, was born in Sharpsburg, Illinois, in 1888, the son of a farmer and one of ten children. He grew up (six feet, four inches) in central Illinois, fifteen miles southeast of Springfield, where a young Abraham Lincoln (also six feet, four inches) had practiced law. Angleton graduated from Christian County Normal School and taught grade school in Illinois before coming to Idaho in 1911 in search of a summer job in the wheatfields.

A fine horseman, he was soon employed as a teamster, his address a room at the Oxford Hotel on Main Street in Boise. At the time, the city and its outskirts had a population of about 25,000 persons, and the Idan-ha Hotel, just up the street from the Oxford, at six stories was the tallest building in the state and rented rooms for one dollar a day.

By 1914 Angleton was a wagon driver for the American

Laundry and had moved to West State Street. Another year, and he was working as a salesman for Pugh-Jenkins Furniture Company.

The following year, distant political events in Mexico altered his life and require some explanation. The Mexican Revolution was underway. Venustiano Carranza, a landowner from northern Mexico with extensive holdings, took over the presidency and was given American recognition. He tried to crush one of his leading generals who had helped him to power: Francisco "Pancho" Villa.

On March 9, 1916, Villa crossed the border with 485 men and made a surprise attack on the little desert town of Columbus, New Mexico, which happened to have a U. S. cavalry garrison. Villa's band killed eighteen persons, half of them soldiers, while suffering losses of almost one hundred of their own. Villa was angry about the recognition of his rival, but also may have been an agent of German intrigue seeking to preoccupy the United States, or simply may have been in need of fresh supplies.

American reaction was prompt. Senator Ashurts of Arizona summed up national sentiment when he said, referring to Secretary of State and teetotaler William Jennings Bryan, "We need less grapejuice and more grapeshot." On March 10, President Woodrow Wilson directed Secretary of War Newton Baker, who had taken office the previous day, that an armed force, displaying scrupulous regard for the sovereignty of Mexico, be sent into Mexico with the sole object of capturing Villa.

General John "Blackjack" Pershing was selected to command the so-called Punitive Expedition into the state of Chihuahua— empty and unknown terrain to Americans at the time. In mid-March, assisted by infantry and artillery, the campaign moved south with the hope that the campesinos would assist it—about as likely as the Sheriff of Nottingham entering Sherwood Forest expecting the peasants to help him hang Robin Hood.

The cavalry marched as much as sixty-eight miles in a day, but their quarry eluded them. After chasing false rumors for weeks, bogging the supply trucks in alkali, and discovering that the eight planes of the First Aero Squadron were unable to fly over 12,000-foot mountain passes, the expedition of 10,000 soldiers came to a halt 300 miles inside Mexico. The Americans were caught in the middle of a family quarrel, hated by both sides more than they hated each other.

In mid-June, to dissuade Carranza, who had not agreed to the invasion, from attacking U. S. towns, President Wilson called up the entire National Guard, 110,000 strong, and deployed it on the border with Mexico.

At this point, Hugh James Angleton joined the Idaho National Guard, Second Idaho Infantry, and was dispatched to Arizona. He did not, as has often been reported, ride with Pershing—no National Guard units crossed the border into Mexico.

With both sides awaiting developments, July to December was a quiet period. January 28 the expedition finally withdrew to New Mexico without Villa.

James Hugh Angleton, however, while stationed on the Arizona-Mexico border, met a vibrant Mexican girl, dark-haired and diminutive Carmen Mercedes Moreno, born in the state of Sonora of a family engaged in mining and ranching.

In May, 1916, Carmen had turned eighteen; in mid-December she and James, age twenty-eight, married at Sacred Heart Church in Nogales, sixty-five miles south of Tucson.

The Angletons returned to Boise in early 1917—a momentous year: the Bolshevik Revolution flamed in Russia; the United States declared war on Germany; postal inspectors in New York, on grounds of defeating the enemy, opened and read all correspondence leaving the United States; and the Angletons' first son, James Jesus, was born December 9 at St. Alphonsus Hospital in Boise. Four days later, he was baptized Catholic at St. John's Cathedral in Boise.

An extrovert, James Hugh Angleton continued to work as a salesman, now for Idaho Candy Company, and the family lived at 102 South 17th at Main Street in Boise (the house, with slight alterations, is at present the Zurcher Building). In 1920 a second son, Hugh Rolla, was born.

In 1922 Angleton took employment with the National Cash Register Company, again as a salesman (the company had opened a Boise office in 1913). He prospered, and the family moved to 1515

Sherman Street in Boise's North End. By 1925 the Angletons had moved to a larger house at 1809 West Washington at North 17th, and then, with the births of daughters Carmen and Dolores, to a white frame, two-story house on the corner at 901 North 16th.

By 1927 Angleton had advanced to branch manager and sales instructor of the Western Division for National Cash Register. In 1929 the family moved to company headquarters in Dayton, Ohio, where Angleton was promoted to manager of the Northeastern Division and, eventually, to vice-president in charge of the company's European operations.

In 1933, when NCR threatened to close down Italian operations, Angleton bought the Italian franchise and moved his family to Milan. As a Mason and head of the American Chamber of Commerce in Italy, he became the best known and connected businessman in the country, paying off the franchise in a few years. In 1941, just as Japan entered the war, Angleton moved to New York with his wife and two daughters. The family business was subsequently confiscated. He enlisted in the Army and attended the School of Military Government in Charlottesville, Virginia, then joined the Office of Strategic Services, working for the executive officer of Special Operations. He saw action in five campaigns during the war, including the invasion at Anzio. (He nearly lost a leg when a shell exploded next to his jeep, killing two of his fellow officers.) Among other duties, he served as aide to General Mark Clark, gradually rising to the rank of colonel. By the war's end, he held the Bronze Star and Italian Military Star for valor in the field of combat.

After the war, Angleton and his wife returned to Milan and later Rome to rebuild the NCR franchise. Then in 1964 he sold his interest back to the company (since purchased by AT&T), and retired with his wife to Boise, where he lived in an apartment on Crescent Rim Drive until his death in 1973.

James Jesus (a common name among Hispanics and pronounced in the Spanish manner) Angleton, oldest of the four Angleton children, spent his first ten years in Boise's North End. His childhood friend, Dr. Richard Forney, has fond memories of him.

The boys lived a block apart on North 16th and went to Whittier School. Afternoons they played baseball, football, and basketball on the vacant lots along Harrison Boulevard; evenings they played kick-the-can and pompom pullaway. But Forney's brightest memories are of playing marbles.

"Jim was a real crackerjack shot with one particular marble—it was an agate. So I'd loan him the agate, and he'd pay off my rent with part of the marbles he won. He was the scourge of the neighborhood. He won every marble game he ever got into," Forney recalls with a grin and a twinkle. "Jim was a crack shot, by golly. He never missed with that one particular agate. He was deadly," Forney says with a laugh. "So I kind of rented the agate to him. He wanted it; I should have given it to him, I guess. I thought it was more fun to watch him win and divvy up with me. He was good, he really was."

Forney has kind memories of the Angleton household. "Mrs. Angleton had a very interesting custom, which she must have brought from Mexico. There were four kids—two boys and two girls—and by giving each one of them a birthday every three months that would make one birthday party a month year-round." He elaborates, "She'd have Jim's birthday party one month, and one month later would be Delores, and the next month it would be Carmen, and then Hugh, and then Jim again. Each of them had a birthday party four times a year." He smiles. "The neighborhood kids were invited. We'd all come, bring something wrapped up." He laughs at the recollection. "Presents and ice cream. She liked to have a party, and without a reason, a birthday sounded good, so she had a lot of them. It was just practically a routine: a birthday party at Angletons."

Forney recalls a memorable outing as a child with the Angletons. "They had a nice car, when everybody didn't have a car. I remember one time they took us up to what's now Hulls Gulch—at that time it was called Slaughterhouse Gulch—full of weeds, and there'd been an old brick factory up there. One of the things Idaho Candy Company made was horehound cough drops. Horehound is a little weed. Mr. Angleton worked for Idaho Candy," he continues, "and they rounded up ten of us kids and took us in Angleton's car up to the gulch and gave us all knives, and we all went around and cut horehound so they could make candy from it." He concludes with a smile, "Yeah, you remember those things."

Forney bought his *Liberty* magazine subscription route from Jim Angleton; at 1,000 copies a week, it was the second-largest such route in the country at the time. The routine was for the delivery boy, on a bicycle, to pick up copies downtown at Sixth and Main, load his bags and go door to door collecting a nickel, of which he kept a cent and a half. Much of the weekly route was run in the morning before school.

When the Angletons left Idaho in 1929, the marble games in the North End were never the same. The Angletons moved to Dayton, Ohio, a rapidly growing city of 200,000, where the family lived first on Stone Mill Road and then on Southview Road in a prosperous suburb of the city, with outskirts rural enough that James would have vivid memories of raccoon hunting with his father.

As mentioned earlier, when James, in 1933, was sixteen, the family moved again, to Milan, Italy, where NCR manufactured its cash registers. That summer James attended the international Boy Scout Jamboree in Gondollo, Hungary.

In the fall, he was sent to board for a year at Chartridge Hill House in Buckinghamshire, an agricultural area in central England, about seventy miles northeast of London.

Thereafter he entered Malvern College, founded in 1865, a boarding school for boys ages thirteen to eighteen. The hillside campus overlooks the Severn Valley between Bristol and Birmingham. The school curriculum—English, mathematics, science, history, language, economics, art—prepares students for rigorous university entrance examinations. James studied English, French, German, and history. In addition, he also played soccer, and served as a house prefect, and as a corporal in the Officers' Training Corps. In December of his third year, he left Malvern College.

Almost forty years later, in an interview with Thames Television, he remarked, "I was brought up in England in my formative years, and I must confess that I learned, at least I was disciplined to learn, certain features of life, and what I regard as duty."

During these years, the young Angleton spent summers in Italy, but he also camped in the mountainous Haute-Savoie in southeast France, just south of Geneva. The summer of 1936, he worked as an apprentice mechanic at the NCR factory in Paris. The following summer, at age twenty, he attended the Boy Scout Jamboree in Holland, as well as the World Boy Scout Jamboree at Camp Birdsong, Scotland.

In fall, 1937, Angleton enrolled at Yale with the class of '41. He was tall (six feet, one inch), slender, athletic, handsome, brilliant, somewhat shy, "friendly and generous," literary, and well-traveled. English and Italian were his major subjects, yet he was an undistinguished student, graduating in the lower quarter of his class, and holding the class record for incompletes.

Outside the classroom, however, he excelled. He roomed with Reed Whittemore, a future poet of some distinction. Bothered by chronic insomnia, Angleton kept long hours: he wrote poetry in his room, listened to jazz, played poker and dice until dawn, handicapped horses, engaged in chess games, played tennis and golf, mastered bowling, studied photography, grew orchids, and worked on the *Yale Literary Magazine.*

He was one of the founders of the *Freshman Weekly,* and editor of the class publication, *'41.* The following year, he edited *Vif,* a sophisticated inter-university French review, and there published a pair of his own poems in French. They reflect his abiding interest in the poets Baudelaire, Rimbaud, and Verlaine; and one of those poems, "Caresse Primordiale," about lips, reveals the Imagist influence:

> Brushstrokes
> sketched in vermilion
> two silent petals
> seeking
> their
> intimates

in little flames...
this fruit
of knowledge,
she whispers
softly,
it's very good,
isn't it?

In the summer of 1939, Angleton and Whittemore launched *Furioso*, a non-campus magazine of verse that would, the editors promised, "give the public the real poetry that has been kept from them." It opened with an introduction by Archibald MacLeish, poet and future Librarian of Congress, and printed work by poets of such standing as Richard Eberhart, William Carlos Williams, Wallace Stevens, e e cummings, and Ezra Pound. (The quarterly survived until 1953.)

While summering with his family in Italy, Angleton had managed to visit Pound in Rapallo in 1938 and take pictures of him playing tennis, and thus was able as a sophomore to induce Pound to come to Yale for a visit. Pound stayed with the Whittemore family, and altogether he made three contributions to *Furioso*. He did write a letter describing Angleton as "one of the most important hopes of literary magazines in the U. S." Pound's and Angleton's paths would cross again in a few years under circumstances neither of them could have foretold.

Oddly enough, Pound was a fellow Idahoan by birth, having been born in Hailey in 1885, and although his family moved before he was two years old because his mother could not abide the altitude and lack of manners, at times he referred to himself as "The Idaho Kid." In 1908, when his first book of verse, *A Lume Spento*, was published, he wrote his father, "Sound the trumpets, let zip the drum and swat the big bassoon. It pays to advertise...ergo spread this precious seed. Hailey shall read my biography. The Chippewa war eagles [his grandfather settled in Chippewa Falls, Wisconsin] may summarize my glorious career...in firing up that press notice in the Hailey papers, you might have them suggest that there is a vague chance of the University of Idaho securing my services if they run hard enough."

And in 1931, when Hailey celebrated its fiftieth anniversary, Pound wrote *The Hailey Times:*

> Am I to congratulate the town on being five years older than I am? ...The only thing I have against my native state is Senator Borah as head of a senate committee to deal with foreign countries about which he knows nothing and where he has never set foot. As for a message to my native town—How can I tell what the citizens want to know? I suggest they study agricultural credits and that the town library tank up on books dealing with same. There is also a chapter on the "Working Day" concealed in a long book [*Das Kapital*, Chapter X] by an unpopular author [Karl Marx]. That would be good stuff to give the young boys in the schools. It would make good insides for your paper. I can never understand why local editors in America can't run just as good literary stuff as we run in our little Cenova paper. Are the mountaineers less capable of mental effort than the swarthy Italians?

Angleton played varsity soccer for three years at Yale, until he broke his ankle and just missed winning his varsity Y by a point. He was active in the Political Union and a member of the Italian Club. He spent countless hours hunched over pinball machines in the student restaurant across the street from Silliman College. Sometimes he would inveigle a friend into driving him to the beach to watch the sun come up. Often he would borrow Whittemore's car to drive to New York or Mount Holyoke, or simply to the tranquil reaches of the Housatonic River, ten miles east of New Haven, or the Farmington, forty miles to the north, where alone he cast his hand-tied flies over shadowy pools for trout unknown.

He dressed well in English-cut suits, parted his black hair in the middle, and smoked three or four packs of cigarettes a day. He went through books like a silverfish: Milton, Pound's early *Cantos*, I. A.

Richards' criticism, T. S. Eliot's poetry, Benedetto Croce and Dante in Italian. Among his favorite works at the time was William Empson's *Seven Types of Ambiguity*, published a few years earlier—a book, according to one critic, "readable only to those who make out of poetry a whole world of sensibility and a chief interest in life"—but one that differentiates types of poetic language according to the mental processes which cause them.

He lunched with novelist Thomas Mann, met poet Marianne Moore, visited with poet Wallace Stevens, who worked for Hartford Life and Fire and insisted they both go outside on the front porch to smoke. He had dinner with the writer James Agee in Greenwich Village while they went over Agee's manuscript of *Let Us Now Praise Famous Men*. Angleton began his own literary magazine, *The Waif*, delivered secretly to student rooms at night, slipped beneath their doors.

Later he would name as his best friends in college: Reed Whittemore; Andrew Wanning, who taught a course on the problems of poetry; Richard Ellmann, future Joyce scholar; and Eugene O'Neill, Jr.

He remained in New Haven for the summer of 1941—the war precluded passage to Italy or England—and worked on the next issue of *Furioso*, while studying for a failed departmental examination.

In September, 1941, Angleton began Harvard Law School, with the intention, after courses in contracts and international law, of entering the family business.

While in Cambridge, Massachusetts, he met Cicely d'Autremont, a "bright and vivacious" English major and junior at Vassar, who would take her Ph.D. in medieval history in 1984. Cicely was from a wealthy family in Duluth, Minnesota.

Angleton took summer law classes in 1942, and continued through the fall semester; then in January, 1943, he received his draft notice. (Harvard gave him credit for the full semester.) In mid-March at New Haven, he was inducted into the army. The following month, he and Cicely became engaged.

Angleton underwent infantry training at Fort Lawton, Washington, then was selected for Provost Marshal General's School at Fort Custer, Michigan. When his troop train, whose movements were secret, halted at a railroad station, he peered beneath the shade and announced to his fellow soldiers they were in Boise. He recognized the Spanish-revival architecture of the station tower of his boyhood.

In mid-July, despite his father's disapproval, James and Cicely were married in Battle Creek, Michigan. Two weeks later, he selected—the records indicate he was probably recruited by Yale professor Norman Holmes Pearson—the Office of Strategic Services School and Training course. The OSS was the national foreign-intelligence agency, the same one in which his father served. On completion, he was assigned as an Army corporal to the Italian desk in Washington, D. C.

At this time, e e cummings wrote to Cicely, "What a miracle of momentous complexity is The Poet," and further to Pound, "Jim Angleton has been seemingly got hold of by an intelligent prof and apparently begins to begin to realize that compulsory military service might give the former a respite from poisonal responsibility...maybe he's developing?"

In December Angleton sailed from New York for London to handle Italian matters for X-2, the counterintelligence unit of the OSS, which prior to D-Day directed most of its western European operations from London. Counterintelligence has been described as "a Dantean hell with ninety-nine circles." The ways a spy's message may be read are almost as numerous as the ambiguities written about by Empson:

It is written by a loyal agent and its information is accurate.

It is written by a loyal agent but its information is only partially accurate.

It is written by a loyal agent but its information is entirely inaccurate.

It is written by a double agent and its information is completely false.

It is written by a double agent but its information is partially true, so that the false parts will be believed.

It is written by a double agent but its information is entirely true, so that the allegiance of the agent will not be uncovered.

The X-2 section of the OSS was established in March, 1943, with a staff of three; by February, 1944, it had expanded, like a fist into a hand, to seventy-five persons. When Angleton arrived at the handsome brick and stone, five-story building at West End Ryder Street, X-2 occupied the entire first floor and shared the rest of the building with MI5, British intelligence, and MI6, British secret service. Here began a federal career that would make him, in the words of one informed writer, "as singular a man as ever worked for the U. S. government."

Angleton was given a tiny office with windows that—except for being shattered by bombs twice in two months—were kept closed at all times. Although he lived in a small flat near Paddington Station, he installed an army cot in his office, and according to his secretary, Perdita Doolittle, daughter of the poet (H)ilda (D)oolittle, "Nobody else in the OSS was quite so single-minded in his work." He pored over intercepts "as though they were the Dead Sea Scrolls."

Angleton had high intelligence, undying curiosity, endless patience, a predilection for the complex; he had a mind that dealt with subtleties and arcana—poetry, after all, being messages coded in conscious ambiguities, intertextual allusions, and associational connections. And he was a quick learner. A formidable combination. Within six months, he had his second lieutenant bars and was chief of the Italian Desk for the European Theater of Operations.

In such hours off as he took, he traveled with his boss, Norman Holmes Pearson, an English and American Studies professor from Yale, to visit T. S. Eliot, E. M. Forster, Graham Greene, Benjamin Britten, and the Sitwells. Other than the men he worked with, however, he had few friends in London, and naturally enough immersed himself in his job and its solitude.

In October, 1944, Angleton was transferred to Rome as the commanding officer of Special Counterintelligence Unit Z. The Allies were driving north up the Italian peninsula in pursuit of the retreating German army. In March, 1945, he was promoted to first lieutenant and chief of X-2 for the whole of Italy. At twenty-seven he was the youngest X-2 Branch chief in the OSS, and he was also the only non-Briton in Italy cleared to share top secret Ultra—the breakthrough by British cryptologists into German military codes. In London he had learned theory, in Rome practice; by now he was an accomplished counterintelligence agent.

He was an entrepreneur of intelligence in Italy, a "practitioner of detail," pursuing potential recruits, even representatives to the Vatican. Reputed to know every street and bridge in his field of operations, he located resistance centers and tracked down German agents. He sent men to every photography studio in Rome and assembled mugbooks of German officers. He developed forms, techniques, and evaluations of interrogation. He snagged a warehouse of important documents on the Soviets—"a fantastic amount of code stuff." He even found papers recording the conference in 1940 between Hitler and Mussolini. And he recaptured valuable art objects.

Wherever he was assigned, Angleton refused free army billeting because he believed gossip in shared quarters was risky and time-consuming; he preferred sleeping in his office, awaiting new intelligence materials.

In May, 1945, Germany surrendered. Angleton received the Legion of Merit from the U. S. Army for his exceptionally meritorious wartime service. The citation credited his X-2 units with the apprehension of over a thousand enemy intelligence agents. He was also awarded the Order of the Crown of Italy, the Cross of Malta, and the Italian War Cross for Merit. General William Donovan, director of the OSS, called him the OSS's "most professional counterintelligence officer." The legend had taken root—one that would grow into "an awesome reputation nurtured over the years by word of mouth."

The war was over, but Angleton refused his father's offer of a partnership in reviving the NCR business in Italy and dismissed all thought of returning to Harvard to finish law school. Promoted to captain in 1945, he stayed on in Europe for two more years, working for the Strategic Services Unit of the War Department, consumed by the world of counterintelligence. He was the senior intelligence officer in Italy, and his chief in Washington referred to him as "a jewel."

A renascent Communism had become the new enemy, but, appalled by the atrocities committed against the Jews, Angleton was also busy collecting evidence for the Nuremburg trials. He established ties with the Jewish underground, which was shuttling Holocaust victims to Palestine. He preserved the assets of the OSS and built an Italian intelligence network for the postwar world, assisting in the reconstruction of the Servizio Informazione Militare.

Angleton's first child, James, was born in summer, 1944, but his wife and son, receiving but irregular communications from him, continued to live in Arizona, where they had moved shortly after he left New York for London in 1944. In 1947, however, Italian operations were closed down, and Major Angleton resigned from the army. In early 1948, he was reunited with his family. He took a leave of absence for seven months, and they lived together in Tucson while he recovered from the enormous stresses of his particularly hellish work.

In July, when the Soviet Blockade had begun in Berlin and the West had initiated its airlift, the Angletons moved to Washington, D. C., and he began his career with the newly formed Central Intelligence Agency, whose footings were poured under the National Security Act of 1947 in order to centralize intelligence efforts. Because President Truman had reservations about an "American Gestapo," and peacetime rivalry with the military and the FBI, the CIA was specifically barred from having police, subpoena, law-enforcement, or internal-security powers; its only espionage authority lay outside American borders—the task at home falling theoretically only to the FBI. As part of the Executive Branch, the CIA reports to the President through the National Security Council and is shielded by secrecy. For the next twenty-five years, the new organization was dominated by OSS veterans.

Again Angleton was, according to his secretary, "totally consumed by his work, there was no room for anything else." His first job, as a GS-15 paid $10,000 a year, was as top aide to the director of the Office of Special Operations, a branch formed from remnants of the OSS Secret Intelligence and Counterespionage branches, responsible for counterespionage. Intelligence is evaluated information, and strategic deception persuades the foreign evaluator to arrive at the wrong estimate. Counterintelligence is defined as all efforts to neutralize, disrupt, or eliminate the activity of hostile persons, groups, or governments to secure intelligence, the obtaining of which adversely affects the national security. Penetration (the placing or recruiting of agents inside hostile services), Angleton said repeatedly, "is the key to counterintelligence." Counterespionage, the distillate of counterintelligence, involves human agents, and their efforts to eliminate spying or employment of secret agents by the enemy to secure intelligence which would adversely affect the interests of the United States. It has been likened to "putting a virus into the bloodstream of the enemy." Angleton was involved with both; he was never, as has been frequently misstated, a spy; he was a spy-detector or spycatcher.

The Angletons lived in a three-bedroom house in Alexandria, Virginia, where their second child, Helen, was born in summer, 1949. Since college, Angleton had been something of a loner. A classmate at OSS training said, "Angleton impressed me the most...a very exceptional man...a strange genius...I would have liked to have been one of his friends, but he never gave me the chance because he was so secretive." As though in a witness protection program, Angleton now largely dropped from public view, his identity better known to his adversaries in the Kremlin than to his countrymen.

The National Security Act, and consequently the CIA, was a child of the Cold War: in the period after World War II the primary concern of American foreign policy was Soviet expansion in Europe, and it is almost impossible to recapture the atmosphere in which those policymakers operated. A mood of foreboding and apprehension hung over Europe. Communists seized power in Poland, Hungary, Rumania. Czechoslovakia had fallen to a Communist coup d'etat; Italy, Greece, and Turkey had been threatened by local Communist parties. The Truman Doctrine announced that the U. S. would help non-Communist countries resist takeover "by armed

[Communist] minorities or by outside pressure." In 1949 Russia exploded its first atomic bomb, and the same year the State Department conceded that China had fallen to the Communists. The Western allies were convinced that a Soviet attack was imminent. Newspaper reports revealed that the Soviets had highly successful spies at the British Embassy in Washington, D. C., inside the Armed Forces Security Agency, and at Los Alamos, New Mexico.

Yet it was in 1949, just before leaving for Europe on CIA business, that Angleton wrote a three-page holographic will, allowing a rare glimpse of his code: "You who believe or half believe, I can say this now, that I do believe in the spirit of Christ and the life everlasting, and in this turbulent social system which struggles sometimes blindly to preserve the right to freedom and expression of spirit."

In this same will Angleton requested that "a bottle of good spirits be given to the poet [Ezra Pound]." This, despite the fact that in 1942 Pound had made ranting, sometimes incoherent broadcasts in Italy espousing Fascism and anti-Semitism. The U. S. Grand Jury in Washington, D. C., indicted him for treason. In 1945 Pound had surrendered to the first American soldier he encountered and was held at an army detention training center in Pisa for six months. Angleton provided the Department of Justice with information on Pound's regard for Mussolini and Fascism, carefully distinguishing between the man and his work. Although working in Rome at the time, 150 miles to the south, Angleton did not visit him. Pound was flown to the U. S. for a lunacy enquiry, and the jury found him of unsound mind and unfit to stand trial. In 1949, the year of Angleton's will, Pound was in Washington, D. C., in St. Elizabeth's Hospital for the criminally insane, where he would remain for another nine years, before returning to Italy and ten years of reclusive silence. Whether during those years Angleton ever went south four miles across the Anacostia River and up the hill to visit Pound in Chestnut Ward at St. Elizabeth's is a question of darkness. Poets Archibald MacLeish, T. S. Eliot, William Carlos Williams, e e cummings, Marianne Moore, Langston Hughes, Elizabeth Bishop, and Charles Olson did; so did Angleton's former boss, Norman Holmes Pearson. At least at home, over an archway, Angleton hung a photograph of Pound.

By early 1950, the Angletons purchased a four-bedroom house and its adjoining lot on a quiet, anonymous street in Arlington, Virginia. Angleton's hours and work at "L" building in Washington withdrew him from his family. While his wife knew his occupation, his son thought he worked for the post office. Cicely recalled later, "You could never ask him any questions about his work...he was a person who wanted to be alone, yet he would get terribly lonesome when the family wasn't around. He was a loner, but he wanted us there."

The following year, Angleton became the CIA's exclusive liaison with Israeli intelligence, Mossad. Because of his ties and broad contacts, going back to his service in Italy, he was a natural choice for the Israeli "account," as it was known, but the decision did not sit well with the agency's Middle Eastern Division.

In 1953 the House Un-American Activities Committee was threatening universities, labor unions, and Hollywood, contemptuous of the individual rights of individual Americans. With Senator Joseph McCarthy, whom Angleton despised, hunting Red bogies under every American bed, President Eisenhower selected Allen Dulles, younger brother of Secretary of State John Foster Dulles, to head the CIA. Dulles was the first civilian head of the agency; he had, however, been the OSS officer who brokered the surrender of Axis troops in northern Italy, and he had headed political operations for the CIA. Dulles believed in covert action. In December, 1954, the perma-frost period of the Cold War and the year of the Communist Control Act, he created a larger, secret unit called the Counterintelligence Staff, and appointed Angleton, for whom he had a high personal and professional regard, to run it. The CIA charter covered the activities of the Soviet Union's Komitet Gosudarstvennoy Bezopasnost—the Committee of State Security, or KGB.

Dulles remained as Director of Central Intelligence for eight years, the longest tenure ever, and Angleton always had direct access to Dulles' office. He was nicknamed "No Knock" Angleton. Dulles' aide Tom Braden recalls that Angleton "always came alone and had this aura of secrecy about him...he was a loner who worked alone."

Angleton's job was to ensure that foreign intelligence agencies did not infiltrate the CIA; to do this, his methodology required penetration of Soviet intelligence services. He had studied defectors, deception, and the techniques of surveillance. Now he applied his knowledge exclusively to the KGB.

Code-named "The Poet," "Kingfish," and "Orchid," Angleton was aware that complete integrity of communications was vital, as were compartmented operations. "Need-to-know" was the test for shared information.

He divided the staff into units: operations (clandestine agents and suspected agents); research and analysis (file archives); special investigation group (penetrations by the KGB); liaison (to other United States departments and agencies and friendly foreign intelligence services); international Communism and front organizations; international police; and special operations (Israel). These sections eventually were staffed with nearly 300 officers, assistants, translators, and clerks.

At the end of his second year as chief of counterintelligence, Angleton recommended to Richard Helms, the number two man in the Operations Directorate, that "we gain access to all mail traffic to and from the USSR which enters, departs, or transits the U. S. through the Port of New York." Angleton argued that opening the mail—about 14,000 letters a year—would provide "an entirely new avenue of information in the field of counterespionage."

The program, known as HT-LINGUAL, operated out of La Guardia Airport in conjunction with a laboratory in Manhattan, and with the knowledge of the Post Office Department. Before the operation was concluded in 1973, over 200,000 letters were opened, and a watchlist assembled of 600 groups and individuals, such as the American Friends Service Committee, the Ford Foundation, the Rockefeller Foundation, Justice William O. Douglas, Senator Hubert Humphrey, Congressman Richard Nixon, Linus Pauling, and John

Steinbeck. Information was shared with the FBI.

The action was clearly illegal, clearly an unconstitutional invasion of privacy. Furthermore, the agency was treading in territory forbidden by its charter: domestic operations. As the Inspector General for the CIA conceded, "it is improbable that anyone inside Russia would wittingly have sent or received mail containing anything of obvious intelligence or political significance...there was no recent evidence of it having produced significant leads or information." Russian spycraft had to be assumed to be as good as our own, with their agents having channels more secure than regular mail. The operation was a bad idea based on a worse premise, and when uncovered, brought substantial discredit upon the CIA. Worst, it was the betrayal of the form of government Angleton was fighting to preserve from subversion.

In February, 1956, Soviet premier Nikita Khrushchev, in a six-hour speech at the Twentieth Party Congress, denounced Stalin's dictatorship. Among the more remarkable slants of his speech, aside from confirmation of a ruthless regime, were the implications of a loosening of controls on the Communist party in satellite countries and the possibility of non-revolutionary paths to power.

John Foster Dulles and Allen Dulles wanted copies of the text. Angleton produced one on April Fool's Day. Artful guesses say he obtained it from Poland by way of the Israelis.

Allen Dulles released it in its entirety to the *New York Times*, where it appeared June 4, and then, through Italy, to Eastern Europe. Printing of the speech sparked riots in Poland and the Hungarian uprising in October. Dulles considered it "one of the major coups of his tenure," and it added considerably to the Angleton mystique.

Angleton and his unit also developed the evidence that in 1957 helped lead the FBI to the KGB agent Colonel Rudolf Abel, who for ten years had been operating as a spy from a photography shop in Brooklyn. (It was Abel who was traded for U-2 pilot Francis Gary Powers.) His indefatigable efforts also led to the apprehension of George Blake, a senior officer in the British Secret Service; Georges Paques, the deputy press officer working for NATO (the subject of the book and film *Topaz)*; and Heinz Felfe, chief of counterintelligence operations against the Soviet Union for the West German Federal Intelligence Agency.

In 1958 the Angletons celebrated the birth of their third and last child, Lucy. At this time, Angleton's frantic pace and chain-smoking caused him to be hospitalized for treatment of emphysema, or incipient tuberculosis. Before long, however, he was back in his penumbral world. He was married to his job, a former subordinate observed. "He often worked all day Saturdays, and used to come in Sunday afternoons."

In his private hours at home, Angleton carved and stamped leather belts, and polished gemstones he collected in Arizona, incorporating them into jewelry: tie pins, cuff links, buckles, bracelets, necklaces.

He kept a hive of bees and harvested their honey. And he cultivated prize-winning orchids. "After the war, I started raising tomatoes. It was a gradual transition to orchids; they're the most perfect flower." He added, "The Lady's Slipper is my favorite because it's the hardest to grow." He knew every orchid grower in Europe and sometimes used that title as a cover when he traveled. Altogether he had 700 orchids in two greenhouses in his backyard. His hybrid cattleya, "Cicely Angleton," was registered in 1973 with the Royal Horticultural Society.

He liked music—Italian opera, pop vocalists from Carole King to Elvis Presley—and he liked to dance. He did not care for the theater, but he was fond of films, especially westerns.

He was a connoisseur of wines and savored good food wherever he was stationed or visiting, dining at La Nicoise, L'Escargot, the Rive Gauche, the Shanghai, the F Street Club, the Army and Navy Club, and Harveys.

At times he would go duck hunting along the Potomac River, where he owned a small tract.

His real and lifelong passion, however, was dry-fly fishing for trout, and as any such fisherman worthy of his cast, he tied his own flies. In his handwritten will of 1949, he bequeathed his fishing gear to his young son, "in order that he might have some small inclination to follow this sport." He was a member of the Tobique Salmon Club and loved to fish the Miramichi River in New Brunswick, a tributary of the St. John and accessible by a gravel road east from Maine.

He also was a member of the Brule River Sportsman's Association and owned sixteen acres in northern Wisconsin on the Bois Brule River, which flows into Lake Superior. He fished there alone for rainbows, brookies, and German browns.

Poet and neighbor Caroline Marshall recalled a summer visit on the Brule with Angleton when he shared his ardor:

> He hints at why he likes the dank secrecy of darkness to play the game when he describes how the great browns come out then. "They're shy," he says. "Be one feeding during the day, and the mere suggestion of a shadow passes—gone."
>
> The patient game of waiting, silent, for the trusting quarry to expose itself, that is the game of fishing Jim Angleton played in the summer....
>
> I saw him one night when I was a child—coming suddenly wet, slippery, and silent as a huge brown in from the dark, trailing rain, his fedora pinched and dripping, pulled low over his eyes, a fisherman wholly unlike others.

He was not a fisherman wholly unlike others, except that he was an accomplished master of his crafts. His friend and admirer Charles Murphy, *Time* editor and *Fortune* correspondent, described the fisherman in action:

> I had never fully appreciated some of his qualities until a fishing trip to the Adirondacks fourteen years ago [1961]. It was a bonechilling early spring day, and with another member of the party, I had retired fishless to the bank for a consoling drink and to wait for Angleton. Finally, he came into view, waist-deep in the icy water

and feeling for safe footing among the slippery rocks. He was using a 2¾-ounce Leonard rod and casting with easy grace, the tiny fly landing lightly eighty or ninety feet below him. He took one and a half hours to draw abreast of us, never quitting a run or a pool until he had tested every inch of the surface with one or another of some dozen flies. In the end, though, he had five fine native trout in his creel.

Sam Papich, an ex-Montanan, was the FBI liaison man with the CIA for nineteen years and knew Angleton well. He recalls, "Jim had the hands of a surgeon, and he made beautiful trout flies. Sometimes we'd go fishing together. Jim would walk up and down for a quarter of a mile studying the water, vegetation, the insects. Then he'd decide what to do. He could give you a lecture on the life of a mayfly from the larval stage up until it's a fly. I'm a trout fisherman, too, but he was a master at it. He usually released the fish he caught. To him, it was the challenge."

Another friend, Cord Meyer, who worked with Angleton at the CIA and fished with him regularly, said, "[Jim] came to understand the entire ecology of the stream in the end, right down to the life phases of the bugs. He could fish on the surface, or he could cast upstream with a nymph fly, allowing the line to drift back so he could just feel its tip. Fishing was not a superficial effort...it was a total effort to understand the ecology and win."

Robin Winks, Yale professor and author, has stated, "Virtually everyone who has written on Angleton has been attracted to the image of the chief of counterintelligence, alone, patiently and silently angling for some still, deep-rising fish. The image is fine, and accurate enough, but it misses the real point. Angleton was a fly fisherman. The devoted fly fisherman may carry a hundred or more flies with him and can choose from a thousand patterns. Some flies are literal imitations of real flies while some imitate nothing at all."

Angleton himself remarked to his daughter Lucy, "A fly fisherman is a purist. The classic way to fish is that you enter the life of the trout, and you try to see the world that he lives in, in terms of his world. The art of fly fishing is not just to go out and throw a fly on the water...it is to observe. You can give the illusion of a real fly with the coloring of your hackle and wings and all the feathers you put on it. And it will float down the river with its hackles cupped up, and you give it a little twitch, and the trout really believes that it is a fly...."

Included in his library were four shelves of books on the art of trout fishing. In recommending one of them to an interviewer Angleton said, "It doesn't matter whether you hook him [trout]. It only matters that he take the line. Even when he later drops it, you've beaten him. And he knows he's been beaten. That's the whole point of the game."

Angleton—a name the poet made felicitous—cast his flies with fluidity on streams in England, and on the Matapedia River in Quebec, and at Silver Creek near Hailey when he visited Idaho.

No stream Angleton waded, however, had a shoreline more slippery than that of counterintelligence. In 1962 Anatoly Golytsin defected in Helsinki. He said he was a major in the First Chief Directorate of the KGB. Brought to Washington under wraps, he appeared to be a source of accurate information. Angleton, who regarded most defectors as plants, debriefed him. Golytsin insisted that the KGB already had an agent inside the CIA Directorate for Plans: he did not know the agent's name, but he knew the content of certain reports made by the agent, he had a physical description, and he knew the agent met with the KGB in London on a certain date. Angleton decided the defector was genuine, and the revelation triggered The Great Mole Hunt.

A mole is someone recruited prior to entry into intelligence service, or a "defector in place" recruited after having attained a post. Golytsin's information and Angleton's belief in it launched the hunt to uncover the Soviet Union's penetration of the CIA. For the next ten years, Angleton devoted a substantial part of the resources of his staff to verifying Golytsin's claim.

An earlier episode had left Angleton peculiarly predisposed to take the hook of doubt. As a green X-2 agent in London in 1944, he had come to know and like Harold "Kim" Philby, who in 1940 had joined the counterespionage division of Britain's MI6. Although Philby was five years older than Angleton, the two had much in common, and Philby became Angleton's primary tutor in counter-intelligence.

The two were friendly enough that in 1945 Philby stopped off to visit Angleton in Rome, and their relationship deepened in 1949, when Philby was dispatched to Washington as MI6 liaison to work with the FBI (and CIA) on identifying Soviet agents on the basis of code interceptions. Philby later told an interviewer, "We [he and Angleton] used to lunch about three times a fortnight, and we spoke on the telephone about three to four times a week." In 1950 Philby had Thanksgiving dinner at the Angletons'; in 1951 Angleton attended a dinner party at Philby's house with a large number of FBI and CIA officers. The pair logged thirty-six formal meetings at "L" building. Angleton's memorandums concerning those meetings disappeared, and the import of these exchanges may never be known.

In reality, Philby was a traitor and a Soviet spy—according to Allen Dulles, "the best spy they ever had"—whose eleven years of betrayal did enormous damage to American-British interests during the postwar years. In the end, he was uncovered in 1951 by CIA agent Bill Harvey and fled to Russia in 1963, where he remained until his death.

Everyone was duped, including Angleton. In Philby's memoir, *My Silent War*, he wrote of Angleton:

> Our close association was, I am sure, inspired by genuine friendliness on ·both sides. But we both had ulterior motives. Angleton wanted to place the burden of exchanges between CIA and SIS [British Secret Intelligence Service] on the CIA office in London—which was about ten times as big as mine. By doing so, he could exert the maximum pressure on SIS's headquarters while minimising SIS intrusions on his own. As an exercise in nationalism, that was fair enough. By cultivating me to the fullest, he could better keep me under wraps. For my

part, I was more than content to string him along. The greater the trust between us overtly, the less he would suspect covert action. Who gained most from this complex game I cannot say. But I had one big advantage. I knew what he was doing for the CIA and he knew what I was doing for SIS. But the real nature of my interest was something he did not know.

Angleton, who would later remark that he had his doubts about Philby, never credited him with being a mentor, since he did not regard him as more intelligent, simply clever. But Philby's treachery—part of the ring of four so-called Cambridge Apostles who betrayed their families, friends, and country—stunned and devastated Angleton. It impelled him into a state of ultrasuspicion ever after. The eddyline between obsession and paranoia is not all that wide under normal circumstances. Within the deep waters of the CIA, as John Ranelagh has written in *The Agency*, "In due course, paranoia will overwhelm every counterintelligence officer, and this fact is taken advantage of in every conflict with them. All forms of reality begin to blur in such conditions."

To pursue Golytsin's revelation, Angleton established the Special Investigation Group (SIG), a secret unit of eight laconic officers within another secret unit. "Only a handful of insiders actually understood its work." With the tacit support of the Director and the Deputy Director of Operations, and contacts with the Office of Security and the FBI, SIG investigated no fewer than forty senior CIA officers. All of them were cleared. For several crucial years, however, Operation HONETAL virtually paralyzed the CIA's Soviet Division, which backed away from its Soviet contacts because it was told, in light of Golytsin's warning, that it had been "contaminated" or compromised. Angleton, pursuing the case with the obsession of a comet hunter, did find a suspect, and Dulles agreed the suspect had to go, but he was a suspect only because he had been in London on Golytsin's date.

In the first forty-eight hours of his debriefing, Golytsin delivered a great deal of useful information, including identities of KGB agents in Britain, France, Germany, and Italy. He also cautioned that the mole would be assisted by other Soviet agents passing as defectors or double agents, who would provide disinformation that would bolster the mole's credibility while discrediting Golytsin's own information.

Six months later, February, 1964, Yuri Nosenko, purportedly a captain in the KGB Second Chief Directorate and son of a former top Soviet minister, defected to the CIA in Geneva. Debriefed by the Soviet Division, his information countered Golytsin's in many instances and raised doubts about the likelihood of a Soviet mole. Aspects of Nosenko's story—self-contradictions, inconsistencies, discrepancies—strained credulity, however, and made him suspect. He claimed, for example, to have seen the files on Lee Harvey Oswald that showed that the KGB had no association with him. The task of evaluating his credibility was not simple; nonetheless, the Soviet Division believed it had the most important defector to date.

Angleton showed Golytsin the transcript of Nosenko's interrogation. Golytsin, perhaps fearful he would lose his status because Nosenko was a defector of higher status, tried to cast aspersions, saying Nosenko was a KGB provocateur. Then Angleton, who never met Nosenko, persuaded Pete Bagley, the senior Soviet Division officer, that on the basis of Golytsin's debriefing, Nosenko was a fake and a major deception.

The FBI believed Nosenko's story sufficiently to want him to testify in front of the Warren Commission investigating the assassination of President Kennedy; the CIA decided not to let him testify.

An egregious abuse of human rights followed. Nosenko was flown to Washington, imprisoned, and subjected to hostile interrogation. With the approval of the Justice Department, he was denied alien status in order that the CIA could detain him, since the agency had no legal power to detain anyone. He was considered a "visitor," and was held in solitary confinement without charge or trial for a year—poorly fed, allowed to shave and shower once a week, given no toothbrush, no blankets, no communications or reading materials of any kind. Questioned incessantly, Nosenko stuck to his story. In all, he was held in isolation for three and a half years, most of it at Camp Peary, Virginia, in a windowless ten-by-ten foot concrete cell without heat or air conditioning.

In mid-1966, new CIA Director Helms, recognizing that the case was an operational disaster and contained the seeds of equally disastrous publicity, told the Soviet Division senior officers to resolve it within sixty days. But it dragged on and on.

Leonard McCoy, a respected and experienced CIA officer, wrote a memorandum evaluating a 900-page CIA study of Nosenko, and argued that "no fake defector in the history of postwar intelligence has ever given away such vital information as Nosenko."

The case was reviewed independently of the Counterintelligence Staff and the Soviet Division, and after another year of interviews and polygraph tests, a new 300-page report concluded Nosenko was who he claimed to be. He had simply told some minor lies to increase his importance to the CIA. Angleton, however, refused to accept the report's conclusions. As A. L. Rowse wrote, "It is astonishing the foolish things one can believe if he thinks too long alone."

In 1969 Nosenko finally was given his full freedom. He was employed by the CIA as an independent consultant, retroactively paid $25,000 a year for the years 1964-1969, and given a resettlement allowance of $50,000. He changed his name, married, and bought a house in the Sunbelt; he expressed no bitterness: "I am proud to be an American. This is my country." In 1975 at CIA headquarters he gave a two-hour lecture on KGB counterespionage against Americans in Moscow, and afterwards received a standing ovation.

The consensus of knowledgeable CIA officials now is that as of 1964 Nosenko was the most valuable KGB defector to the West. In 1990 the chairman of the KGB (1961-1967) admitted in an interview that Nosenko's defection caused utter consternation inside the KGB.

The possibility of Golytsin being an agent sent to spread suspicion and confusion was meticulously reexamined. The final report concluded he, too, was genuine.

Was there a Soviet mole, or did Angleton overdo it? The answers to the question are buried somewhere in the counterintelligence maze. Unarguably, Angleton's suspicion was not irrational. He may have been right. Certainly the KGB penetrated the intelligence services of the other Western countries: in the early 1960s there was a scandalous penetration of French intelligence; both chiefs of counterintelligence in Britain and West Germany were working for the KGB at various times.

Nevertheless, because it corrupted the stream of intelligence collection and analysis for so long, The Great Mole Hunt has been called "the single most corrosive episode in the CIA's history." As Director Colby would write later, "This fixation on penetration so preoccupied us that we were devoting most of our time to protecting ourselves from the KGB and not enough to developing new sources and operators that we needed to learn secret information about the Soviets."

At about this time, Angleton became at least peripherally entangled in another CIA activity. In summer, 1967, President Johnson suspected that protest groups opposing the war in Vietnam were Communist-inspired. Top-secret Operation CHAOS (MH-CHAOS) began in response to a directive from Johnson ordering the CIA to determine whether the anti-war movement enjoyed financing or was manipulated by foreign Communist governments.

The CIA charter, as mentioned, prohibits it from operations within the U. S. The FBI was already involved in collecting information on protest groups and infiltrating them. Regardless, Director Helms used Special Operations Groups hidden within Angleton's Counterintelligence Staff to infiltrate protest groups in order to provide cover stories for infiltration of foreign anti-war groups, and the effort included surveillance of American dissenters, not American spies. Moreover, thousands of files on peace movements, campus radicals, and black nationalists were collected in a central registry within counterintelligence, although the operation was not run by Angleton, and he had little to do with its functioning.

In November, when Helms delivered to President Johnson at a cabinet meeting the results of his study, which found student activism was a worldwide trend fueled by the draft and Vietnam, without foreign involvement, Johnson and Secretary of State Dean Rusk indignantly refused to accept the findings. The CIA, they were persuaded, just had not looked hard enough. A revised paper followed, and then another. Still no Communist connection. Sometimes the mind concocts spider webs where there are no spiders. The investigation expanded, growing as fast as the peace movement.

The operation continued under President Nixon. The CIA repeatedly delivered the same conclusion: antiwar activists and domestic protests were homegrown. But Nixon wanted to know what his domestic opponents were up to so that he could harass and discredit them. What Nixon never understood, perhaps because he knew nothing about sports, is that when people cannot trust the score, any game goes to hell. The CIA had sought to establish a tradition that it was apart from domestic politics: "it served the President, not the politician." Within the agency, however, there was a feeling that Nixon wanted to use it for partisan political purposes and that CHAOS was a prime example. In 1973 Director James Schlesinger terminated CHAOS. Later, its purpose and duration would explode like a timebomb in the national news, wounding Angleton in the process.

Through the late 1960s and early 1970s, Angleton went on working with permutations and operations as remote and unknowable to most persons as the language of the Navajo Code Talkers of World War II. Like the epicycles of deception, directors changed: McCone, Raborn, Helms. Angleton enjoyed the confidence of each, even if none fully understood his autonomous enclave or all its doings. His name weighed heavily in meetings, where "he had a genius for argument which forced his opponents to attempt to prove a negative." Helms gave him high marks, and he was a tough grader.

Angleton arrived every morning at his second-floor office at Langley, Virginia (the new headquarters after 1962). A large reception room accommodated three secretaries. Large black safes paneled the outer office walls, and a special vault room was maintained just across the corridor.

Angleton's inner office was twenty-by-twenty-five feet. He sat in a high-backed chair at a commodious wooden desk; stacks of paper piled up like deep snow. The window blinds were always closed when he was there, and visitors, submerged in cigarette smoke, reported a Dantean gloom in which even a *Ficus benjamina* would not live.

Joseph Smith, a covert-action specialist in Clandestine Services for twenty-two years for the CIA, left a vivid description of his visit to the office:

> I remember the first time I ever went to Angleton's office. It took me a day to get over the experience. I found Angleton tucked away in an inside office which was completely draped in very heavy curtains. His desk sat amid a dozen various gadgets. Some of them I could identify as photographic apparatus, but I had no idea what purpose most of them served. Angleton himself was peering at some documents under a strong desk light. He was very pleasant and we had a good business talk, but I felt I had been admitted to an inner sanctum whose existence I must never mention to anyone.

In February, 1973, Director Richard Helms departed the CIA to become ambassador to Iran. President Nixon appointed James Schlesinger as his replacement, but he left after five months to become Secretary of Defense and was followed by William Colby, head of all clandestine operations.

Colby and Helms were opposites in approach and temperament, and Colby and Angleton were as different as plow and plane. Their mutual dislike was no secret in the CIA. They had first clashed in Italy during the late 1950s, when Colby supported the Christian Democrats' (Socialists) "opening to the left." Angleton feared the Socialists and Communists would reach an accommodation, and then the Communists would triumph. When Colby served the CIA in Vietnam as Chief, Far East Division, for five years, Angleton pushed for establishment of counterintelligence operations to staunch the hemorrhage of secrets to the North Vietnamese. Colby refused, and Angleton vehemently criticized him for it. (As eventually revealed, North Vietnam had nearly 40,000 informers in the south.) As Deputy Director of Operations, Colby also had relieved Angleton of liaison with the FBI. Further, convinced Angleton's "wilderness of mirrors" view of Soviet foreign policy was the product of woolly logic—"I confess that I couldn't absorb it"—he had urged Schlesinger to fire Angleton. Schlesinger dismissed the suggestion.

Once in the saddle, Director Colby took a "corporate management by directives" approach. He soon exercised his authority to terminate HT-LINGUAL. A few months later, Colby removed the Israeli account from Angleton's office, rerouting communications from Israel through the Near East Division. Then in December, 1974, he called Angleton to his office and informed him that he wanted him to give up the Counterintelligence Staff as soon as possible. He offered the choice of consultancy or retirement. Angleton refused his offer.

The next day, *New York Times* reporter Seymour Hersh, who had won a Pulitzer Prize for uncovering the My Lai massacre of 450 unarmed civilians in Vietnam, telephoned Colby to say he had a bigger story than My Lai. They agreed to meet in Colby's office.

At their meeting two days later, Hersh revealed that he had learned of Operation CHAOS. He intended to write that the CIA had engaged in widespread spying against American citizens, in violation of its charter. Colby confirmed many of Hersh's allegations and toned down some of his exaggerations. He also mentioned HT-LINGUAL. Hersh concluded incorrectly that Angleton was responsible for both.

Once the reporter left, Colby summoned Angleton to his office and explained that the *Times* story was going to appear, alleging Angleton had broken the law. He concluded by telling Angleton, "You will leave, period."

Colby was within his prerogatives. For obvious reasons, employees of the CIA are not protected by the Civil Service Act, serving at the discretion of the Director, who can dismiss them without stated cause. Angleton drove off in his black Mercedes.

Two days later, Hersh's story ran under a three-column head-

line on the front page of the Sunday _Times_: HUGE CIA OPERA-
TION REPORTED IN U. S. AGAINST ANTIWAR FORCES,
OTHER DISSIDENTS IN NIXON YEARS. Since Angleton's firing
coincided with the _Times_ story, the press and public assumed he was
responsible for Operation CHAOS, and the misapprehension was
some time in being corrected. The perils that operate at the
intersection of public and private life are considerable. Angleton
could hardly be blamed for assuming Colby orchestrated matters in
order to force him out. This man who avoided having his photograph
taken, who had sought to be as inconspicuous as a watermark in
paper, was the object of intense public scrutiny. Reporters camped
on his lawn. His wife flew East from their second home outside
Tucson to be with him.

At the CIA, in a meeting called by the internal Deputy Director
for Operations, announcement of Angleton's "retirement" was
greeted with shocked silence. "The father of Western counterintelligence" had been replaced. His top two deputies resigned. And
Colby went to work hacking the Counterintelligence Staff from 300
down to 80.

Before Schlesinger, Colby's predecessor, left office, he learned
that the CIA had furnished assistance to E. Howard Hunt in his
burglary of a psychiatrist's office while employed by the Nixon
White House. Concerned about other possible illegal activities,
Schlesinger ordered all senior officials of the agency to report to him
on present or past activities which might be construed as outside the
legislative charter of the CIA.

The list, compiled largely by his assistant Colby, consisted of
693 typed pages and came to be known as the "Family Jewels."
Most of the actions were legal, but all of them carried potential
embarrassment.

Colby had provided the top secret list to the chairmen of
Congressional committees responsible for oversight of the CIA, and
someone had leaked the CHAOS item to Hersh. For the entire last
week of December, 1974, the _Times_ ran daily CIA-expose articles.
Public scrutiny of the CIA had begun, and the public, reacting
against secrecy and duplicity in the wake of Watergate, viewed the

CIA with disfavor. Any coverup was a quick ticket to trouble.

Nixon's successor, Gerald Ford, was informed in a telephone call from Colby that all activities revealed by the expose had been terminated. It was a bit like the captain of the *Titanic* telling passengers the ship had merely stopped to take on ice

Meanwhile, an unclassified version of the "Jewels" was released by the House Armed Services Committee, and the Senate Appropriations Committee. Unauthorized wiretaps, warrantless break-ins, psychological profiles of student leaders, infiltrations of ethnic groups, media operations and surveillance, secretly funded American publishing houses such as Praeger, they all came to light. Colby later said he was "privately delighted" by the uproar because he thought it the best way to counter misconceptions fostered by Hersh's stories: full disclosure rather than plausible denial.

January 3, 1975, Colby met with President Ford at the White House and gave him the classified edition of the "Jewels," which made it clear that the CIA had been involved in assassination plots or attempted coups against eight foreign leaders.

The next day, Ford, who as a Congressman had been a member of a committee that was supposed to be an informal watchdog of the CIA, announced the appointment of the Commission on CIA Activities within the United States, chaired by Vice-President Nelson Rockefeller. Ford was attempting to defend the Executive Branch, to whom the CIA had always been accountable, by preempting the field from a more hostile probe by Congress, but he was also running for election and wanted to distance himself from the sins of the agency.

Two weeks later, however, in a private dinner with senior executives of the *New York Times*, Ford let slip that he had confined the Commission, whose membership included Ronald Reagan, to domestic operations because if it dug too deeply it might uncover more disturbing skeletons. "Like what?" inquired one editor. "Like assassinations," replied Ford, and thereby became the most notorious lid-lifter since Pandora.

Revelations soon rivered out. In late January, the Senate, not to be denied, established the Select Committee to Study Government

Operations with Respect to Intelligence Activities. It would func-
tion for the next fifteen months.

In February, Angleton testified in closed session for two and a
half hours before the Rockefeller Commission, saying that CHAOS
was only nominally under his control—that the unit reported
directly to Helms.

In June the Commission released its report, and although
emphasizing that the U. S. faced an estimated 500,000 Communist-
bloc intelligence agents, it criticized the CIA for "plainly unlawful
and improper invasions upon the rights of Americans—activities
that should not [be] permitted to happen again, both in light of the
law and as a matter of public policy." In the Commission's view, the
mail openings fell into this category. The report offered thirty
recommendations for reform, recommendations Angleton felt acceptable.

The Senate Select Committee had a much broader charter than
the Rockefeller Commission, one that included the full intelligence
community (all federal agencies), and scrutiny of foreign as well as
domestic activities. It wanted to know everything about the CIA, or
as the staff put it, "bugs, drugs, and thugs."

The Committee was made up of eleven white males, the better
known being Barry Goldwater, Howard Baker, John Tower, Gary
Hart, and Walter Mondale. Senator Frank Church, Democrat from
Angleton's home state, Idaho, was appointed chair.

Born and raised in Boise, a Stanford and Harvard Law School
graduate, Church had a well-furnished mind and a way with
rhetoric.

In April, 1943, he was called to active duty in the Army and went
through the Military Intelligence Training Center at Fort Ritchie,
Maryland, where he completed a course in photographic intelligence and Japanese Order-of-Battle. He was then sent to Asia, drove
over the Burma Road into Kunming, China, and was assigned to the
intelligence staff of the Chinese Combat Command, serving with
distinction until the end of the war.

In Boise, in 1956, at thirty-two he was the fourth-youngest
person ever elected to the U. S. Senate. Two years later, he won a seat

on the prestigious Foreign Relations Committee.

Church received the chairmanship of the Select Committee because he sought it and he had paid his dues. Although he made no mention of his candidacy until mid-November, he was considering a run for the presidency at the time. It would be unfair to say that he was motivated principally by political ambition—the sensitive investigation could easily backfire. He had served sixteen years on Foreign Relations, and in 1973 he had scrutinized covert actions in Chile; however, he was not unaware of the publicity potential for someone seeking a White House residency.

In mid-July, after a half dozen closed formal hearings intended to determine responsibility for possible illegal operations by the CIA, Church told the press that the CIA might have been behaving "like a rogue elephant on a rampage," carrying out plots without anyone else's knowledge. The larger question still remained: to whom were the intelligence agencies responsible? Who, in other words, was the elephant trainer?

From Angleton the Committee wanted to know which of the CIA operations he ran and just exactly what constituted counterintelligence. Reluctantly Angleton emerged from cover. In August, 1975, he testified in secret executive-session. Loch Johnson, a staff investigator for Church, remembered taking Angleton's deposition:

> Questioning him was like trying to find a new planet through an earthbound telescope: it took constant probing, a sensitivity for nuance, and a willingness to endure vast oceans of silence. Angleton might begin an important story, then let it trail out like a vanishing comet, and disappear into a black hole of ambiguity.

For Idahoans, though, the most riveting scene took place in late September at the public hearings in the ornate Senate Caucus Room, crowded with reporters and television crews under hot lights.

It was Angleton's first public testimony ever, and here he was, confronted by Frank Church: both from Boise, both fishermen, both from the same law school, both having served in military intelligence, both loners—Church being apart from good-old-boy politics and a bit distant—both within a dozen years of being levelled by cancer and sharing the same cemetery.

Yet that was as close as they would ever be; as far as national intelligence was concerned, they were never on the same page. Church, although only seven years younger, looked boyish compared to Angleton. Church wanted a national focus on outrageous agency abuses, leading to corrective legislation and greater congressional responsibility; Angleton sought to shield his life's effort within an agency he believed responsible to the president for national security. "The way the president designs the hat is the way people wear it," he once remarked. One man hoped he was on the rails to the presidency; the other knew his career was derailed.

Angleton, called unexpectedly and before he had time to review his secret testimony, was permitted an opening statement:

> I am mindful of the serious issues facing the committee, and I know of your concern that they be resolved prudently and expeditiously.
>
> My years of service have convinced me that the strength of the United States lies in its capacity to sustain perpetual yet peaceful revolution. It is the ultimate function of the intelligence community, as part of our Government, to maintain and enhance the opportunity for peaceful change.
>
> I believe most strongly that the efforts and motivations of the intelligence community have contributed to the sustaining of a Nation of diversity and strength.

As the hearing proceeded, some sparring occurred between the questioners and the questioned. The senators were apparently unaware that Angleton wrote the book on interrogation for the OSS. Getting transparent answers from someone whose work had depended on being oblique most of his life was like prizing stone out of a rock quarry.

The probe turned inevitably to HT-LINGUAL, and Angleton

admitted he understood it to be illegal.

> Senator Mondale: How do you rationalize conduct-
> ing a program which you believe to be illegal?
>
> Mr. Angleton: To begin with, I was taking over an
> ongoing operation...From the counterintelligence point
> of view, we believe that it was extremely important to
> know everything possible regarding contacts of Ameri-
> can citizens with Communist countries.
>
> And second, we believed that the security of the
> operation was such that the Soviets were unaware of such
> a program and therefore that many of the interests that
> the Soviets would have in the United States, subversive
> and otherwise, would be through the open mails, when
> their own adjudication was that the mails could not be
> violated.
>
> I believe very much...that certain individual rights
> have to be sacrificed for the national security.

Eventually the proceeding took up CHAOS theory.

> Mr. Angleton: It was technically under my supervi-
> sion for 'rations and quarters.' I was not familiar with all
> of the operations...those I knew about, I was approving
> of.

Angleton's greatest difficulty during his public testimony arose
over an offhand comment he had made at the conclusion of his
closed executive session a month earlier. In open session the
question had arisen about why the CIA had failed to comply with
a presidential order to destroy deadly shellfish toxin used to coat the
needle darts fired by an electronic pistol, giving rise to numerous
questions about procedure, morals, and ethics. After being questioned on other subjects, and believing his testimony was concluded,
Angleton stood up and remarked, "It is inconceivable that a secret
intelligence arm of the government has to comply with all the overt

orders of the government." The court reporter took down the comment, and when Senator Schweicker reviewed the interview, he entered it into the record.

Angleton had simply meant that if a high-level government official were thought to be working for the Soviets, the agency might resist his order; more significantly, there might well be overt orders from the Executive Branch that would be countermanded by covert ones from the same branch.

Persuaded that Angleton had said that the CIA was free to ignore or lie to the government, Schweicker now unexpectedly confronted him with the remark. Angleton, seeking to avoid any discussion of whether or not the government was issuing covert orders, withdrew the statement. He said the remark was "imprudent," that "the entire speculation should not have been indulged in." As the proverb goes, "All truth is good, but not all truth is good to say." It was a commentary on the difference in language spoken by intelligence and senators.

In late April, 1976, the Committee published its final reports. Two weeks later, Church won the Nebraska primary, then Oregon, Montana, and Idaho, only to fade in California and Ohio.

In May, 1976, in response to the Committee reports, Senate Resolution 400 established a Select Committee on Intelligence, to be kept fully and currently informed with respect to intelligence activities. The House established a similar committee the following summer.

Much can be said, and has been said, about the Church Committee. Beyond argument, revelations at the hearings damaged liaison arrangements between the Clandestine Service and friendly intelligence services abroad. Morale at the CIA was eroded. Too, executive powers were diluted by the increase in congressional oversight, restoring a constitutional balance, according to some historians.

Secrets, however, have a limited shelf life; they are only valuable for a few years. Almost all of those exposed were already "dead." No real operational changes resulted. Colby, fired by President Ford, acknowledged that the investigations had actually strengthened the CIA and clarified the boundaries "within which it should, and should not, operate." Historian Henry Steele Commager expressed the public view well, saying, "It is the indifference to constitutional restraints that is perhaps the most threatening of all the evidence that emerges from the findings of the Church Committee."

CIA Deputy Director Lieutenant General Walters reflected, "Americans have always had an ambivalent attitude toward intelligence. When they feel threatened they want a lot of it, and when they don't, they tend to regard the whole thing as somewhat immoral." Perhaps the CIA had misunderstood presidential instructions at times, with good grounds for misunderstanding. Harm done and lessons learned were temporary: under Ronald Reagan and William Casey the CIA staff would grow by more than 2,500 persons (to 16,000 today); one million square feet were added to Langley headquarters; and Congress increased the CIA budget by twenty-five percent. Then came the Iran-Contra scandal, with CIA involvement and lies to the House Intelligence Committee.

In 1980, however, Frank Church's bid for reelection to a fourth term was defeated by less than one percent of the vote. Conservative groups brought former intelligence officers, such as Daniel Graham to Idaho, who accused Church of undermining the American intelligence capability. Hired-gun Richard Viguerie prepared a direct-mail flier describing the Senator as "the radical...who singlehandedly has presided over the destruction of the FBI and CIA." (FBI crimes proved far more extensive and serious than those of the CIA.)

But the world goes around and the other side comes up. For some time after the hearings, Angleton again retreated into privacy. Lines from Eliot came to him: "Years of living among the breakage / Of what was believed in as the most reliable— / and therefore the fittest for renunciation /...dark dark dark. They all go into the dark, / Distinguished civil servants." At home on his mantel, however, he cherished a photograph of former Director Richard Helms, signed, "To Jim, the nonpareil among all the pros." And in April, 1975, with Colby conveniently out of town, Deputy Director Walters at the CIA presented Angleton with the coveted Distinguished Intelligence Medal, the highest honor the CIA can offer a living employee. The citation noted his "outstanding contribution to the security of the United States...and his contributions to the most critical and significant counterintelligence activities of the past twenty-five years, upholding the finest tradition of the Agency."

Gradually, Angleton surfaced more frequently, attending a class reunion at Yale, seeing friends, eating at the Army and Navy Club or the Blue Ridge fishing club. In May, 1976, he returned to Boise for his mother's birthday and for a dinner honoring 600 distinguished Idahoans.

He attended the Episcopal church with Cicely in Arlington, and spent more time communicating with his family. Their son had earned a B.A. in Middle Eastern studies at the University of Arizona, then had volunteered for military service in Vietnam, where he was promoted to Army corporal. Their daughters had converted to the Sikh faith, one living in the Washington area, the other in New Mexico.

In 1978 Angleton sued CIA Director Stansfield Turner in order to get access to his own former files and rebut testimony given to the House Assassination Committee about the handling of the Nosenko case. At March-end, 1979, a settlement allowed him to go back into CIA headquarters to read the secret documents. He was there for four hours, but he had to wear a visitor's badge. Soon afterward, he completed his classified testimony to the Committee.

In Washington rumors circulated that Angleton considered Colby the mole. Possibly he remarked that Colby could not have done more harm to the agency if he had been working for the other side—more damage than any mole. In any event, in early 1981 Colby received a call from Angleton saying, "*The New Republic* says this week that I said you were a Soviet mole." Colby replied he would write *The New Republic* that Angleton never said such a thing. Angleton agreed, Colby wrote, the letter appeared, the matter closed.

Angleton was now gray-haired, slightly stooped, with shadows under his eyes. He wore horn-rimmed bifocals tinted gray. One CIA officer who knew him well said his mouth "often wore a small, mysterious smile, the smile of a man who had a secret he would not share."

In 1986 he gave up alcohol; he switched from filter-tip Virginia Slims to Merits, four to five packs a day, then gave them up completely. He read books (he was a character in at least a dozen spy novels) and poetry; tended and exhibited his orchids. He took a three-week fishing trip to New Brunswick.

Along with other former CIA officials, he established the Security and Intelligence Fund, initially a legal defense fund for former intelligence agents, that became the Security and Intelligence Foundation. He served for a while as chairman, promoting understanding of and support for a strong American intelligence community. He was also editor of *The Journal of International Relations*. Along with his friend Charles Murphy, he wrote a piece about the Senate hearings wryly titled, "On the Separation of Church and State." He made some spirited backcasts at Church:

> Church is a blown-in-the-bottle, copper-riveted, 24-carat example of the rough diamond from the frontier polished into a political celebrity within Washington's liberal left-wing Establishment.
>
> Let us give the muckraker his due. The CIA and the FBI in their arcane and overlapping responsibilities did engage in some illegal and ill-advised operations, although these were by no means altogether reprehensible when weighed in light of the national security considerations prevailing at the time. The CIA did briefly consort with political assassins who appear to have been recruited from "the gang that couldn't shoot straight," and it did allow itself to be briefly drawn into unworthy technologies associated, among other things, with explosive cigars [for Fidel Castro]. It has all been laid out for the rest of the world to see—the crumbled skeletons rooted out of the closets of six administrations.
>
> Be that as it may, the intellectual boundaries that

separate Church from the real world in which the CIA
until recently operated so spiritedly and the one that fills
his private vision are as stark as the mountains that wall
off his native heath in Idaho. One has only to examine the
Committee's findings on the CIA's intermittent intru-
sions in Chile, between 1963 and 1973, to appreciate
how successful the man from Idaho has been in raising a
fantasy to match his mountains.

Angleton granted interviews, selectively and cautiously: Thames
Television, *London Daily Telegraph*, the *Boston Phoenix*, the *New
York Times*.

Among the more interesting was an interview given in Idaho in
May, 1976, the day after the Teton Dam Disaster, to a reporter from
the *Lewiston Morning Tribune*. Some of his comments bordered on
bitter:

> [Church] never once said, 'You did a good job, but
> you strayed from the reservation.' There was never an
> accolade given to any member of the intelligence commu-
> nity. He used the term 'rogue elephant' on the intelligence
> community. History will show he was the rogue elephant.
> The pendulum will swing against what has transpired in
> the last year and a half.
>
> The intelligence issue is bipartisan. One would have
> hoped the president [Ford], both as it affected the intel-
> ligence community and the multi-national corporations,
> would have taken the issue in terms of separation of
> legislative and executive powers, to the Supreme Court
> for a decision.

As for the abuses in covert operations, he said, "It is better to
have imperfect democracy than a totalitarian state."

At least one persistent freelance reporter, Aaron Latham, was
able to get Angleton to talk on the record about some of his literary
friendships and opinions. He regarded *Moby-Dick*, with its

monomaniacal Captain Ahab, who in his search for the cunning whale, declares, "All visible objects are but as pasteboard masks," the greatest American novel.

> [I didn't pursue a literary career after the war] because I found out the war wasn't over.
>
> I go to the writers I like. I don't find any new ones I like.
>
> [T. S.] Eliot is my favorite without any doubt, but Pound probably had the finest ear as far as the English language is concerned. But he never stayed with one style and developed it. He was an innovator, but his philosophy didn't really hang together. The fact that he called one book *Personae* or *Masks* is reflective of his poetry and the different facades he had.
>
> I don't think anyone ever took Pound's politics seriously. It was another mask. I think it was part of that kaleidoscopic side of Pound. I don't think he was an integrated man.
>
> Eliot was a whole man. Good sense of humor. Fairly dry but very good. Eliot was simply monumental. I have a tremendous respect for his consistency. But I think Eliot killed poetry.
>
> I knew Robert Frost. I don't think he was a big man in the sense that Pound or Eliot were.

Angleton, having once been a talented photographer himself, submitted to having his picture taken by Richard Avedon for publication in *Rolling Stone*. But he refused six-figure offers from publishing houses to write his memoirs, honoring his oath of secrecy as a former employee of the CIA in sharp contrast to several former directors.

In 1987, at age sixty-nine, Angleton's chain-smoking finally caught up with him. The morning of May 11, after several days in Sibley Memorial Hospital in Washington, D. C., comforted by the presence of his wife, he died of lung cancer.

Four days later, the funeral service was held at Rock Spring Congregational Church in Arlington, and was attended by hundreds of mourners. His friend Reed Whittemore recited from "Gerontion" by T. S. Eliot, in which the mind of an old man becomes lost in a "wilderness of mirrors." The closing hymn at the service was "My Country, 'tis of Thee."

Walking out afterward, news commentator Daniel Schorr, who had done two lengthy interviews with Angleton over the years, remarked, "There was no eulogy." Someone nearby turned and quipped, "It's classified."

Angleton's ashes were buried in Boise. Since he was not a practicing Catholic, his parents' remains were moved from the Catholic section of the cemetery to a plot alongside their eldest son's. Angleton's grave is about 200 yards north of the five-foot granite prism that memorializes Senator Frank Church, who died three years earlier.

Six months after Angleton's death, Israel dedicated a public memorial corner within sight of the King David Hotel in Jerusalem, where Angleton enjoyed staying when he visited Israel. A large stone was inscribed in English, Hebrew, and Arabic: "In memory of a dear friend, James (Jim) Angleton."

Any appreciation of a man might be justly measured by the size of the hole his going leaves. Angleton lived long enough to see the beginnings of radical change in the Soviet Union—he was, of course, suspicious. But after his watch, he also witnessed national security scandals coming to light like secret ink held over a candle, with the greatest number of spy trials in American history reported in the newspapers. Among the more notorious liars and thieves:

In 1976 David Barnett, a career CIA officer, began spying for the Soviets.

In 1977 Edwin Gibbons, a former CIA officer, offered hundreds of classified documents for sale to the Soviets.

In 1977 Chris Boyce and Andrew Lee stole secret satellite information from TRW Corporation and sold it to the Soviets, doing such damage that the Project Pyramider covert-communications system for CIA agents was cancelled.

In 1977 William Kampiles, a CIA watch officer, sold the manual for the KH-11 photo-reconnaissance satellite to the Soviets for $3,000.

In 1984 Karl Koecher, a former CIA employee, was charged with spying for the Czechoslovak intelligence service.

In 1985 former CIA officer Edward Hopper, "a recipient of the best espionage training the U. S. could provide," sold information about CIA operations in Moscow to the KGB, then escaped from the FBI and was granted asylum in the Soviet Union—the first CIA agent to defect.

In 1985 Larry Wu-Tai Chen, a former broadcasting analyst for the CIA, was discovered to have been passing secrets to Chinese intelligence for thirty-three years.

In 1985 the Walker family and communications specialist Jerry Whitworth's Navy spy ring, in operation for seventeen years, were revealed by Walker's ex-wife, after the FBI repeatedly ignored tips. More than a million messages and the keys to decipher them, as well as 1,500 secret documents, had been fed to the KGB. The damage was catastrophic, jeopardizing the nation's ability to defend itself—so great its full extent may never be known.

In 1987 Jonathan Pollard was given a life sentence for spying for Israel. He had been rejected for employment by the CIA, but the agency failed to advise naval intelligence when he started working there. Defense Secretary Caspar Weinberger wrote the trial judge, "It is difficult for me to conceive of a greater harm to national security than that caused by the defendant"—he estimated repairing the damage could cost one billion dollars. Worse, the Pollard case cast a shadow of distrust across U. S. and Israeli intelligence.

In 1994 Aldrich Ames, CIA chief of the Counterintelligence Branch of the Soviet Division, was arrested, along with his wife, once a paid CIA informer, for selling secrets to the KGB and its successor, the Ministry for Security of the Russian Federation. Ames accepted more than $2.7 million over twelve years. He was portrayed as the worst traitor in the Agency's history. The CIA had come to resemble the *Pequod*.

The cases were proof, if anyone needed it, that "espionage is not merely an inconsequential game played by inveterate cold warriors...but a deadly business that can affect the survival of the nation."

Before this waterspout of traitors, whose lowest common denominator was money, David Phillips was able to write in *The Night Watch*, "CIA has the best record of any intelligence service in history in defending itself against penetration by hostile services. Perhaps that will be Angleton's monument."

In an ironic twist, Angleton died shortly before a scheduled meeting with Senator David Boren, chairman of the Senate Intelligence Committee, just when the government which had rejected him was expressing an interest in him and his ideas once again.

Several of his obituary columns written in Washington newspapers attempted to vindicate Angleton. One in the *Washington Post* observed, "Perhaps he was too suspicious, but as we have seen, his successors have often not been suspicious enough. His faithless vigilance might well have prevented United States marines—semper fidelis—from giving KGB agents guided tours of the American Embassy in Moscow. Sometimes paranoia is just what the doctor ordered."

Hooking spies is a business that requires a balancing act between liberty and security. Any evaluation of James Jesus Angleton must include his flaws. As Pulitzer Prize-winning reporter Thomas Powers has observed, no one outside the CIA is ever going to know if Angleton overdid it, because no one outside the CIA will ever have access to his files, or all the other intelligence agencies' files—"your successes are unheralded; your failures are trumpeted."

Necessarily, an impartial judgment must consider the problem inherent in Angleton's position. Writer John Ranelagh has set it out clearly:

> Angleton was the director's preventer, and many recognized that he had to pay a penalty for the position: his suspicions would always be matched by the suspicions of others about him, and since his job was about suspicion, it was inevitable that some suspicions would be

wrong and hurtful. He represented a lesser disease inoculating against a greater one, but a disease despite that. There was also an inevitable tension between those who are doing the recruiting for the agency and those, like Angleton, who were attempting to see to it that those recruited were not penetration agents. Many people felt there had to be somebody like Angleton in the agency—even if at times the effect was overdone.

Powers makes a further point. "The primacy of security explains a lot of the hocus-pocus of intelligence, the back-alley mucking about, the dangles, the doubling and redoubling of agents, which leads most casual tourists of the profession to throw up their hands in despair. But it is better," he admonishes, "to have no intelligence service at all than to have one which is insecure."

Angleton would have been of one mind about that, as well as another of Powers' estimates: "Counterintelligence is wearing work, demanding a prodigious memory, patience, great psychological sensitivity, and the capacity to live with uncertainty forever. Yet not having it, for a lot of CIA people, makes as much sense as walking barefoot through a snake farm."

According to scholars, Angleton is assuredly a legitimate claimant for the title of theoretician of American intelligence. He was, according to Robin Winks, "the person who brooded longest, and perhaps with the greatest penetration, over the specialized methodology of counterintelligence." Former director Richard Helms, who did not think the core of the agency was ever penetrated, at least while he was there, told a reporter, "James Angleton was to American counterespionage what Thomas Edison was to the development of electricity."

And now, back where he was born, he rests, unheralded, in rectangular solitude; in Eliot's words, "in the world of perpetual solitude / Shuttered with branches, dark in the afternoon." In a sense, the nation will never be out of debt to him.

AGE —   48
HEIGHT —   6'1"
WEIGHT —   160
EYES —   Hazel
HAIR —   Gray

SIGNATURE

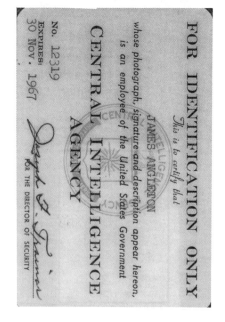

69 ANGLETON'S BOYHOOD HOUSE IN BOISE.
70 ANGLETON'S CIA IDENTITY CARD.
71 ANGLETON AFTER RETIREMENT.

CARESSE PRIMORDIALE

par J. J. Angleton

Trait de pinceau
esquissé en vermeil,
deux pétales muets,
cherchant,
ouvrent à trouver
les siens
intimes
en flammettes...
ce fruit
de la connaissance,
elle chuchote
doucement,
c'est très bon,
n'est-ce pas?

PIANOLA A 2 FRANCS

par J. J. Angleton

Pousse un bouton
salaud,
seulement un jeton
de deux francs,
une salée pour cinq,
écoute ça salaud?
C'est oripeauswing-
musique
sensuel mouvement.
Vois-tu ces hanches
en poire,
balançantes?
Allant retournant
une tournée, une tournée
tappant et battant
duvet-lèvres
flouchantonnant—
si doucereux sente...

Salaud, c'est toi
qui l'a fait,
toi et ton
sale petit jeton.

72 ANGLETON'S POEMS AS A COLLEGE FRESHMAN.
73 ANGLETON AT HOME IN 1975.

74 ANGLETON IN HIS STUDY.

HERMITS

The more I see of people, the more I like my dog.
And this would be good country if a man could eat scenery.

The lake's ice gives light back to the air,
Shadows back to water.

In wet years the land breathes out,
And a crop of limber pines jumps into the open
Like green pioneers.
In dry years
Beetles kill them with roadmaps
Under the skin.

The land breathes in.
The sun goes down,
And the whole sky cracks like rivermud in drought.

A few trees make it each time,
As if some tide carried them out, away from the others.

They say a tree that falls in timber
Goes down in good company:
Snow drifts in and it all goes soft.

They say a ghost is a ghost
That doesn't know it's dead yet.

Those limber pines die standing, lightning-struck, wind
  broke,
And enough good pitch
For a hermit's winter.

The cabin stood; the man was long dead.
Packrats nested in the firewood,
And a crowd of medicine bottles held forth on the shelf.

When hermits die
They close their eyes. They never hear
The parson sermonize how somewhere
There is hope where no hope was.

Tanglefoot,
Dead-On-Your-Feet,
A chance to be alone for a chance to be abandoned,
Everything is lost or given.

Hermits never know they're dead till the roof falls in.

—James Galvin
Imaginary Timber

ACKNOWLEDGMENTS

I wish to thank John Conley and Peter Donovan, whose editorial assistance did for me what I could not do for myself.

I am especially grateful to Diane Raptosh, Art Schoenfeldt, Johnny and Pearl Carrey, Roger and Julie Sliker, Roger Cole, Sandy Lopez, Jim Maguire, Tom Trusky, Roy DeYoung, and Ernie and Laurie Houghton.

Among librarians, I would like to thank those of Albertsons Library, Special Collections, Boise State University; and those on the second and third floors of the Boise Public Library.

The opening poem by Galway Kinnell is one stanza from the title poem of his book, *When One Has Lived A Long Time Alone,* and is used with permission (New York: Alfred A. Knopf, 1991).

The closing poem, "Hermits," by James Galvin, is from his collection, *Imaginary Timber* (New York: Doubleday, 1980), and is used with the kind permission of the poet. Galvin's prose work, *The Meadow* (New York: Holt & Co., 1992), will claim any reader who opens it.

Sources and Further Reading

RICHARD LEIGH

The single best source is Edith and William Thompson's, *Beaver Dick: An Historical Biography of Richard Leigh*. (Laramie, Wyoming: Jelm Mountain Press, 1982.) Leigh's diary is part of the American Heritage Center collection, University of Wyoming, Laramie. Photograph of the diary courtesy of the American Heritage Center. Other photographs are used with the permission of the Smithsonian Institution, Washington, D. C.

WILLIAM HISOM

I am indebted principally to *Prospects: Land-use in the Snake River Birds of Prey Area, 1860-1987*, edited by Todd Shallat. (Boise: Boise State University Social Sciences Monograph One, 1987.) The transcript for the Warren Mace trial was made available from the files of the Bureau of Land Management in Boise. Photographs are from Albertsons Library, Special Collections, Limbert Collection; and from Theresa Wagers, Amos Burg, and Pat McShane (gloves).

DAVID LEWIS

Johnny Carrey, of Riggins, Idaho, generously provided most of the information and photographs in this chapter.

CLYDEUS DUNBAR

Without the assistance of Jim Van Cleave, of Baker, Oregon, this chapter would have been impossible. Shirley Smith Edmundson, of Pine Creek, Oregon, provided additional sources of information and photographs.

EARL PARROTT

I owe many of the facts about Parrott's life to several persons. Specific thanks to Hack Miller, Johnny Carrey, Willis Johnson, Rae W. Parrott, Bill Bernt, and Bob Sevy. Photographs courtesy of Hack Miller.

WILLIAM MORELAND

This chapter could not have been written without the work of Richard Ripley, of Spokane, Washington, since it is based in considerable degree upon the facts in his more complete biography, *The Ridgerunner* (Cambridge, Idaho: Backeddy Books, 1986). Photograph courtesy of Lewis Jacobsen.

SYLVAN HART

I am indebted to Arthur Hart (no relation), Boise, for information about Sylvan Hart's family and his school years. In 1969 Rosita Artis and Nikki Stillwell conducted an invaluable oral interview with Hart, and the transcript is on file at the Idaho State Historical Library. The ISHS also granted permission for excerpts from Hart's unpublished manuscript, *800 Yarns*. Sylvan Hart provided me with many anecdotes and a brief autobiography. *The Last of the Mountain Men*, by Harold Peterson (Cambridge, Idaho: Backeddy Books, 1984) may be of interest. Photographs by Verne Huser, Kay Kiler, and Ted Streshinsky.

LYDIA COYLE

The single collection of Zaunmiller's own writing is *My Mountains: Where the River Still Runs Downhill*, edited by Donna Henderson. (Grangeville, Idaho: Idaho County Free Press, 1987.) I am grateful to the *Idaho County Free Press* for permission to quote from Zaunmiller's columns; and to Donna Henderson, Mary Crowe, and Mary Houston for shared information. Photographs courtesy of Steven Shephard, Glenn Oakley, Mel Reingold, and Richard Forney.

RICHARD ZIMMERMAN

I am indebted to William Studebaker for permission to quote from his poem, "What Salmon River Dick Said," from *Eight Idaho Poets* (Moscow, Idaho: Univ. Press of Idaho, 1979); to Ron McFarland for the excerpt from his article, "The Art of the Eccentric"; and to Zimmerman for enduring multiple interviews. Photographs by Dave Fross.

HELENA SCHMIDT

A Wild Cowboy, by Heidi Bigler Cole (Payette, Idaho: Rocky Comfort Press, 1992), contains useful information and valuable photographs of Henry and Helena Schmidt, and provides a larger context for their lives on Cuddy Mountain. In 1979 Louis Attebury did an oral interview with Schmidt which is on file with the Idaho State Historical Society. Helena Schmidt patiently answered my innumerable questions. Photographs courtesy of Kevin Clark and *The Idaho Statesman.*

CLAUDE DALLAS

In writing this chapter, I have made much use of *Outlaw,* by Jeffery Long (New York: Morrow & Co., 1985), and *Give a Boy a Gun,* by Jack Olsen (New York: Delacorte Press, 1985). Of the two, Olsen's is the less romantic, more even-handed and thorough. The transcript of the trial, "State of Idaho versus Claude Lafayette Dallas, Jr.," is on file at the Idaho Supreme Court building in Boise. Special thanks to Tim Nettleton, Ray Lyon, Bill Mauk, Lance Churchill, and Glenn Johnson. Photographs with the permission of *The Idaho Statesman.*

JAMES ANGLETON

Facts about Angleton's career are drawn freely from *Cloak & Gown: Scholars in the Secret War, 1939-1961*, by Robin Winks; *Wilderness of Mirrors*, by David Martin; *Cold Warrior, James Angleton: the CIA's Master Spy Hunter*, by Tom Mangold; *The Man Who Kept the Secrets: Richard Helms and the CIA*, by Thomas Powers; *A Season of Inquiry: The Senate Intelligence Investigation*, by Loch Johnson; and *The Agency: The Rise and Decline of the CIA from Wild Bill Donovan to William Casey*, by John Ranelagh. I am grateful as well to Richard Forney for recollections, and to E. Reed Whittemore for the poems from *Vif*. Photographs by Dennis Brack, with permission from Black Star.

These are only a few of the numerous sources drawn upon in this book; I single them out for mention because my debt to them is especially large.